Everyone Is Wrong About China

The Myths and Realities of Sino-US Competition

Other Titles by This Author

50 Things You Didn't Know About China
ISBN N/A

Shanghai (Panda Guides Shanghai)
978-0992026813

The Transcendent Harmony
ISBN N/A

The author is solely responsible for the analysis presented in this work; this analysis does not reflect the viewpoints of any of the author's employers, past, present, or future.

When the way prevails in the empire, fleet-footed horses are relegated to ploughing in the fields;
When the way does not prevail in the empire, war-horses breed on the border.
Lao Tzu

Everyone Is Wrong About China

The Myths and Realities of Sino-US Competition

Brendan O'Reilly

CHANGEMAKERS
BOOKS

London, UK
Washington, DC, USA

CollectiveInk

First published by Changemakers Books, 2025
Changemakers Books is an imprint of Collective Ink Ltd.,
Unit 11, Shepperton House, 89 Shepperton Road, London, N1 3DF
office@collectiveinkbooks.com
www.collectiveinkbooks.com
www.changemakers-books.com

For distributor details and how to order please visit the 'Ordering' section on our website.

Text copyright: Brendan O'Reilly 2024

ISBN: 978 1 80341 887 2
978 1 80341 903 9 (ebook)
Library of Congress Control Number: 2024912354

All rights reserved. Except for brief quotations in critical articles or reviews, no part of this book may be reproduced in any manner without prior written permission from the publishers.

The rights of Brendan O'Reilly as author have been asserted in accordance with the Copyright, Designs and Patents Act 1988.

A CIP catalogue record for this book is available from the British Library.

Design: Lapiz Digital Services

UK: Printed and bound by CPI Group (UK) Ltd, Croydon, CR0 4YY
Printed in North America by CPI GPS partners

We operate a distinctive and ethical publishing philosophy in all areas of our business, from our global network of authors to production and worldwide distribution.

Table of Contents

Introduction	1
Section One: Myths	21
Fallacy Number One: China Is Poor	23
Fallacy Number Two: Chinese Economic Statistics Are Wildly Inaccurate	39
Fallacy Number Three: China Is Rich	45
Fallacy Number Four: Chinese Economic Policies Are Inherently Predatory	53
Military Fallacies	65
Fallacy Number Five: China Is Uniquely Aggressive	67
Fallacy Number Six: The PLA Is Weak	82
Fallacy Number Seven: The PLA Is a Major Threat to the United States	96
Diplomatic Fallacies	107
Fallacy Number Eight: Chinese Diplomacy Is Ideologically Driven	109
Fallacy Number Nine: Beijing Has Foreign Enemies	124
Fallacy Number Ten: Beijing Seeks to Undermine the Global Order	133
A Brief Synopsis of Current Trends and Likely Future Developments	143

Section Two: Predictions — 149

First Prediction: Controlled Competition Continues — 151
Second Prediction: Both Governments Overstate the Extent of Bilateral Contention — 161
Third Prediction: China Overtakes the US Nominal GDP by 2030 and Maintains Higher GDP for the Rest of the Century — 167
Fourth Prediction: China and the US Will Never Purposefully Go to War — 171
Fifth Prediction: US Alliance Systems Continue; China Does Not Form NATO-Style Partnerships — 189
Sixth Prediction: US Allies Support Geopolitical Countering of China but Not Economic Crippling — 204
Seventh Prediction: A Traditional Arms Race Is Unlikely; If It Does Occur, Washington Will Lose — 208
Eighth Prediction: The Chinese Government Retains Relative Edge in Domestic Political Effectiveness If It Remains Rational and United — 212
Ninth Prediction: India-China Contention Supplants US-China Rivalry — 219

Section Three: Grey Swans — 227

Grey Swan Number One: Nuclear War — 229
Grey Swan Number Two: European Countries Form a Geopolitically United Global Power — 236
Grey Swan Number Three: Climate Change Majorly Undermines Global Agriculture — 241

Table of Contents

Grey Swan Number Four: (Another) Pandemic
 Disrupts the Global Economy   246
Grey Swan Number Five: Technology
 Undermines Mutually Assured Destruction   249
Grey Swan Number Six: Various Internal
 Disasters   253
Grey Swan Number Seven: Civil War   257
Conclusion: So What?   268

Introduction

China and the United States share the most important bilateral relationship in the world. Washington and Beijing's increasingly acrimonious struggle for global dominance is altering, and in some cases upending, long-standing global dynamics from the Taiwan Strait to Africa, Central America, and everywhere in between. Every person alive today is exposed to the impacts of contention between the US and Chinese governments. However, false narratives and mistaken assumptions undermine a comprehensive understanding of China and its relations with the world. The widespread ignorance among our decision makers and general population is especially dangerous as US-China relations enter a new realm of uncharted competition.

The rivalry between the world's strongest military, economic, and diplomatic powers continues to unfold across a wide range of regional and categorical fronts. Serious miscalculations by either side could escalate into an extinction-level event for the human race. At the same time, significant areas of mutual interest lurk under the surface of an obvious rivalry. Deep economic ties bind the countries together. Social and cultural exchanges remain robust.

Various dynamics driving Sino-US relations are enormously important in the international sphere and for every national government on our planet. They also help shape domestic political, social, and economic conditions in both China and the US. The shift in relative global power and the opening up of new frontiers of rivalry create unprecedented risk and opportunity for nations, businesses, and individuals. A basic grasp of the dynamics underlying relations between China and the US is crucial for understanding political and economic trends in both countries, along with the broader human condition in the 21st century.

While the main driver of increased contention is straightforward, the implications of the trend of confrontation are multifaceted and complex. Rivalry between Beijing and Washington has intensified primarily because China has rapidly expanded its relative power at the expense of a historic US advantage. The US has been the most powerful country since at least the 1940s, but China now challenges the key spheres of Washington's once seemingly insurmountable global dominance. Beijing wouldn't even necessarily need to adopt any explicitly aggressive policies against Washington in order to make the US government nervous; rather, the basic realities of China's increasing relative power effectively limit Washington's global influence. A dominant power almost invariably feels threatened by a rival with expanding capabilities. At the same time, Beijing fears that the US government may use its lingering dominance to attempt to stop, or even reserve, the trend of rising Chinese power. The changing relative strength in terms of economic output, military capabilities, and influence over third countries are driving Sino-American contention. Other factors, such as differences in culture, worldview, and political systems, play a role in the rivalry, but they are far less important than the brute realities of economic resources, military strength, and to a lesser extent, diplomatic influence.

There has never been a bilateral relationship as complex, as multifaceted, as potentially transformative, and as dangerous, as the ties and tensions that now exist between the US and China. Because of economic globalization and the nearly instantaneous flow of information, the competition between the two powers impacts every country on the face of the Earth. While US-Soviet competition also had global implications, the Soviet Union was never well-integrated into the economies of most countries outside its immediate periphery. No major US companies ever derived a plurality of their profits from Soviet consumers; the Soviet Union was never the largest trading partner of any US treaty ally. Direct bilateral trade and investment between the USSR and US was negligible. Furthermore, the relative balance of economic influence between two leading global powers has never shifted so rapidly as it has in recent decades.

There is also a historically unprecedented cultural element coloring Sino-US contention. Despite their obvious political differences (and decades of concerted US and UK propaganda efforts to paint Moscow as an "Asiatic" power) US-Soviet rivalry took place between two broadly defined "Western" states with roughly comparable worldviews. Washington and Moscow have a shared cultural lineage tracing back to the Roman Empire and ancient Greece. China comes from an entirely different and equally rich civilizational landscape with its own philosophical, literary, historical, theological, linguistic, and conceptual frameworks.

Nuclear weaponry is another factor that makes US-China competition unique when compared to all previous bilateral global or regional great power confrontations — barring, of course, the Cold War. Unlike the national governments that jockeyed for relative advantage during previous rounds of major shifts in geopolitical conditions (such as the run-up to and during the First and Second World Wars) both Beijing and Washington face an existential constraint on the use of direct military force against each other and other major powers. Ongoing efforts made by both Beijing and Washington to strengthen their strategic nuclear deterrence are extremely likely to remain primarily defensive. Despite the ebb and flow of tensions, both governments are extremely unlikely to risk their own survival by intentionally launching a nuclear first strike, or even a large-scale conventional attack that could be misconstrued by their adversary as a nuclear first strike. While this dynamic cannot rule out minor clashes or accidental escalations, Beijing and Washington remain strongly incentivized to avoid direct, full-scale military conflict.

For these and other reasons, it is difficult, and perhaps misguided, to compare US-China rivalry with previous global struggles for dominance. Patterns that occurred previously do not necessarily apply to a novel scenario. The US, China, and humanity in general are facing an unprecedented situation.

US-China competition is a unique and vital development in human history, and it is therefore a trend that is at once difficult but also vitally important to analyze with a dispassionate, objective viewpoint. Despite its obvious importance, widespread falsehoods and fundamentally illogical analysis hinder a clear understanding of the key drivers of the bilateral relationship. These misrepresentations, misunderstandings, and in some cases, outright fabrications, exist throughout the politics, media, and popular discourse in both countries.

Government censorship in China constrains the extent to which the actions and motivations of the US government can be understood and analyzed. Some outdated notions of exceeding US preeminence also continue in Chinese society. Nearly all Chinese people have some exposure to popular US media, and many have relatives or friends who have emigrated to the US. Popular movies and television programs rarely depict poverty in the US, and Chinese migrants are unlikely to tell tales of significant hardship when they speak to family and friends. Additionally, the US remains relatively prosperous when compared to China on a per capita basis, with the rapid advance in living standards in China only occurring within the previous two decades. On the other side, many Chinese motivated by a sense of nationalism *overstate* US problems and the extent to which relative global power has shifted in favor of their national government. In state-controlled media, US policy is almost always interpreted through the lens of the perceived interests of the Chinese government. In China, public understanding and academic scholarship about Beijing's bilateral relations with Washington are warped by misperceptions and limited in scope.

At the same time, misunderstandings of China are even more pronounced in the US, despite the country's lack of official media controls. Generally, common misperceptions of the US competition with China stem from two fundamental misunderstandings. First, many in the US underestimate the current, and likely future, capabilities of the Chinese government. Simultaneously, many in the US *overestimate* the extent to which the Chinese government wants to use these capabilities to directly undermine the US. This creates a dangerously distorted narrative in which Beijing is seen as simultaneously too weak to challenge key areas of global US hegemony (it is not), and also nefariously intent on destroying US prosperity and exporting its version of authoritarian government to North American shores (it isn't). Nationalism and ideological bias lead many US citizens to overstate their government's relative capabilities and the degree to which rival governments are inherently hostile. At the same time some Americans, based on their own personal or political grievances with the Federal Government, overestimate the problems faced by Washington in its competition with Beijing.

As in China, many of the common misunderstandings within the US are a result of the rapid pace of change in relative economic power between the two countries. In 2008, China's economy, when measured in nominal terms (that is to say, not accounting for generally cheaper prices for the same goods and services in China), was smaller than Japan's, and less than one-third that of the United States. In 2024, China's nominal GDP is over four times Japan's and worth over two-thirds that of the United States. Going back further — but not actually very far at all in the grand scope of human development — nominal Chinese economic output was worth only 11% of that of the US in 1999. All adults in the United States can remember a time when the US was overwhelmingly dominant when compared to China in terms of relative global economic influence. Economic capabilities have huge implications in other fields of contention. A larger economy allows for greater military spending, and more money to invest in education and technological development. It also allows for increased leverage against third countries. Therefore, China has shifted from having roughly one-tenth or one-fifth of overall US capabilities to roughly matching — or in some key fields clearly exceeding — US dominance. This transformation occurred over a period of less than an average contemporary human generation. Such a rapid change in overall power dynamics has helped propel increased bilateral antagonism, as Washington belatedly realized the legitimacy of the threat to its overall global dominance, and Beijing was no longer able or willing to bide its time and hide its capabilities.

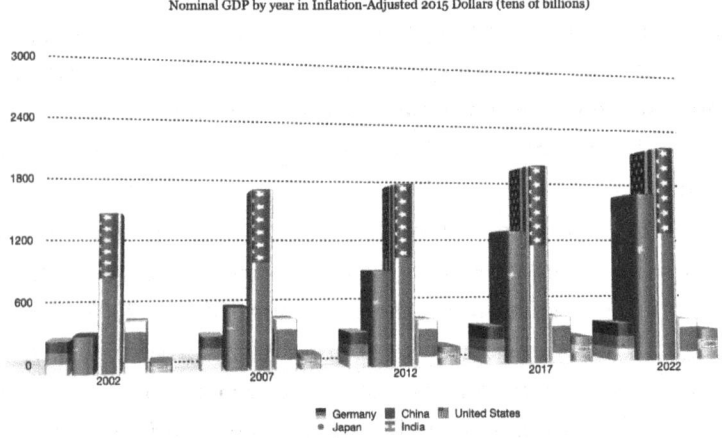

While underestimating China's economic, military, and diplomatic influence stems from a worldview grounded in outdated perceptions and chauvinistic overconfidence, overstating China's inherent threat is largely the result of institutional bias. The US Federal Government, and various interests within and parallel to US government bureaucracies, have a clear and likely long-term interest in exaggerating threats emanating from China for the purposes of increasing their funding and political influence. Playing up China's economic, military, and political threats is also a proven method for electoral grandstanding. Many mainstream media outlets are also keen to exaggerate Chinese threats for ideological or nationalistic reasons, along with their desire to attract viewers. A grounded look at Beijing's capabilities and interests, along with the abilities and goals of our own government, and the resultant interaction between the two governments, is almost entirely absent from popular discourse.

Key Drivers of National Policy

The ruling Communist Party of China (CPC) has four key goals driving its major policies. First and foremost, China's rulers want to maintain their domestic political power. The Chinese government also wants to continue economic growth, as such growth helps solidify internal stability, and also increases Beijing's global influence and leverage. Chinese leaders want to secure the integrity of Chinese territory — an imperative that often puts them at odds with various regional separatist movements and some neighboring states that have claims on the same land as Beijing itself. The CPC also wants to maintain sufficiently credible military forces to secure its trade routes, deter against an attack, maintain domestic tranquility, and pressure other governments when needed.

The essential and consistent goals of the US government are harder to define. The US political system is less monolithic than that of China, and specific policy objectives may shift from administration to administration, and within the various groups that effectively create and enact US government policy. Unlike China, where all political power is effectively monopolized or at least subsumed by the CPC, there are three main entities that effectively craft and/or execute national-level policy within the US. These systems overlap significantly in terms of the individuals who direct them, and the interests they seek to perpetuate, but key differences also exist within the groupings. A brief overview of each group and its interests is therefore necessary for understanding how they shape Washington's approach to China and the rest of the world.

First, and most obviously, are the elected politicians in the executive and legislative branches of the Federal Government. Effectively, they come from one of the two main political parties. Controlling the Presidency is the most important, especially in terms of foreign relations, but the House and Senate also play key roles in drafting policy. The main and overriding goal of these politicians and their political parties is to expand or maintain their power by winning elections. In practical terms, this is achieved by ensuring decent economic conditions for the electorate (or at any rate avoiding major catastrophes during one's term) and promoting popular domestic and foreign policy agendas. Economic growth, or at least the continuance of normal economic functions is vitally important; any administration that faces a severe economic crisis is highly likely to lose its power. Of course, the two major parties also have an interest in highlighting the failures of the rival party. While foreign policy is usually a secondary or even tertiary concern in US elections, apparently successful military campaigns can boost the reelection prospects of an incumbent administration and its party, while prolonged conflicts, especially those that result in significant US military casualties, can drastically decrease a politician's or party's electoral performance.

The second key group that creates and implements US policy is an unelected bureaucracy. Individuals serve in decision-making capabilities within the various US intelligence, diplomatic, and domestic agencies, along with the various branches of the US military. They tend to remain consistently employed from administration to administration. People within the bureaucracy may rotate positions within various Federal agencies, academia, think-tanks, internal party leadership positions, and major corporations. The professional bureaucracy tends to take a longer viewpoint in terms of advancing perceived US national interests. Bureaucrats also seek to advance their own careers, but for institutional and ideological reasons they want to expand, maintain, and perpetuate the domestic and global power of the US Federal Government. Elected politicians, based on personal, institutional, and ideological factors, also want to ensure US global dominance, but their scope for effective long-term planning and action is limited by the realities of election cycles. Most bureaucrats do not directly face such constraints.

Large corporations are the third category of key institutions effectively shaping US government policy. Corporate influence within the US political system is so pervasive and enduring that the interests of powerful corporations cannot be rationally ignored when examining the strategies and policies of the US Federal Government. Corporate lobbying strongly influences (and in many instances essentially drafts) key US legislation. Elected politicians depend on corporate campaign contributions to help them win elections. Representatives of corporate outfits receiving large contracts from the Federal Government, and industries heavily subsidized by the Federal Government, have effectively embedded themselves within most of the key organizations that collectively comprise the Federal bureaucracy. As with the other two institutional entities, many individuals shift between the corporate, bureaucratic, and elected systems of the US policymaking superstructure. However, the collective interests of corporate entities are generally the least congruent with the other decision-making entities. Simply put, all corporations naturally seek to maximize their profits.

The various entities that create and draft US government policy have essentially three overriding interests. Elected politicians — and the two political parties with an effective duopoly on national political power — want to win elections. The bureaucracy seeks to strengthen and perpetuate the influence of the US Federal Government. Corporations want to maximize profits. These various, and sometimes contradictory, motives have shaped, currently shape, and will continue to shape US policy to China.

The dynamic of contention between Washington and Beijing is driven by the fundamental incompatibility of only one of the key strategic goals of each power. The US government seeks to remain the world's most powerful nation. The Chinese government seeks to expand its global influence. While Beijing may or may not aim directly at supplanting the US in the globally preeminent position, the CPC does want to help ensure its monopoly on political power at home by growing its influence abroad. Naturally any organization, and especially national governments, seek to strengthen and expand their influence. In many key areas, the fundamental goals of the decision-making powers in the two countries are not necessarily contradictory. Power brokers in Washington are not necessarily *directly* threatened by the perpetuation of the CPC's domestic political monopoly, Chinese economic growth, or a Chinese military capable of projecting regional influence. Beijing's fundamental interests are generally not undermined by a particular US candidate or political party winning an election, US Federal Government influence (at least in most areas), or profit making by US corporations. Some key drivers of government interest overlap; Beijing and Washington benefit from overall economic growth, and both governments also have a clear interest in avoiding existentially threatening nuclear or environmental catastrophe.

Nevertheless, in one vital area — relative global power — the interests of the Chinese and US government are clearly at odds. This was not always the case; historically, the US and China have been perfectly willing to cooperate against mutual rivals or enemies, namely Japan from 1937 to 1945, and the USSR from around 1979 until the collapse of the Soviet Union. Now, though, because the US and China are the world's two most influential countries, they are clearly in competition with regards to relative global influence.

Economics, diplomacy, and military capabilities are the three main fields in which China and the US simultaneously exert and extend their global power. Competition between Beijing and Washington takes place within these arenas. All three of these levers of influence are interlinked, with strength in one aspect usually boosting capabilities in the other two.

Military power is easy to define — it is the power brought to bear on other countries through the use or potential use of conventional and nuclear armaments and the ultimate means through which a national government deters direct attacks on its territory. Major global powers generally utilize the threat, whether explicit or implicit, of military power far more often than they actually employ the weapons to directly attack other countries. This is especially true for major, nuclear-armed nations such as the US and China in their dealings with other significant global powers. Military strength helps protect territorial integrity and can help secure trade routes against potential adversaries. Military power is the most important means of overall global power *when and only when countries engage in direct military conflict.* Additionally, military power arises nearly entirely from economic and technological prowess, and in the event of a protracted war, it must be sustained by domestic productive capabilities.

Economic power comes from national capabilities in production, technology, trade, and finance. Influential governments can use their economic heft to boost their diplomatic and military power. Trade ties with other countries help create bonds of common interest and generally disincentivize direct conflict. Possession of a strong, enticing, and growing domestic economy also provides national governments with leverage in terms of setting the rules for investment from abroad. Whether in terms of trade or investment, national governments use access to domestic markets as a bargaining chip. Meanwhile, outbound investment spreads a country's power and influence without resorting to costly and dangerous military adventurism.

Diplomatic power is the influence that national governments have over other countries. It takes many forms, including formal treaties, the perception of common interests between national governments, domestic political lobbying, informal ties between leaders, and the ability to shape public opinion. Diplomacy is usually a mix of cooperation, quid-pro-quo dealmaking, and coercion. Of the three main avenues of international power, it is the most difficult to quantify. Skeptics may argue that diplomatic power is only useful to the degree that it can be used to enhance a government's military and economic capabilities. Similarly, some may argue that diplomatic power is largely a *result* of economic and military might. Nevertheless, there are real-world political diplomatic influences apparently parallel to, though outside, the realms of pure military and economic power.

The Present Dynamic

Washington and Beijing are the world's two most influential global powers, and they are therefore positioned in a dynamic of overall strategic confrontation. Two key events have made this reality obvious in recent decades. First was the collapse of the Soviet Union, a common foe of both the PRC and the US.

Introduction

Prior to its collapse, the Soviet Union was widely regarded as the world's second most influential global power. China, though developing rapidly, was still poor by global standards when the USSR dissolved, and in no position to directly challenge US global preeminence.

In the 1990s many people naively believed that Washington would never again face a credible rival for overall global leadership. This faith was based in part on the (largely correct) observation that the US was far ahead of other national governments in terms of its military, economic, and diplomatic influence. Many also believed the US-centric system of capitalism, democracy, and generally unrestricted international trade was so obviously superior that Washington would never again face a credible competitor with an alternative domestic system. They assumed any potential competitor would, of course, need to adopt US-inspired systems in order to grow its power, and the adoption of such systems would naturally mean that common ideological frameworks would smooth out, or even completely prevent, any major apparent divergence in national interests. With regards to foreign policy, the US government spent most of the 1990s in a sense of self-satisfied hubris.

The 9/11 attacks undermined, but did not destroy, official US complacency. Nevertheless, Washington's global reaction to the attacks set the stage for a sustained and rapid erosion of relative US power in comparison with China. Instead of focusing on the perpetuation of its dominance against an ever-increasingly obvious great power rival, Washington expended significant military, financial, and political capital in costly "War on Terror" conflicts, most notably in Afghanistan and Iraq. Many US actions during the course of the post-9/11 conflicts, including increased cooperation with several authoritarian Middle Eastern governments, significant civilian casualties, and the torture of detainees, undermined Washington's international prestige. Meanwhile, Beijing was largely following a doctrine of "biding time and hiding capabilities." Except for a brief show of force in the Taiwan Strait during Taiwanese elections in 1996, since 1979 Beijing had been notably quiet with regards to openly threatening interstate conflict. The Chinese government has instead focused nearly exclusively on improving infrastructure, attracting foreign investment, expanding trade ties, and otherwise improving its domestic economy.

In addition to the collapse of the Soviet Union, the other major event illustrating the dynamic of increased Sino-US global competition was the 2008-2009 Global Financial Crisis. In 2007, the nominal GDP of the United States was almost exactly four times larger than that of China. However, China, which still had so much low-hanging economic fruit and was less exposed to complicated and risky financial shenanigans, emerged from the crisis almost entirely unscathed. In 2009, China overtook Japan as the world's second largest economy in terms of nominal GDP. In 2012 China surpassed the US in terms of having the world's largest volume of international goods trade. In 2016, China overtook the US in terms of price adjusted, purchasing power parity GDP. Because of the crucial importance of economic power in determining overall global influence, each year that Chinese economic growth exceeded that of the US was another year in which the overall relative power shifted in Beijing's favor.

This unprecedentedly rapid shift in relative global economic power caught the US political elite largely unawares. Washington had been distracted by its unending conflicts in the greater Middle East and its lingering contention with Moscow on the fringes of the former USSR. Some US policymakers also apparently internalized their own system-justifying propaganda, and based their approach to China on two psychologically reassuring fallacies. The first was that an increasingly prosperous and globally integrated China would naturally become more democratic. The second was that an autocratic government could not maintain rapid economic growth over multiple decades, and that a massive economic correction, or even collapse, in a stubbornly authoritarian China was inevitable. Incidentally, a third fallacy — that a democratic China would be less nationalistic and more inclined to accede to US global influence — also underpins the current US approach to China, though circumstances have not disproven it yet.

From around 2011, the US government began implementing policies out of an increasing awareness and fear of expanding Chinese power. Washington has sought to strengthen its system of military alliances and expanded its military footprint in the West Pacific. The Obama Administration announced a "Pivot to Asia" aimed at systematically deploying "a substantially increased investment — diplomatic, economic, strategic, and otherwise — in the Asia-Pacific region." Although US officials claimed their aim was not to counter growing Chinese power, the effort was clearly a reaction to Beijing's expanding influence. The Obama Administration also launched regular naval patrols within areas of the South China Sea claimed by Beijing. US officials said such patrols are merely aimed at establishing freedom of navigation under international law. However, given the fact that the US did not regularly conduct and publicly broadcast such exercises in the South China Sea during previous administrations, such efforts clearly have an element of power projection in response to increasing Chinese military capabilities and deployments.

The US government has also sought to undermine, or at least somewhat disrupt, China's growing global economic influence and technological capabilities. Policies within this framework have included tariffs on Chinese imports introduced under the Trump Administration, along with various unilateral US sanctions against Chinese tech companies, most notably ZTE and Huawei. Washington has blocked specified Chinese companies from acquiring US technology, limited Chinese investment in key sectors within the US, and even put restrictions on the subjects that Chinese nationals can study at postgraduate levels in US universities.

Meanwhile, the Chinese government has also shifted its policy approach in recent years, both domestically and in the international sphere. After Xi Jinping assumed power as General Secretary of the CPC in 2012, he boosted his overall popularity within Chinese society and solidified his control within the Party through an intense crackdown on corrupt officials and government waste. Under Xi, the Chinese government also reversed a trend which had prevailed since around the late 1990s of moving extremely slowly towards marginal political liberalization. Instead, Xi's administration has moved — slowly — toward *decreased* liberalism and increased government control over media, culture, society, and some areas of the economy.

The trend towards greater centralized control under Xi Jinping has been especially pronounced in China's outlying areas. Chinese officials responded to the 2019-2020 protest movement in Hong Kong by effectively curtailing some of the territory's political autonomy and reducing the range of acceptable political activity to stymie "anti-national" elements. In the far northwest region of Xinjiang, authorities responded to ethnic separatist agitation and bouts of violence with mass surveillance and widespread preventative detention aimed at "reeducating" potentially subversive individuals. From around 2017, officials in Xinjiang detained hundreds of thousands of individuals (nearly all of whom were members of predominantly Muslim ethnic groups) possessing certain characteristics and actions deemed to indicate potential militancy — such as overt religiosity, unemployment, and ties to people living abroad. These moves have provided the US and some of its closer allies with stronger political justification for confronting an increasingly powerful, and apparently increasingly autocratic, Chinese government. They have also undermined one of the key assumptions of Washington's former approach to China — that increasingly close global economic interconnections would inevitably lead to political liberalization.

Beijing has also been more assertive on the international stage under Xi Jinping. China has expanded its investments in infrastructure in other countries, especially under the One Belt One Road initiative launched in 2013. Various branches of the People's Liberation Army (PLA) have increased their presence and patrols in the South China Sea and near Taiwan.

While some observers believe that the PRC's increased assertiveness on the global stage is due to a new approach driven specifically by the personality Xi Jinping, it is more likely that the changing position of China itself on the international stage is prompting Beijing's increased assertiveness. Simply put, the Chinese government under Xi Jinping is more intentionally assertive because its growing economic power gives Beijing the capabilities and confidence to act assertively. Recent Chinese shifts in Chinese government policies are broadly consistent with a shift of power in its favor. Some Chinese officials have directly stated this perception — during a heated public exchange with US counterparts in 2021, Yang Jiechi, a top-ranking Chinese diplomat, responded to perceived US criticism by saying, "the United States does not have the qualification to say that it wants to speak to China from a position of strength."

US officials have openly called on other countries to shun, or at least reduce, technological and economic engagement with China. In late 2021, Commerce Secretary Gina Raimondo stated, "If we really want to slow down China's rate of innovation, we need to work with Europe." Previously, President Biden said, "China has an overall goal ... to become the leading country in the world, the wealthiest country in the world, and the most powerful country in the world.... That's not going to happen on my watch because the United States is going to continue to grow." However, maintaining US global preeminence simply through growing overall US power is extremely unrealistic, given its relatively smaller population, engrained political deadlock, and the fact that, barring technological miracles that could somehow be monopolized within the US, its period of rapid economic growth is almost certainty over. Realistically, perpetuation of total US dominance over a country with four times its population and apparently easier avenues for sustained economic growth almost certainty entails somehow holding China back from its natural potential.

The institutions that effectively create and implement US policy are constrained in their approach to rising Chinese power. The professional bureaucracy, with its ability to engage in longer-term strategic thinking, is the keenest on ensuring US global dominance by constraining Chinese influence. For personal and ideological reasons, various elected administrations also generally share that same goal. However, since China is so integrated into the global economic system, and since Beijing itself has a significant degree of economic leverage it could use against Washington, no elected US government is willing to implement policies — such as universal restrictions on US trade and investment with China — that could forcibly curtail China's economic growth. Such policies would almost invariably result in a severe and prolonged economic crisis within the United States. Additionally, essentially all major US corporations have a clear interest in keeping profitable trade and financial ties between the US, China, and various third countries. Despite the escalated rhetoric on both sides, these contradictions create and will likely ensure the trend of a limited contention between the US and Chinese governments.

There are key aspects of the US government's goals and policies regarding China that are vital to the US, China, and the broader world, which are effectively taboo in popular and political discourse. Should the US try to perpetually maintain a larger nominal GDP than China? Does Washington need to deploy additional military assets in the West Pacific to contain Chinese conventional military capabilities? Should the US undermine China's relations with third countries? Should, and can, the US perpetuate its global dominance by undermining the CPC's political monopoly? If these are to be US goals, how can they be achieved? If such efforts succeed, what are the likely unintended consequences? Are they reasonable, and worth the likely costs? How is Beijing likely to respond to perceived US efforts to constrain its potential? What are the common interests of Beijing and Washington? Can the two powers cooperate in some fields while maintaining competition in others? Should the national governments of China and the US agree to voluntarily limit their weapons systems in order to reduce the likelihood of accidental nuclear exchange? There is a dangerous lack of dispassionate analysis examining these questions, especially considering the fact that any major miscalculation on these fronts could significantly increase the probability of global economic collapse, environmental catastrophe, or nuclear warfare.

Section One

Myths

To successfully analyze the current trends and likely outcomes of US-China contention, it is first necessary to dispel common misconceptions that hinder US understanding of its relative position compared to China. These misconceptions can broadly be categorized into the three key areas of bilateral competition, namely the Economic, Military, and Diplomatic spheres. Because of the centrality of economic trends in driving US-China rivalry, it will be useful to first examine US misconceptions about China's economy.

Fallacy Number One
China Is Poor

Many people in the US believe the majority of the Chinese population is poor. The perception of underfed Chinese factory workers earning five cents an hour permeates national discourse. While China is, on a per capita average, significantly less materially prosperous than the US, Western Europe, or Japan, it is no longer an especially poor country. Instead, China is almost exactly in the middle in terms of average global material prosperity. Yet common perceptions of widespread Chinese poverty persist.

The roots of this fallacy are quite understandable — up until quite recently, China *was* poor. China's recent relative poverty was a historical aberration. While comparative economic history prior to the early 1800s is difficult, China, with its massive population, a relatively effective government, and a historic advantage in technology, likely had the world's greatest national economic output during most periods from ancient times to the early Industrial Revolution. Even in terms of per capita output, China did not start falling behind Western Europe until around the late 1700s. However, as the Industrial Revolution swept Europe, the United States, and then Japan, the leaders of the Qing Dynasty were blinded by China's long and illustrious history of relative cultural and political dominance. Chinese leaders did not embrace the new opportunities presented by industrial technology until they were in a far inferior position to relative upstarts.

The following paragraphs attempt to briefly outline the main reasons for China's poverty and instability prior to around 1980. Historical context is needed to provide broad explanations of general economic conditions. The key point to remember is that

China has only recently emerged from a long period of poverty brought about largely by misguided government policy and a period of prolonged warfare.

Much of China's relative economic decline on the international stage from around the 1700s was due to the policy of *haijin* — literally, "Ocean Ban." *Haijin* effectively prohibited most oceanic trade from around 1500 until the 1680s. Before *haijin*, China had the world's largest and most sophisticated ocean-going vessels. Massive Chinese fleets engaged in trade and military shows of force in the Western Pacific and the Indian Ocean as far as modern-day Mozambique. However, China's rulers effectively ceded the Age of Exploration to Western European powers through the purposeful restrictions in long-distance ocean trade under *haijin*. The trading ban was aimed mostly at cutting off pirates and Taiwan-based rebels, though internal court politics also likely played a role. China turned inward and remained primarily agricultural, missing out on the rapid increases in productivity and technological development brought about first through transcontinental trade, and then through the Industrial Revolution.

A lack of modern weaponry resulting from its technological and industrial backwardness was a primary factor that caused the Qing Empire to lose a series of embarrassing conflicts against newly industrial rivals. Chinese armies lost conflicts to Britain (1839–1842 and 1856–1860), France (1884–1885), Japan (1894–1895), and Russia (1900). Further compounding China's relative economic and political decline was a string of major civil wars, including the Taiping Rebellion, which killed up to 30 million people from 1850–1865. Concurrent uprisings by various groups in northwest and southwest China killed over a million more.

Britain, France, Germany, Russia, and Japan forced a weakened and divided Qing Empire to sign a series of "unequal treaties," granting the countries free access to ports and exempting their citizens from prosecution under Chinese law. The Qing Dynasty lost its control over the foreign affairs of vassal kingdoms in Vietnam and Korea, and also direct control over some of its internal territory. Beijing was forced to give up Hong Kong to Britain in 1842. Japan defeated China in the First Sino-Japanese War, forcing the Chinese government to give up control of Taiwan in 1895. Elements of the Qing government supported the nationalistic Boxer Rebellion (1899–1901), which sought to drive out the foreign imperialists (and killed many Christian Chinese converts). Growing resentment by the majority Han population against the Manchu-led Qing hindered the war efforts. Many governors in eastern and central China refused to aid the central authorities and fight foreign forces during the Boxer Rebellion. The conflict ended with an Eight Nation Alliance of Britain, France, the US, Germany, Japan, Italy, Russia, and Austria-Hungary dictating terms of peace after their armies seized Beijing and looted ancient artifacts.

Overthrow of the Qing in 1911 did not solve China's economic backwardness and political turmoil. The new Republic of China (ROC) could not effectively control much of the country's territory. Warlords set up their own enclaves in multiple provinces. Reformers founded the Nationalist Party, or Kuomintang (KMT), in 1919 with the aim of effectively unifying the country and driving out imperialist forces. The Communist Party of China (CPC), founded in 1921, also sought unity and freedom from foreign domination, but its cadres blamed China's weakness primarily on feudalism and outdated cultural norms. In 1926 the KMT and CPC, with their power bases in the south, cooperated against warlords during a successful military campaign known as the Northern Expedition. However, KMT leader Chiang Kai-shek betrayed his former Communist allies in 1927, initiating the Shanghai Massacre and driving the Communists into an underground and primarily rural insurgency.

Japan, recently industrialized and hungry for additional territory and markets, took advantage of the deepening chaos and seized northeast China's Manchuria in 1931. Guerrillas, aided by patriotic forces, resisted the Japanese occupation and its puppet state. However, Chiang Kai-shek preferred to use most of his limited military resources to fight the CPC rebels instead of the foreign enemies. Chiang famously explained his choice by saying, *"the Japanese are a disease of the skin; the Communists are a disease of the heart."* The civil war between the Nationalists and Communists continued until 1936, when Chiang was kidnapped by a former warlord's son, who forced Chiang to sign an agreement to form a united front with the CPC against Japanese incursions.

In 1937, Japan reacted to this Second United Front by launching a full-scale invasion of the main population centers of eastern China. Despite the obvious mutual threat, the alliance between the KMT and CPC remained tenuous, and was often broken. Around 15 million Chinese died in the War of Resistance Against Japan. Chinese forces fought Japan in a full-scale conventional and guerrilla conflict for over eight years; during four of those years, China resisted alone, barring some foreign (primarily Soviet) support. After making rapid gains over the first year of the war — seizing Beijing, Shanghai, Nanjing, and most other major cities — Japanese forces were bogged down by Chinese resistance along largely static fronts that lasted for most of the conflict. US entry in the war in 1941 quickly changed the overall trajectory of the wider conflict in East Asia.

Soon after Japan's defeat in 1945, the CPC and KMT forces resumed armed hostilities. Roughly four million more Chinese died during the fighting. The KMT, plagued by corruption, inflation, and a lack of sense of purpose, lost the war. The remnants of the ROC government fled to Taiwan in 1949, while the CPC took Beijing and declared the new People's Republic of China (PRC).

Mao Zedong won control of a country that had been devastated by a series of deadly conflicts which had killed tens of millions of people and displaced countless others over the previous hundred years. The PRC was a government that, for the first time in decades, effectively united Chinese territory under one administration — with the exception, from their perspective, of Taiwan, Hong Kong, and Macao. The CPC sought to improve the country's economic conditions through central planning. These methods led to some achievements in terms of advancing basic literacy and industrialization. Soviet support helped greatly, although there were enormous inefficiencies arising from the command economy. Government spending on military efforts during the Korean War (1950–1953) put a further strain on resources.

A series of historically unprecedented mistakes in basic governance soon obliterated most of the fragile social and economic improvements following the founding of the PRC. Mao Zedong was a savvy and flexible guerrilla leader. From the Northern Expedition through both phases of the Chinese Civil War and the War of Resistance Against Japan, Mao had shifted alliances when necessary and maintained ties with disparate groups to advance the practical interests of the CPC (and of course his own position at its head). However, as a ruler he was tragically ideological, placing far too much trust in Stalinist interpretations of Marxist theory and refusing to change course until far too late.

Stalin died in 1953. In 1956, Soviet leaders officially condemned Stalin's cult of personality, his violent and often irrational crackdown on other Communists, and other excesses of his rule. Mao strongly disagreed with this new appraisal from Moscow, and he accused the new rulers of his most important ally and China's vital technological and economic lifeline as "revisionists." The alliance between China and the Soviet Union began to strain, and then break.

Then things got worse. In 1958 Mao initiated the "Great Leap Forward," an effort to rapidly industrialize the country by directly harnessing China's massive labor force. The goal of this movement was to "catch up" to the level of industrial output of the United Kingdom, a geopolitical adversary and major economic power at the time. Specifically, Mao sought for China's steel production to surpass that of the UK by the early 1970s. The chosen methods for achieving this ambitious goal were based nearly entirely on the CPC's ideological vision. Mao relied primarily on top-down mass mobilization, believing that China's enormous population and enlightened leadership would allow the country to leap past normal stages of industrial development.

Authorities forced peasants into massive collectives and effectively outlawed private farming. Rural farmers could only eat surpluses from what they grew after officials appropriated significant portions of their harvests to feed the swelling urban population of industrial workers. Under Mao's orders, CPC cadres launched a movement to facilitate the mass killing of sparrows, which were condemned as parasitical grain-eating pests. However, sparrows also eat insects, and soon growing swarms of locusts were gorging themselves on Chinese grain. Officials, facing the pressure of quotas from Beijing, forced peasants to make steel in agricultural areas. During the Great Leap Forward, authorities established roughly 600,000 "backyard furnaces" in rural communities that were meant to function as small-scale steel plants. Laborers amassed various sources of raw iron, including dining utensils, cookware, and family heirlooms, and melted them down in an effort to produce more "steel." Wanton deforestation supplied wood to keep the flames burning. Such furnaces made a product that was inferior to actual steel, and was practically worthless for any actual industrial purposes.

While the human tragedies of the Great Leap Forward are almost entirely because of impractical policies, natural disasters further contributed to the misery of the era. Relatively little rain fell in much of China's agricultural heartland in 1958 and 1959. When the rains finally came, there were not enough trees to soak up the water in many hilly and mountainous regions, and the resulting floods killed hundreds of thousands. Between twenty and fifty million Chinese people died, primarily from starvation and disease, during the Great Leap Forward, and China's economy significantly contracted during the three-year campaign. The disaster was sufficiently disruptive as to convince the government to end the project, and Mao lost some authority within the Party in its aftermath. Relative economic moderates began to consolidate increasing influence within the CPC. Officials relaxed some collectivization programs, and introduced more practical economic measures. Mao even stepped down as State Chairman, although he remained leader of the Communist Party of China.

Mao's period of reduced political responsibilities and quiet introspection was tragically short-lived. In his mind, the failures of the Great Leap Forward were not due to his own unrealistic economic goals and methods, but rather on the sabotage of hidden counterrevolutionary elements, and China's "backwards" culture. To rectify these perceived problems — and to solidify his internal power — Mao launched the "Cultural Revolution" in the mid-1960s. During the Cultural Revolution, Mao again relied on mass mobilization of the Chinese population. Common people were encouraged to violently struggle against "rightist elements" and "capitalist roaders." Mao said the masses must destroy the "Four Olds" — Old Ideas, Old Customs, Old Habits, and Old Culture — and replace them with New Ideas, New Customs, New Habits, and New Culture. Mao strengthened his cult of personality through the study of Mao Zedong Thought, specifically the quotations in Mao's *Little Red Book*.

Volunteer "Red Guard" brigades carried out Mao's orders. Youth formed armed groups to "uncover" the backward political and social elements in society and destroy the old traditions that Mao believed were hindering China's progress. Gangs of teenagers, wielding Chairman Mao's *Little Red Book*, and improvised weapons, beat up and sometimes killed their teachers for perceived "counterrevolutionary" deeds, words, or thoughts. Relatively prosperous farmers were denounced by their neighbors and publicly murdered. Teenagers formed groups to go out to the countryside and smash the tombstones of their ancestors. Red Guards defaced or burned numerous artifacts (some hundreds or even thousands of years old). In some areas Christian priests were killed, Buddhist monks were forced to eat meat, and Mosques were converted to pigsties.

Ubiquitous paranoia and violence during the Cultural Revolution nearly ruptured the fabric of Chinese society. Children denounced their parents; different factions of Red Guards vied for revolutionary purity, and fought running gun battles in the streets of major cities. In several instances the People's Liberation Army had to deploy to suppress sustained gun battles between Red Guard factions in major urban centers. Dozens of top Communist party leaders, who had dared to criticize Mao's policies, were publicly humiliated, tortured, and exiled to remote provinces. Many resorted to suicide rather than face sham trials and horrific physical and psychological abuse. The government sent seventeen million "intellectual urban youth" "up to the mountains and down to the farms" to live as peasants in poor rural communities. Colleges and universities admitted no new students during the most intense years of turmoil. University education effectively ceased for nearly a decade, and even education at lower levels suffered due to instability and social breakdown.

The terror of the Cultural Revolution only came to a complete end following Mao Zedong's death in 1976. After a brief internal struggle, Mao loyalists were thrown out of power and replaced with more practical voices, led by Deng Xiaoping. Deng enacted a series of market reforms, which created the environment needed for China's massive economic growth starting in the early 1980s. Unlike Mao, Deng was flexible with regards to domestic policy. Once, when another senior CPC leader criticized Deng in an internal Party meeting by saying his policies were straying from the path of socialism, Deng famously replied, "It doesn't matter if a cat is white or black, a cat that catches mice is a good cat." The message was clear — while the Communist Party of China would maintain its name and monopoly on political power, its leadership was willing to implement policies centered on practical results, as opposed to ideological purity.

The motivations for Deng's reforms were clear. China was among the poorest countries in the world when he took power. According to World Bank figures, in 1980, China's per capita GDP was about $195 measured in 2020 US dollars. This was less than half the per person economic output of the Democratic Republic of the Congo in the same year. Even in terms of total nominal GDP, China, despite its massive population, had lower national economic output than Italy, Brazil, and Canada in 1980. The country, facing widespread and severe poverty, along with significant strategic contention with the Soviet Union, needed to improve its material standing. Luckily for China's rulers, clear examples of far more successful economies were in the periphery of the People's Republic of China. In 1980, Japan's per capita nominal GDP (again, measured in 2020 USD) was about $9500, Hong Kong's $5700, and South Korea's $1800.

The economies of Japan, Taiwan, and South Korea had significant elements of central government planning, but corporations and individuals operating with self-interested profit motives guided the majority of economic activity. Beijing's prosperous East Asian neighbors had based their growth in large part on export-oriented industrial development, with the United States — which Beijing had established official relations with in 1979 — serving as the main export market. Furthermore, South Korea and Taiwan were, at the time, effectively one-party autocracies, and Japan, while democratic, was also in practice ruled by one party. Deng saw clear models for how the CPC could maintain power while gradually opening up the economic system. Indeed, improving the people's livelihood would help ensure social and political stability after over a hundred years of upheaval.

Among the first policies that Deng enacted was allowing markets to function in the agricultural sector. It was relatively low-hanging fruit, given the gross inefficiencies which had defined the system previously, and the results were nearly immediate. Farmers, incentivized to increase their yields through personal economic interest, rapidly increased production.

Another key area that Deng opened up was foreign investment. China clearly had massive potential for industrial development with a huge population of industrious and literate workers, and an apparently stable and rationally self-interested political system. Many major investors outside mainland China had political misgivings, but if the CPC would not suddenly appropriate assets or collapse into anarchy, the potential rewards on investment were enormous. The overall political situation seemed sufficiently stable to many investors, especially ethnic Chinese in nearby territories. In 1979 the Chinese government established four Special Economic Zones (SEZ) in which foreign — and from Beijing's perspective, not-quite-foreign — investors could take advantage of China's massive and, at the time, ridiculously cheap labor force.

The first SEZs were strategically located in areas along China's southern coast — Xiamen, Shantou, Zhuhai, and Shenzhen. Xiamen, a colonial-era port located about six miles west of the ROC-controlled island of Kinmen, was ideally located, both physically and culturally, to attract investment from Taiwan. Most inhabitants of Taiwan and Xiamen spoke a variety of Minnan, a regional language, at home. Shantou, further down the southeastern coast, is situated in the ancestral region of many ethnic Chinese in Thailand, Malaysia, Indonesia, and Singapore. Zhuhai is adjacent to Macau, which at the time was a Portuguese-administered territory on the western edge of the mouth of the Pearl River. Finally, Shenzhen was a sleepy fishing village of some 30,000 inhabitants on the eastern edge of the Pearl River directly north of Hong Kong. While the SEZs helped open up China to the world, much of the crucial first investments came from Taiwanese, Hong Kongers, and ethnic Chinese residing in Southeast Asia — people who had clear cultural, linguistic, familial, and in many cases personal ties with the mainland, and who, indeed, the Chinese government did not consider "foreign."

Government investment in transport infrastructure also contributed to China's rapid economic growth from the early 1980s. Transportation is an area in which the PRC's top-down, centralized political monopoly can benefit efficiency and long-term planning. While there are occasionally competing interests between various city, county, and provincial governments, centralized CPC control means that such differences are usually smoothed out quickly. Once policy decisions have been made, they are not slowed or hindered by the various interests of specific interests or lobbies. While this dynamic was disastrous during the Great Leap Forward, in terms of providing basic transport infrastructure this system has obvious advantages. Between 1990 and 2020, 32 new subway systems began operating in Chinese cities. China first began operating high-speed rail systems in 2007; by 2020 the country had more miles of operational high-speed rail lines than all other countries in the world combined. Since 1980 China has opened dozens of new commercial airports and built tens of thousands of miles of new highways. State-owned enterprises (SOEs) have primarily been responsible for this construction spree. While the government has curbed the power of SOEs in many industries, they remain vital in critical strategic sectors, such as transport infrastructure.

Since the market reforms of the early 1980s, significant foreign investment, growing international trade, adequate education, improving transport infrastructure, and relative political stability have contributed to a mutually beneficial economic environment, with each major factor aiding the others. In the past several decades, there has been one major shock that threatened this system, and therefore the CPC's political monopoly. From 1988 to 1989, China experienced a relatively short-lived economic crisis. Consumer prices increased around 25% within a year, sparking panic-buying in many areas. The resultant social unease caused many blue-collar workers to join student protesters who were demanding free speech, competitive elections, and other political reforms. The showdown between protesters and police in and around Beijing's Tiananmen Square ended in a military crackdown on entrenched protesters. The initial causes of the protest campaign were essentially political, but the movement only came close to actually overthrowing the CPC's political monopoly because of economic hardship. Protests, and in places riots, did not only occur in Beijing, but also in several other major cities. Beijing's strategy of increasing material well-being while maintaining strict control of assembly, media, and force, has remained essentially constant since 1989.

China's ascension to the World Trade Organization (WTO) in 2001 further accelerated the country's economic engagement with the rest of the world and its related development. Now, China is not only a source of labor, but also a key market for a variety of international companies. Indeed, the initial advantage of cheap labor that initially brought much investment to China has largely dissipated as increased opportunities have led to higher wages. Many labor-intensive, relatively low-skilled industries are shifting out of China to areas with lower costs of labor, such as Vietnam, Cambodia, and Bangladesh. Despite this trend, China maintains some crucial manufacturing advantages in terms of transport infrastructure, education, reliable utility systems, industrial concentration, and, in many cases, access to the Chinese consumer market. Despite competition from countries where labor is less expensive, China remains an industrial powerhouse.

China currently is, when compared to a global average, almost exactly in the middle in terms of economic output per person. In 2022, China's per capita nominal GDP was about $12,720 USD, ever so-slightly above the global average of $12,690. For comparison, per capita nominal GDP was about $73,320 in the US, $34,000 in Japan, and $2410 in India. Even when accounting for inflation, average per capita economic output in China in 2022 was over 24 *times* higher than it was in 1980.

Given China's huge population, its middling per capita output means the country has a massive economy. In 2000, nominal US economic output was about 8.7 times larger than China's; in 2010, it was about 2.4 times larger, in 2015 1.6 times larger, and 1.3 times larger in 2020. For comparison, the US economy was about twice as large as Japan's in 2000, and four times larger than Japan's in 2015. In nominal terms, US GDP was over 20 times larger than India's in 2000, and over seven times larger in 2019.

Keep in mind, the preceding GDP figures are in nominal units, which do not account for the disparity in prices between different countries. On average, roughly equivalent goods and services are significantly cheaper in China than in the US, Western Europe, and Japan. At the same time, prices of most goods and services in China are generally higher than they are in India or most of Africa. As an overall rule, items and labor are more expensive in richer countries. Economists use power parity (PPP) to account for these differences, giving the same nominal unit of currency higher "value" in countries where prices are lower. Three dollars might not buy much food in a restaurant in New York, but it might provide a decent meal in Nanjing, a delectable feast in Kolkata, and a week's worth of groceries in Malawi. Nominal GDP is best at measuring the relative financial power of countries, while PPP GDP is better at comparing the physical economy. Per capita PPP GDP is the best of the various imperfect methods for comparing the relative standards of living for populations in different countries.

China overtook the US in terms of PPP GDP in 2016. This means China has an overall greater productive capacity than the US. It can (and does) generate more electricity, extract more minerals, produce more manufactured goods, and grow more food (or at least more valuable food) than the US. Given the fact that China has over four times the population and labor force of the United States, this shouldn't come as too much of a shock, though, comparatively, average productivity remains significantly higher in the US than in China. GDP can simply be thought of as the product of a country's labor force multiplied by its overall productivity. Once China overcame its hundreds of years of instability, technological inadequacy, and mismanagement, its reemergence as the preeminent global economy was almost inevitable. Although this subject is out of the scope of the current chapter, a similar transformation has apparently begun in India and will likely continue over the coming decades.

PPP GDP in Constant 2017 Dollars (tens of billions)

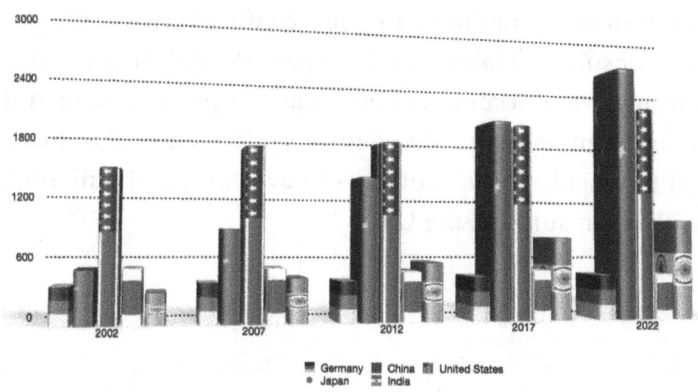

Regardless of whether it is measured in nominal or PPP terms, China's large, and growing, economic influence is the key factor driving increased competition between Beijing and Washington. China's expanding economy means the Chinese government has more money to spend on military capabilities, diplomacy, foreign loans, education, and technological development. Relative economic might has been the key lynchpin of US global dominance following World War Two. China's economic growth has undermined, and continues to undermine, this relative global dominance. Now, a rapid increase in spending power makes China an indispensable export market for a variety of countries, providing Beijing with an increasingly effective source of leverage over foreign corporations and governments. Every year that China's economic growth outpaces that of the US is another year in which the overall balance of relative global power shifts from Beijing to Washington. The fact that this development has occurred so rapidly in recent years means that both China and the US, along with other concerned powers, consistently underestimate Beijing's capabilities when compared to Washington.

There are, of course, other key levers of international prestige and influence, such as military capabilities. However, nuclear weapons and intercontinental ballistic missiles have largely rendered direct, intentional military conflict between the great powers obsolete. Unless an unexpected, and likely utterly disastrous, event occurs, raw economic output will remain the most important measure of a country's relative global influence, and in this field, China continues to overtake, and will almost certainly soon surpass, the US.

Fallacy Number Two

Chinese Economic Statistics Are Wildly Inaccurate

A degree of skepticism towards official economic statistics from China is perfectly reasonable. Economic growth has been the key lynchpin underlying China's recent decades of relative political stability and expanding international influence. The Chinese government imposes significant controls over the flow of information. Indeed, China's top leadership is itself sometimes somewhat doubtful of economic figures reported by local and provincial authorities. When calculating national GDP growth, the central government's estimates tend to be slightly lower than the average reported figures from various provinces, provincial-level municipalities, and ethnic autonomous regions. The CPC assesses the job performance of municipal, county, and provincial officials primarily through quantifiable indicators, such as crime rates, pollution readings, the recorded frequency of large-scale protests or other mass disturbances, public health outcomes, student performance, and, especially, economic growth. Officials have a clear motive to exaggerate economic performance, on the local, provincial, and national levels.

While some skepticism is entirely rational, there are nevertheless publicly available figures from a variety of apparently neutral sources that generally corroborate China's reported economic growth in recent years and decades. It is therefore illogical to assume that China's reported national economic statistics are *wildly* inaccurate — say, by a degree of over 10% or so. Despite the existence of significant evidence to the contrary, many public figures, including some key policymakers in the US, have essentially deluded themselves into believing that China's rapid economic development in recent decades is an illusion or fabrication. They assume that the relative weakening of Washington's global economic influence is merely a mirage conjured by an authoritarian competitor. This belief is essentially a psychological coping mechanism that provides mental comfort to politicians and others who would prefer China's economic growth, and related increase in international power, to be untrue. However, psychological defenses do not necessarily correlate with objective reality. Again: a degree of skepticism of official economic figures from China is absolutely logical, but the fairly widespread belief in *enormously* exaggerated figures is not.

China's rapid reported economic growth could only be mostly the result of deliberate fabrication if the CPC has successfully co-opted the Ford Motor Company, Toyota, the Australian Department of Foreign Affairs and Trade, and immigration officials in the United Kingdom in a nefarious conspiracy of global deception. Statistics from these various organizations, which are presumably not operating at the behest of top-ranking cadres in Beijing, generally support figures that the Chinese government presents regarding overall economic growth in the country. It is therefore logical to assume that, from a macro perspective, national GDP growth statistics from China generally conform to objective reality, although undoubtedly some inaccuracies, including possibly intentionally incorrect, politically driven exaggerations, likely exist at some level.

According to World Bank figures, China's overall nominal GDP grew from $2.77 trillion in 2000, to $4.42 trillion in 2005, $7.55 trillion in 2010, $11 trillion in 2015, and $14.62 trillion in 2020. These figures are measured in 2015 US dollar equivalences, so monetary inflation is already factored into the statistics. In other words, China's reported economic output in 2020 was about five times larger than it was in 2000, *even after accounting for inflation*. Annually, China's GDP grew at a reported average of around 8% per year during this period. This notably rapid rate of apparent growth also contributes to widespread skepticism of China's economic figures.

Nevertheless, there are numerous third-party statistics that generally correlate with the official reports. Take, for example, figures from international automakers based outside of China. Toyota reported selling about 147,000 vehicles in China in 2005, and 1,409,000 in 2019 — an over nine and a half times increase during a period in which the Chinese government reported a roughly fourfold economic expansion. In 2019, Ford vehicle sales in China were about 3.7 times higher than their 2005 annual sales numbers, while Volkswagen sales increased by over 5.7 times during the same period. On average over the first two decades of this century, most major foreign automakers reported sales in China increasing at a more rapid rate than China's overall economic expansion.

According to the UK Office for National Statistics, annual arrivals of Chinese tourists visiting the UK increased from around 186,000 in 2010 to 883,000 in 2019 — a 4.7-fold increase. During the same period, Chinese arrivals in Japan increased over 6.7-fold, from around 1.4 million to 9.6 million. China's reported 2019 GDP was about 1.8 times larger than it was in 2010. Meanwhile, Australian statistics on national exports to China increased from around 7.6 billion AUD in 2001 to 117 billion AUD in 2019. When factoring for inflation, this represents a 9.86-fold growth, over a period when China's economy expanded at a reported factor of roughly 4.7. At the same time, according to the US Census Bureau, the value of US goods exports to China increased roughly fourfold between 2001 and 2019 after accounting for monetary inflation, a rather slower pace than China's reported growth rate during the same timeframe.

To be fair, these various statistics from foreign corporations and government agencies cannot, should not be understood as direct, one-to-one indicators of total economic growth. Chinese trade with certain countries grew faster than its rate of overall economic development, while the expansion of trade with other nations was slower. Also, various policy changes, such as national governments easing controls on visas for Chinese tourists, have certainly influenced tourist arrival figures. Nevertheless, the collective existence of numerous, third-party indicators that generally align with the Chinese government's reported growth figures generally indicate that the official statistics likely generally align with objective reality. Some degree of inaccuracy is certain, but for the figures to be *wildly* off is extremely unlikely.

There are valid reasons to be skeptical of official figures from any country, but especially a massive nation governed by a largely opaque party which relies primarily on improving economic conditions to perpetuate its political monopoly. However, there is no reason to believe that various national governments and international corporations who have reported expansions in trade with and sales in China have been lying for two decades on behalf of the CPC's core interests.

Additionally, the PRC's recent record of several decades of sustained, rapid economic growth has clear historical precedent in the region. Japan's economy expanded nearly fourfold between 1960 and 1980. South Korea's inflation-adjusted GDP expanded over fivefold during the period from 1980 to 2000. Hong Kong's economy grew more than fourfold between 1975 and 1995. While mainland China's reported growth rate during its most rapid years of economic expansion has generally outstripped its earlier-developing neighbors, the overall trends are not wildly different. Also, it is important to keep in mind that mainland China in 2001 was, on average, actually somewhat poorer than Japan in 1960 and South Korea in 1980. The Chinese economy therefore had more low-hanging developmental fruit to harvest. China's growth has also likely benefited from productivity-enhancing technological advances that did not exist in previous decades.

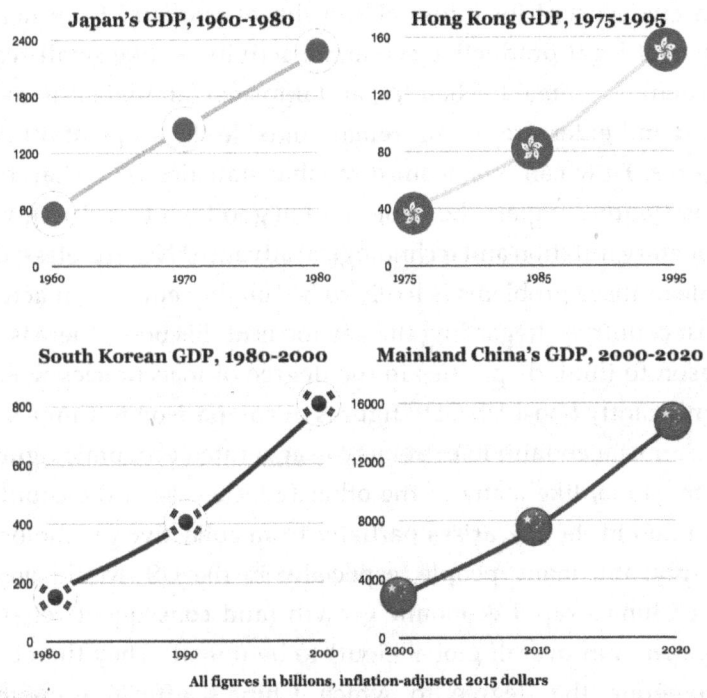

All figures in billions, inflation-adjusted 2015 dollars

Like the PRC itself, East Asian societies experienced rapid growth largely through education, infrastructure improvements, relative political stability, attracting foreign investment, and export-oriented manufacturing. Few Western commentators have cast serious doubt on the record of rapid economic growth in Japan, South Korea, or Taiwan. Only the PRC's recorded economic expansion is singled out as especially dubious. While the PRC is currently more politically opaque and authoritarian than most of its East Asian neighbors, South Korea and Taiwan also experienced rapid growth under autocratic political systems. At any rate, the Chinese government largely followed clear and factually uncontroversial regional precedents to achieve a period of rapid material development.

All national-level GDP figures have their problems, especially in large countries. GDP is difficult to calculate. How can one account for informal and illegal markets? Even many types of legal productive economic activity — like small-scale gardening, animal husbandry, and informal familiar systems of child and eldercare — will remain outside the scope of official figures. How can one acquire reliable statistics? How can one consistently compare the "true" cost of goods and services given monetary inflation and technological advance? Nevertheless, the scale of these problems is likely to be roughly equivalent across most countries. Regarding the key focus of this book, there is no reason to think disparities in the degree of inaccuracies would significantly boost US GDP figures in comparison to China's.

A mistaken faith in extremely exaggerated economic figures from China, like many of the other fallacies about the country common in the US, arises partially from collective psychology. Simply put, many people, especially in the US, would *prefer* that China's rapid economic growth (and consequent relative expansion in overall global clout) to be untrue. They therefore exaggerate the degree to which China's official economic statistics are likely to be inaccurate, and ignore reliable evidence indicating that they are probably roughly correct. These beliefs create a major blind spot for policymakers and the public at large. Self-delusion cannot change reality: China's economic influence, when compared to the US, *has* expanded rapidly. This trend is also likely to continue in the coming decades.

Fallacy Number Three

China Is Rich

China has the world's overall largest economy when measured in Purchasing Power Parity (PPP) terms. It is likely to overtake the US in nominal GDP by the end of the 2020s. The Chinese economy is dynamic and diversified; it is the largest consumer and producer of a variety of goods, including steel, televisions, books, apples, and chicken eggs. China has more miles of high-speed rail than any other country. Chinese cities have more buildings over 300 meters in height than all other countries combined. Chinese tourists and students are the key source of income for numerous hotels, shops, and schools located all around the world. However, China is not rich.

While China's total economic output is undoubtedly massive, and likely to continue to grow significantly, goods produced and services rendered in China are also effectively shared among the world's second largest national population. One must consider averages when accessing the overall economic conditions experienced by individuals in a country. As you may recall from Fallacy One: China is Poor, as of 2022 China's per capita nominal GDP was about $12,720 USD, placing it almost exactly at the global average. When accounting for PPP discrepancies, per person economic output in China was about $21,480. This places China almost exactly on par with the global human average for economic output. China is not rich.

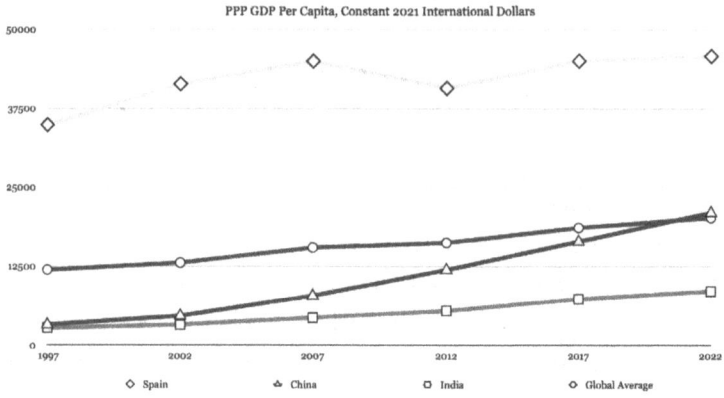

The myth of an overall wealthy China is based partially on the experiential biases of many people from outside the country. Most Chinese nationals studying, traveling, or settling abroad come from Chinese families with the highest 10% or so of income. Furthermore, most foreign nationals who visit or even work in China spend most of their time in larger and wealthier cities. There are certainly millions of Chinese regularly traveling abroad and buying luxury goods. Perhaps two hundred fifty million people in China have material consumption levels approximately comparable with the middle classes of the US, Western Europe, and Japan. However, these people are not necessarily representative of the Chinese population as a whole.

China's material prosperity varies significantly from location to location. The PRC is made up of 22 provinces, four provincial-level municipalities, five ethnic autonomous regions, and two Special Administrative Regions (SARs). The municipalities are Beijing, Shanghai, Tianjin, and Chongqing; with the exception of Chongqing (which is actually larger than some smaller provinces) the municipalities tend to be highly urbanized and have the highest per person economic output of subnational administrative units in mainland China. Of course, they are still less wealthy on average than the Hong Kong and

Macau SARs (and Taiwan, which the PRC claims but does not administer). Macau and Hong Kong are technically part of the PRC, but they have a degree of autonomy in terms of legal systems, currency, and border controls. Despite their title, the five ethnic autonomous regions don't have much effective autonomy at all. The areas, located primarily on China's frontiers, have high concentrations of non-Han ethnic minorities (with minority groups accounting collectively for around 10% of China's population). As with all of mainland China, political control in the regions is effectively monopolized by the centralized bureaucracy of the CPC, albeit with at least some ethnic minority membership and at least token concessions to minority languages and representation.

China's wealthiest and most productive provinces along the Pacific coast are on average far more prosperous than their inland counterparts. Coastal provinces like Jiangsu, Zhejiang, Fujian, and Guangdong, along with the municipalities of Shanghai and Tianjin, have received the lion's share of investment from abroad. These areas have also attracted tens of millions of economic migrants from other areas of China. Large cities in coastal regions have massive skyscrapers, modern shopping malls, and extensive urban mass transit systems. At the same time, hundreds of millions of people still live on small farms in humble villages throughout China, especially in the inland regions. Most of China's rural population, while not suffering dire conditions such as malnutrition common in truly impoverished countries, can nevertheless be reasonably defined as fairly poor from a global perspective.

Even in urban areas there is a large population that could be broadly defined as "working poor." Most are migrants from inland China who have moved to the big cities in search of a better life. Their material conditions, while often challenging, tend to be vastly superior to China's poor of distant and not-so-distant decades. China once had a nearly endless supply of farmers willing to move to cities for low pay, but the laws of supply and demand have pushed wages up significantly over the past two decades. As of early 2024, mandated minimum monthly wages ranged from 2690 RMB in Shanghai to as low as 1450 RMB in parts of Heilongjiang. These figures do not account for employer-provided insurance benefits, and market rates for most types of even low-skilled work tend to be above the minimum wage. Nevertheless, there are millions of people working in urban China with annual incomes of less than 4000 USD in nominal terms.

It is also important to keep in mind that there are vast disparities in the economic conditions of different regions of mainland China. In 2022, GDP per capita was about $28,000 in Beijing, $26,700 in Shanghai, and $21,500 in Jiangsu Province. Meanwhile, per person economic output was only around $7800 in Guangxi, $7700 in Heilongjiang, and a mere $6700 in Gansu. These figures are in nominal terms, and don't account for purchasing power discrepancies within various regions. The cost of living, especially housing, is far higher in Beijing than in Gansu. Nevertheless, the disparities represent a massive gap in economic productivity and prosperity between mainland China's richest and poorest regions. Jiangsu has over three times the per capita GDP of Gansu. For comparison, in 2022, the US state with the highest per capita GDP (New York) had only about twice the nominal per capita GDP of the state with the lowest (Mississippi).

China's middling average per person output has enormous implications for global competition between China and the US. First and most importantly, it should be apparent that China, despite its several decades of largely sustained and rapid development, still has significant potential for economic expansion. While growth rates have slowed somewhat in recent years, they remain fairly robust, especially when compared to countries that already enjoy overall high levels of material prosperity. For decades various observers have forecasted a stalling or crash of China's economy. While such a scenario is possible, it does not appear to be especially likely. Jiangsu, although coastal and fairly urbanized, still has massive swaths of rural land worked by villagers living on small plots. If Jiangsu's annual per capita GDP can reach the nominal equivalent of $21,500, there is no apparent reason why the rest of mainland China cannot eventually achieve at least the same level of average economic output. If every municipality, province, and ethnic autonomous region in China was brought up to Jiangsu's level of per capita GDP (or, in the case of Beijing and Shanghai, brought down!), then China's economy would be roughly 70% larger than it is today in nominal terms, and therefore over 20% larger than that of the US.

China's nominal per-capita GDP in 2022 was roughly the same as South Korea's was in 2001. South Korea's GDP per capita expanded to $32,640 by 2022. To be sure, circa-1990s South Korea may have some advantages that China does not possess. For starters, it was smaller, and even in its mountainous interior, no part of South Korea is over one hundred miles away from the sea. Political autocracy and inefficiencies in government-driven development could hold China back. However, contemporary China also has major *advantages* that South Korea lacked in the 1990s. Unlike South Korea, China is not currently threatened by a rival government with tens of thousands of soldiers occupying mountains 40 miles north of its capital city. China also has access to efficiency- and productivity-promoting technologies and infrastructure (most notably, the Internet and smartphones) which did not majorly contribute to South Korea's economic development in the 1990s. China, while dependent on imports for many crucial materials, nevertheless has far larger reserves of minerals, energy, and other natural resources than

South Korea. China has far more land, and more arable land per capita. Certain global or domestic events could conceivably knock China off its path of growth, but by far the most likely scenario is that, by around 2045, China will have a per capita GDP roughly equivalent to that of South Korea in 2022. This would give China an economy nearly three times larger than the current output of the US. Unless the US, for some unforeseen reason, experiences economic growth at an unprecedently rapid rate for an already-wealthy country, it will almost certainly be economically overtaken by China. Once China's nominal GDP surpasses that of the US, the gap will probably continue to grow significantly, likely for at least several decades.

As with the other economic fallacies discussed previously, the fallacy of a rich China has (somewhat counterintuitively) helped lull many US policymakers into a sense of complacency with regards to China's expanding influence. Influence decision makers in Washington DC assume that most of China's easily plucked low-hanging economic fruit in the country has already been harvested, and therefore China's material development is likely to drastically slow or even stall. More specifically, some observers make comparisons between China's likely near-future economic course and Japan's Lost Decade.

After experiencing rapid growth from the 1950s through the late 1980s, Japan's economy stalled from around 1993, growing only around 1% per year from the mid-1990s. While the causes of Japan's stagnation are complex, and debated between various economists, the collapse of an asset bubble is usually cited as the main factor. Prior to the so-called Lost Decade, many observers saw Japanese economic dominance as inevitable, as Japanese companies dominated many global markets and bought key assets around the world. Japan's nominal GDP reached a peak of around 71% the nominal value of the US economy in 1995. Some observers believe China's recent economic miracle will also soon sputter and stall.

In actuality, comparing the current economic and geopolitical situations of China in the early 2020s and Japan in the late 1980s reveals far more differences than there are similarities. First, and most obviously, China has over ten times the population Japan had in 1990. While significant demographic issues arising from an aging population exist in both countries, they are far more pronounced in Japan. Japan's population peaked sometime between 2005 and 2010, and has been declining ever since. China's population is expected to peak around 2024. Furthermore, Beijing controls territory over 25 times larger than Japan. China has far greater natural resources in terms of minerals, energy, hydropower potential, and farmland. Perhaps most importantly, China has only about half the inflation-adjusted per capita GDP of Japan in 1990. While there may be significant asset bubbles and bad debt within the Chinese economy, it also has greater potential for untapped development.

Another key factor that many experts believe contributed to the asset bubble and other macroeconomic problems that brought about Japan's Lost Decade(s) was the Plaza Accord. The Plaza Accord was an agreement reached between Japan, Germany, France, and the US in 1985. Under the terms of the Accord, Washington essentially coerced Japan and Germany to rebalance their trade with the US by raising the value of their currencies relative to the US dollar. The subsequent increase in the price of the Japanese yen hurt Japanese exporters. It also increased inbound speculative investment, contributing to a major asset bubble in Japan. The eventual collapse of this bubble stalled Japan's economic growth for years.

Part of the reason the US was able to pressure Japan and Germany to agree to the terms of the Plaza Accord was because the US was (and is) a major contributor to the military defense of Germany and Japan, promising to protect them from attack while maintaining significant numbers of armed forces in their territory. China, as a nuclear power possessing a large conventional military force, and with no foreign bases on its soil, has obvious leverage to avoid any such impositions. Furthermore, even if China was somehow compelled by force or circumstance to increase the value of its currency against the US dollar, such a scenario could, among other outcomes, cause the Chinese economy to rapidly overtake that of the US in nominal terms. Japanese yen doubled in value against the USD within three years of the 1985 Plaza Accord; as of early 2024, China's RMB would only need to appreciate roughly 55% against the US dollar for China to overtake the US in terms of nominal GDP.

Mainland China's economic growth rate has slowed, and will likely continue to gradually slow over the coming decades. Similar declining rates of economic growth have been observed in South Korea, Japan, and Taiwan following their periods of rapid expansion. Still, it is important to keep in mind exactly where China is located on the historic curve of economic development in East Asia. China is not rich, and therefore it still has significant room to grow. In the absence of an unexpected development, China is therefore highly likely to continue on its path of overtaking the US economy in nominal terms, with attendant consequences for the balance of overall global power.

Fallacy Number Four

Chinese Economic Policies Are Inherently Predatory

There is a widespread perception in the United States, and especially in government circles, that China's current global economic engagement is invariably exploitative towards other countries. Specifically, US officials accuse Beijing of enacting an effectively mercantilist trading policy that unfairly encourages exports while limiting imports from abroad. Some influential voices charge the Chinese government with engaging in extractive neocolonialism in poorer countries, particularly those in Sub-Saharan Africa. As with most commonly accepted fallacies regarding China's global role, there is some truth behind this oversimplification. Chinese government agencies have no scruples about using any effective mechanisms at their disposal to achieve their core aims, even if they may contradict established expectations. However, this is also true for every other major power, and China's economic engagement with other countries is driven almost entirely by *mutual* self-interest with other relevant parties.

There is a glaring imbalance when comparing annual exports and imports between China and the US. China exports far more to the US than the US does to China. In 2023, Chinese exports to the US were worth nearly three times the value of Chinese imports from the US. This dynamic has continued, with some variation, for over a decade. Many people in the US extrapolate from this bilateral trend to say that China is an inherently predatory trading partner with other countries. However, having a lopsidedly negative balance of trade with China is a uniquely US issue that does not necessarily apply to China's other trading partners.

Overall, China's goods exports are worth about 20% more than its imports, and this ratio has decreased significantly in recent years. In 2023, several major economies, including South Korea and Brazil, exported a greater value of goods *to* China than they imported *from* China. From 2015–2023, the balance of trade between China and Germany, and China and Japan, has been roughly even. Among the other top thirty global economies in terms of PPP economic output, Russia, Australia, Iran, Saudi Arabia, and Malaysia all exported more to China than they imported from China.

It is also important to keep in mind that, while the pattern of trade in material goods between the US and China is particularly imbalanced, the US also has a lopsided balance of trade with many other trading partners. Overall, the US imports are worth around 26% more than US exports. In 2019, the Vietnamese exports to the US were worth over six times the value of US exports to Vietnam; this ratio grew to *over sevenfold* in 2020. In 2023, total US imports exceeded total US exports by over 25%.

Why is trade between the US and China (and the US and many other trading partners) so lopsided? Much of the answer lies in the status of the US dollar as the global reserve currency. In 1971, the Nixon Administration, partially in response to spending pressures prompted by the US war effort in Vietnam, took the US dollar off the gold standard. Previously, US dollars had been "backed" by a fixed exchange rate with gold. Nixon's move increased the flexibility of US macroeconomic policy by effectively allowing Washington to "create" more dollars. It also significantly increased monetary inflation in the US.

In 1971, the US GDP was worth over 35% of total world economic output in nominal terms, far ahead of any other country. Due to its massive economic, military, and political power, other countries were happy to accept the US dollar as payment, even if it was not backed by any tangible asset, and even if US policymakers could, at least in theory, create as many

US dollars as they saw fit. It was only after the abandonment of the gold standard that the US began to experience severe defects in terms of international trade.

The US last had an international trade surplus — a situation in which the value of US exports was higher than the value of its imports — in 1975. When measured as a percentage of total US GDP, the overall trade deficit grew substantially in the early and mid-1980s, driven in large part by growing imports from Japan. After a brief rebalancing in the late 1980s and early 1990s, the trade deficit grew further, peaking at around 5.5% of total US GDP in 2006. Following the 2007–2008 financial crisis, the trend has rebalanced somewhat, remaining at around 3% of US GDP in recent years.

The trend of labor-intensive manufacturing shifting from the US to lower-wage countries — Mexico in the 1990s under NAFTA, then China, then Bangladesh and Vietnam — has also been a factor in the overall US trade deficit as a whole. Nevertheless, China has merely been the most significant beneficiary of a preexisting pattern. After opening China up to foreign investment, the Chinese government benefited from increased access to capital. Many US companies have also benefited massively from access to relatively inexpensive Chinese labor. There was nothing inherently unique, or even inherently Chinese, in this process. Furthermore, China itself is now experiencing some negative impacts from the "race to the bottom" trend in globalization. Wages in apparel factories are around $500 per month in most Chinese cities, while workers in Bangladesh or Cambodia might only be paid the local equivalent of $150 or so for the same type of work. Therefore, many lower-tech, lower-skilled, labor-intensive industries have shifted in recent years from China to China's poorer Asian neighbors.

A cursory examination of China's international trade leads some people to assume that China is increasingly dependent on exports to the US. This is a subsidiary fallacy to the belief that China is an inherently predatory trade partner. Although the balance of trade between the US and China greatly favors Chinese exports, this does not necessarily mean that China is increasingly dependent on exports to the US for its overall economic growth.

True, by nominal measurements China is exporting more to the US than even before, with increasingly large trade surpluses in recent years. However, these figures don't account for monetary inflation. They also don't account for the overall growth in the Chinese economy. In 2007, China exported $321 billion dollars' worth of goods to the US. At the time, Chinese exports to the US were worth roughly 8.6% of China's total annual economic output. In 2023, Chinese exports to the US were to $427 billion in nominal terms, but when counting for inflation, $427 billion in 2023 "only" had the equivalent value of roughly $292 billion 2007 dollars. Additionally, because of overall economic growth in China, Chinese exports to the US were worth only roughly 2.4% of China's total GDP in 2023.

China is still, to a large degree, reliant on exports to the US as a key driver of its national economy. Such exports help to ensure economic activity by boosting employment, investment, and overall growth. However, China is far less *relatively* dependent on exports to the US than it was in the mid-2000s. Undoubtedly, the large volume of imports from China gives the US government a degree of economic and political leverage. Beijing obviously wants to avoid additional tariffs and other policies that can impede Chinese exports to the US. China is willing to grant concessions in order to ensure the flow of trade continues. However, the extent of such US economic leverage against Beijing is limited, and in relative terms, shrinking, as China grows its domestic market and expands trade ties with Southeast Asia, Europe, Latin America, Africa, and other parts of the world.

Like the vast majority of international powers, the Chinese government maintains extensive trade and investment ties with other countries out of perceived self-interest. While Chinese trade with the US is imbalanced, China represents a crucial *export* market for numerous countries. As of 2023, mainland China was the largest export market for South Korea, Australia, New Zealand, Malaysia, Indonesia, Brazil, Peru, Taiwan, Angola, Oman, Iran, and Mongolia.

These patterns of trade help solidify China's global political and social ties. They allow countries that have significant concerns about the military dimensions of Beijing's growing influence, such as South Korea and Japan, to benefit from the economic dimensions of increased Chinese clout. Trade links abroad also provide a network of defense against any sustained US efforts aimed at maintaining Washington's global dominance by seeking to systematically restrain China's economic development. Governments in Tokyo, Seoul, Canberra, Kuala Lumpur, and Taipei may largely share Washington's concerns about Beijing's increasing political and military power. At the same time, they are highly unlikely to sign on to any US efforts that would limit the growth potential of their most important customer.

Its position as the most important export market for numerous countries also gives the Chinese government a degree of leverage against its trading partners. Just as Washington has used the patterns of trade to put pressure on Beijing, Beijing can use trade as a tool if foreign governments engage in policies that are sufficiently odorous to the CPC. Indeed, Beijing has used this leverage before in at least two notable cases.

In 2017, the South Korean government announced plans to host a US-operated Terminal High-Altitude Area Defense (THAAD) anti-missile weapon system. South Korean and US officials said the system was aimed at protecting South

Korea from a potential North Korean missile attack. However, Beijing was concerned that the system could be used to detect, and possibly intercept, China's strategic missile systems, and thereby provide the US a dangerous edge in the unlikely event of a nuclear exchange between the two powers. Beijing first complained to Seoul. When mere complaints and warnings failed, Chinese officials targeted South Korea with a range of economic measures. Chinese authorities limited the number of Chinese tour groups authorized to visit South Korea. Beijing also disrupted South Korea's crucial cultural exports to China, refusing to allow K-Pop groups permission to tour in mainland China and suspending broadcasts of various South Korean movies and television programs.

Beijing has also used economic leverage to put pressure on the Australian government. The CPC views Canberra as too close to the US, and specifically vulnerable to Chinese economic pressure. In 2019, Australian exports to China — mostly iron and coal — were worth over $150 billion, accounting for over 11% of Australia's total GDP. From around 2019, Beijing-Canberra tensions escalated significantly in reaction to a variety of policies and controversies, including Australia's participation in US-led patrols in Chinese-claimed sections of the South China Sea, vocal support for the protest movement in Hong Kong, and laws in Australia meant to curb foreign political influence, which effectively targeted pro-Chinese political activity in Canberra. Beijing responded by restricting Australian exports to China. While the practical results of the policies have been difficult to assess, China's economic targeting of Australia may be as simple as a case of "killing the chickens to scare the monkeys." Such efforts are likely intended, at least in part, to signal to other countries that they are similarly vulnerable to economic retaliation if they are overly vocal or active in their support for US policies that Beijing views as aimed at containing China's rise.

Beijing's leverage of its economic influence to put political pressure on South Korea and Australia might be cited as evidence of China's predatory economic stance. However, such analysis misses a crucial point. The governments of South Korea and Australia sought for China to end its policies and restore trade and economic engagement back to the dynamics that preceded the escalated tensions. The targeted governments were apparently, at least overall, satisfied by the economic patterns that existed before Beijing utilized its economic leverage to put political pressure on them. The fact that Beijing pressured the governments by limiting economic engagement shows that Canberra and Seoul viewed the economic engagement as very much aligned with their own interests. If one cites Beijing's use of China's economic heft in advancing its political interests in Australia and South Korea as evidence of predatory economic policy, then US tariffs and sanctions targeting China could also be seen as proof of the US being the exploitative partner in overall Sino-US economic engagement.

China does not compel various countries and corporations to sell to Chinese customers, invest in Chinese ventures, or export goods from China. Rather, the basic realities of economic self-interest drive this activity. Nevertheless, the Chinese government has several notable advantages in economic dealings with international corporations and the vast majority of national governments. First, China's massive and growing market gives the government enormous leverage. If foreign companies, or the governments of the countries where they are based, do not comply with Beijing's desires, the Chinese government can use a variety of methods to limit, or even cut off, their access to China's markets.

The effective political monopoly of the CPC also allows Beijing to engage in a level of long-term planning that is impossible for most national governments and nearly all corporations. China's leaders do not face short-term pressure from election cycles or quarterly profit figures. Chinese officials are perfectly willing to let foreign companies make significant profits in China, and for other countries to otherwise engage in mutually beneficial trade and economic activity. This engagement has allowed the Chinese people to become more materially prosperous, increasing domestic political stability, expanding Beijing's global influence, and increasing a tax base, some of which can then be used for military purposes. The Chinese government is always mindful of its core interests, and seeks to maintain them over the long term. International trade is used by the CPC to further its own ends, but that does not mean the trade itself was inherently unfair.

Besides being accused of unfair manipulation to intentionally transfer jobs from and otherwise exploit wealthier countries, many policymakers and pundits in the US also accuse China of brutally exploiting poorer countries as a neocolonial overlord. Charges of Chinese neocolonialism abroad, especially in Africa, are based in part on the overall patterns of trade between China and many poorer countries. To oversimplify, China mostly imports raw materials, such as metals, oil, and timber, from these countries, and exports manufactured goods. Sometimes, Chinese companies export products made by Chinese factories "back" to the countries that provided the raw materials for Chinese industrial production. Chinese companies also build roads and rail lines to facilitate this trade. Superficially, there are parallels to these current patterns of exchange and the dynamics that defined the economic relationship between England and India during the British Raj, and between France and much of West Africa during the period of French Colonialism.

Nevertheless, there are more differences than similarities between Chinese involvement in poorer countries and historical colonialism. First and most importantly, China is not imposing these patterns through military force. There are no PLA detachments crushing indigenous rebels in the Congo,

Cambodia, or Sri Lanka. China has exactly one military base abroad — a facility located in Djibouti that supports regional anti-piracy efforts. Djibouti similarly hosts military bases run by the US, France, and Japan. Beijing is no more a colonial power in Djibouti than the governments of these other countries. The Chinese government does not forcibly prevent nations in Africa, Asia, or Latin America from trading with various third countries, unlike the French, Spanish, British, and Japanese in their historic colonial possessions. Furthermore, importing raw materials and exporting finished goods is a pattern of trade that China maintains not only with many poorer countries, but also Australia, New Zealand, Canada, and the United States. No US officials have castigated Beijing for running neocolonial policies in Alberta, Queensland, or Nevada. To call Chinese economic policy in poorer nations inherently "colonial" weakens the definition of colonialism to the point of near-meaninglessness.

Of course, refuting the overall accusations of neocolonialism does not mean that all Chinese economic activity in poorer countries is without fault. Beijing, with its massive economy and ability to provide loans, obviously operates in such countries from a position of relative power. Chinese loans to poorer countries often involve provisions that favor Chinese companies, especially Chinese state-owned firms. Millions of Chinese construction workers, engineers, and various other personnel have worked on Chinese-funded infrastructure projects in Africa, Southeast Asia, and Latin America. This provides an obvious benefit for boosting employment of the Chinese labor force, sometimes to the detriment, or at least the short-term determent, of local workers. Furthermore, many Chinese companies engage in questionable labor and environmental practices abroad.

Nevertheless, similar problems exist, have existed, and will likely continue to exist in nearly every economic relationship that involves significantly richer countries investing into generally poorer ones. Criticizing Chinese economic policies in poor countries as "neocolonialism" is valid if and only if one also labels nearly all self-interested international investment into materially underdeveloped countries as neocolonialism. While this may be valid in some philosophical or political circles, such schools of thought are not meaningfully represented in any major world government, and certainly not in the policymaking circles of Washington DC. For better and worse, the globalized financial system facilitates exploitative — though, in many cases, economically stimulating — capital flowing from the relatively prosperous to poorer countries and regions. Keep in mind this process is similar to what happened to mainland China itself in the 1980s, when wealthy capitalists from Hong Kong, Taiwan, and later the US, Japan, and Western Europe, poured money into China to "exploit" cheap mainland Chinese labor. Whether by coincidence or otherwise, the period of rapid expanding trade between China and various African countries has also seen the greatest and most sustained average rates of economic growth in Africa.

Critics sometimes cite the patterns of China's loans to poorer nations as evidence of Chinese economic aggression. Beijing, flush with foreign currency reserves, has become a key provider of credit to various countries, especially poorer nations in Africa and parts of Asia. Such loans have allowed the Chinese government to effectively compete with Western-dominated international financial organizations, such as the International Monetary Fund (IMF) and World Bank, which also make large loans to the national governments of poorer countries. US officials routinely accuse the Chinese government of unfairly using such loans to expand its political influence in other countries, and even of purposefully positioning Beijing's customers into "debt traps" from which they can only escape by giving China vital infrastructure and other national goods.

Objective analysis of various Chinese loans, when compared to similar loans by other national governments, or institutions such as the IMF, show a rather less sinister overall picture. Out of dozens of loans from 2000 to 2020 totaling, collectively, hundreds of billions of dollars, only two resulted in governments granting national assets — a port in Sri Lanka and some land in Tajikistan — to Chinese interests. In dozens of instances, Beijing was willing to otherwise renegotiate terms or even write off some remaining debt. While Beijing is undoubtedly using international loans to help expand its global economic and political influence, it seems unlikely that China would be setting up borrowers to fail. The IMF and other Western-dominated institutions often demand internal economic reforms in exchange for loans. Beijing may be more lenient in terms of seeking specific fiscal policies, though it sometimes charges higher interest rates. Basic economic law dictates that national governments have improved negotiating power if they are able to "shop around" and secure loans from multiple, alternative institutions. Systematic corruption surely causes wasteful appropriation for some Chinese loans to foreign countries; this is also true for nearly all international loans and aid. US criticism of Chinese loans is clearly based on the perceived self-interest of Washington to curtail China's global economic and political influence, rather than any supposed moral concerns about the well-being of poorer nations.

Another factor notably missing from (primarily) US accusations of Chinese neocolonialism in poorer countries is an examination of the attitudes towards China of the supposed colonial subjects themselves. However, this notable lack of analysis is not due to a lack of data. The Pew Research Center has tracked public opinion in multiple countries on various issues since the early 2000s. Their figures show that, of the African countries surveyed, attitudes toward China tend to be notably positive. In 2019, 70% of Nigerians, 63% of Tunisians, 58% of

Kenyans, and 46% of South Africans had overall positive views of China. Of the 34 countries surveyed globally, Nigeria was ranked second in terms of positivity towards China; only Russia had a higher prevenance of pro-China public opinion. This is not to say that there aren't negative opinions about China, or at the very least certain aspects of economic engagement with China, in various poorer nations; surely, there are. But the overall indicators of public sentiment in various African countries do not show widespread or even notable resentment towards Beijing.

While many specifics of China's economic engagement with the wider world may be subject to legitimate criticism, the broader patterns of interaction are not inherently unfair, or at least they are not especially nefarious when viewed as part of the general system of international trade and investment in which they operate. Beijing engages in trade to directly promote its core interests. International trade and investment with China is voluntary; individuals, corporations, and national governments also have economic relations with China for their own "selfish" reasons. Undoubtedly Beijing is using foreign trade and loans to poorer countries to promote and ensure its goal, long-term policy goals. However, mutually beneficial engagement, even with a degree of power imbalance in many cases, is not the equivalent of exploitation or colonialism.

Military Fallacies

Although economic influence is the most important facet of Sino-US competition, military power also plays an important role. While Washington remains dominant in this area, Beijing has made huge efforts in recent decades to improve and expand its military capabilities. It is extremely unlikely that the US and China will ever purposefully engage in a direct, sustained military conflict. Nevertheless, raw military power is the ultimate method of interstate coercion and guarantor of government survival. A basic understanding of the military facets of Sino-US rivalry, and a dispelling of the misconceptions surrounding this arena of contention, helps build a holistic understanding of the overall dynamics of Sino-US bilateral competition.

Fallacy Number Five
China Is Uniquely Aggressive

US officials and media commonly condemn Beijing's actions and overall strategic stance as aggressive. Undoubtedly, the various branches of the People's Liberation Army (PLA) are rapidly expanding their capabilities and deployments. Chinese warplanes and naval assets have increased their presence in the South China Sea, while making frequent patrols near Taiwan as well as maritime territory disputed between China and Japan. Chinese soldiers regularly engage in standoffs with Indian units along sections of their disputed border in the Himalayas. It would be entirely accurate and fair to describe the Chinese military as increasingly *assertive*. Beijing has more active territorial disputes than any other country on earth. From 2000–2020, nominal Chinese military spending increased roughly tenfold (though military spending as a percentage of total GDP remained almost entirely unchanged). Certainly many PLA actions seem aggressive from the standpoint of governments in Tokyo, Taipei, and Hanoi. However, to describe, without context, China's recent military stance as "aggressive" begs the question — aggressive compared to whom?

Over the last several decades Beijing has used its military in fewer deadly interstate conflicts than every other comparable global power. Given China's vast size, population, and its possession of nuclear weaponry, the only other countries that can reasonably be compared to China on the international stage are Russia, the US, India, France, and the UK. One could arguably add Israel and Pakistan to this list, since they also have nuclear weapons and regional strategic relevance. However, given their relatively constrained global influence and unique geopolitical positions, they can be excluded from this comparison (their inclusion, at any rate, would also show that they have a relatively militaristic recent history compared to the PRC, especially when accounting for differences in national populations). Over the last several decades — indeed, since the foundation of the PRC in 1949 — China has engaged in less frequent and smaller international military conflicts than any comparable power.

When examining the extent to which major powers have been relatively militaristic or aggressive, issues of which side initiated a conflict, or the extent to which a conflict may be justified, are best left aside. Answers to such questions are almost always disputed and may never be resolved objectively. For example, in the Korean War, China's entry into the conflict could be reasonably seen as an aggressive move, or a defensive measure, depending on one's national, historical, and even political perspective. Chinese forces did not participate in the initial North Korean attack, but only intervened in the struggle after US troops crossed into North Korea, took Pyongyang, and continued northwards towards the Chinese border. Politicians and historians, both of the combatant powers and third countries, similarly dispute the proximate causes of escalation that led to open military conflict during China's border conflicts with India and the USSR. Beijing did clearly initiate the 1979 conflict with Vietnam, albeit in response to perceived Vietnamese "aggression" in Cambodia.

The essential aim in this chapter is to examine the frequency and intensity of a government's use of military force in foreign conflicts; moral judgements may better be reserved for another literary venture. A critic may argue that the Chinese government is entirely morally responsible for every single international conflict that it has ever participated in. Another observer could also argue that Beijing was entirely righteous and justified in all its military conflicts. Similar blanket denunciations or justifications could be applied to any other national government, and to endlessly dispute these nuances does little to establish any remotely objective comparison in the relative militarism of various states.

A grim statistical recording and ranking is needed in order to attempt an impartial assessment of the relative militarism of various countries. Which governments have been involved in the most wars? How deadly have these various conflicts been? Where did such conflicts take place? In order to avoid complicated and irreconcilable moralistic arguments over which party started which conflict for which reason, and which side was right or wrong, we will instead look at the raw numbers of international conflicts and deaths. This comparison will overlook minor, UN-approved peacekeeping deployments. Various conflicts in which the major powers did not directly participate through major military deployments, but rather intervened via arming or otherwise aiding combatant forces, are also excluded from the purview of this comparison. This exclusion of interference in indirect proxy conflicts largely *decreases* the PRC's relative lack of military interventionism when compared to the other powers.

That Beijing has been less internationally militaristic than roughly comparable global powers in recent history does not mean that the Chinese government is pacifist in the international sphere. The PRC has fought several international military conflicts. These wars include Chinese intervention in the Korean War in the early 1950s, the Sino-Indian border war of 1962, the subsequent Sino-Indian frontier conflict in 1967, border clashes with the USSR in 1969, an attack on islands in the South China Sea occupied by South Vietnamese forces in 1974, the brief border war with a reunited Vietnam in 1979, and a subsequent series of Sino-Vietnamese clashes along their border from 1979 to 1989. Most recently were the deadly military clashes along the contested Sino-Indian frontier in June of 2020. For the sake of this list, we can include both PRC/ROC clashes in and around the Taiwan Strait (1954–55 and 1958) along with their fighting in the jungles of northern Myanmar (1960–61). Of course, Beijing (and possibly Taipei) would not define such conflicts as "international," but rather maintain that they were merely extensions of the most recent, and technically still unresolved, Chinese Civil War. At any rate, these engagements can reasonably be classified as *interstate* military conflicts. For the purposes of our comparison, the brief PLA campaigns against Tibetan fighters in 1950 and 1959 do not qualify as interstate conflicts since Tibetan forces were not fighting for an internationally recognized government; similarly, successful campaigns by other governments against would-be "internal" rebels will not be counted when comparing the international conflicts of other world powers. For the entirety of its history, the PRC has fought in no more than eleven interstate conflicts, and as few as eight, if one discounts the three rounds of fighting between the PLA and ROC forces after the CPC took power in Beijing.

Now, compare the PRC's record of interstate conflict to that of France. For the sake of fairness and simplicity, let's examine only the military history of France (and other relevant powers) following the 1949 establishment of the PRC. During that timeframe, French military forces fought in the First Indochina War (which began in 1946 and lasted until 1954), the Korean War, the Algerian War (1954–1962), the Suez Crisis (1956), the Ifni War (1957–1958), the Bizerte Crisis (1961), Operation Lamantin (1977–1978) of the Western Sahara War, Operation Manta (1983–1984) during the Chadian-Libyan conflict, the Gulf War (1990–1991), the Kosovo War (1998–1999), the war in Afghanistan (until 2011) and the forcible overthrow of the Gaddafi government in

Libya in 2011. Since 1949, France has directly fought in at least twelve interstate military conflicts. This list does not include French support for the national governments of former French colonies in Africa during civil wars against rebel movements, or (successful) French military efforts from 1947–1948 to suppress a nationalist uprising in Madagascar.

Like France, since 1949 the UK sent military forces to fight alongside multinational allies during the Korean War, the Suez Crisis, the Gulf War, the Kosovo War, the war in Afghanistan, and the 2011 intervention in the Libyan Civil War. Britain also fought during the 1954–1959 Jebel Akhdar War in Oman, the 1963–1966 Malaysian-Indonesian *Konfrontasi*, and the 1982 Falklands War. Among several postcolonial wars were conflicts that resulted in independence for Cyprus (1955–1959), and South Yemen (1963–1967). The UK government also supported the US-led military campaign in Iraq from 2003, and a bombing campaign against the Houthis in Yemen from 2024. Leaving aside semi-international conflicts, such as the Troubles in Northern Ireland, gives a total of the UK participating in thirteen interstate wars during the entirety of the PRC's existence.

US armed forces fought in the Korean War, the Gulf War, the Kosovo War, the war in Afghanistan, the war in Iraq from 2003, the 2011 intervention in the Libyan Civil War, and the campaign launched in 2024 against the Houthi movement in Yemen. The US was also a major belligerent in the Second Indochina War (1955–1975), the Bay of Pigs Invasion (1961), clashes along the Korean DMZ (1966–1969), the 1983 Invasion of Grenada, the April 1986 bombing raids in Libya, and the 1989 invasion of Panama. US military forces have directly fought (without explicit UN Security Council authorization) during civil wars in Lebanon (1958), the Dominican Republic (1965–1966), and Syria (from 2014). Since 1949, the US has fought in no fewer than sixteen direct interstate conflicts, barring minor UN-approved peacekeeping missions and various interventions limited to the deployment of weapons and noncombatant military advisors.

Rounding out the five nuclear-armed members of the UN Security Council is Russia. For the purposes of this comparison, we can include the Soviet Union when recording the various interstate military conflicts fought by Moscow since the 1949 formation of the PRC. These campaigns include the 1956 invasion of Hungary, the 1968 invasion of Czechoslovakia, border clashes with Chinese forces in 1969, and the 1979–1989 war in Afghanistan. Although their participation was limited, Soviet pilots and other forces did directly engage in combat during the Korean War, the 1967–1970 War of Attrition around the Suez Canal, and during the Angolan Civil War. Following the collapse of the USSR, various conflicts broke out among former member states, including major civil wars in and around Chechnya. However, when strictly looking at interstate conflicts, Russian forces fought directly to support separatist regions in Georgia (2009) and Ukraine (from 2014). It is reasonable to consider the 2022 Russian invasion of Ukraine as an additional interstate conflict, though some may argue it was an extension of a war that was launched in 2014. The Russian military has also actively fought in the Syrian Civil War beginning in 2015. Moscow has therefore fought in ten or eleven international conflicts during the existence of the PRC.

Although it is not a UN Security Council member, India is a nuclear-armed country with a massive population. It can therefore be reasonable to compare India to other major powers, including China, when determining the relative frequency and intensity of interstate military conflict. Since 1949, Indian forces were deployed twice to forcibly seize Portuguese colonies in India (1954 and 1961). As discussed previously, Chinese and Indian forces have engaged in one war and two significant clashes along their disputed frontier (1961, 1967, and 2020). Since 1949 India and Pakistan have fought two direct wars (1965 and 1971) along with a series of deadly clashes in 1999, 2016, and 2019. Both sides have engaged in various rounds of cross-frontier shelling in 2001–2002, 2016–2018, and from 2019. A relatively minor and localized border clash between Indian and Bangladeshi forces led to 19 combatant deaths in 2001. Indian military forces also deployed to intervene in the Sri Lankan civil war from 1987 to 1990. Depending on how exactly one classifies various regional conflict, Indian military forces have fought in at least eight and as many as fifteen international conflicts.

For the entirety of its existence, the PRC has directly engaged in at least eight and as many as eleven interstate conflicts. In contrast, the US has fought in sixteen, France at least fourteen, the UK in thirteen, Russia in eleven, and India in at least eight. Of course, this only is a raw comparison of the number of conflicts. Some of these conflicts, like the 2001 Indo-Bangladeshi border clashes and the 2020 Sino-Indian confrontation, were resolved quickly, and resulted in only a handful of casualties, all of whom were combatants. Others, like the Korean War, the Algerian War, and the various Indochina conflicts, were prolonged affairs resulting in the deaths of (at least) hundreds of thousands of civilians.

Among the deadliest wars of the post-1949 era were several in which major global powers did not directly participate in, including civil wars in the Democratic Republic of the Congo, Sudan, and the Iran-Iraq War. In terms of overall death toll, the only *major* conflict that the PRC has fought in was the Korean War. After the Korean War, the deadliest war fought by China was its conflict with Vietnam, which "only" resulted in a maximum of around 50,000 deaths, the majority of whom were combatants. Although all relevant figures are disputed, the

Korean War likely had a roughly analogous total death toll with the Algerian War of Independence, the US-led military efforts in and around Vietnam, the 1971 India-Pakistan war, and the Soviet war in Afghanistan. It is also worth remembering that the US itself was also a major combatant in Korea. Among the major powers, only the United Kingdom could possibly have a significantly less deadly recent history of interstate conflict than the PRC, although even this could be reasonably disputed given London's participation in the wars in Iraq.

The relative deadliness of various international conflicts and the extent to which various powers are responsible for casualties can be difficult to accurately and objectively assess. However, a much clearer, and also relevant, metric is the *duration* of various international conflicts. Taking the broadest possible measure, the military forces of the PRC directly engaged in deadly interstate conflict at one point or another during 19 separate years. During the same timeframe, French forces fought in various deadly interstate conflicts in a total of 30 separate years, British forces during periods in at least 31 years, Russian forces 27, and US during a total of at least 50 years. Only the Indian military has arguably fought in interstate conflicts for a shorter duration than its Chinese counterpart, depending on if one classifies the Kashmir insurgency as an interstate struggle or a purely domestic insurgency.

Location is another key factor to consider when assessing the relative militarism of major global powers. The US, France, and the UK have engaged in multiple major international conflicts thousands of kilometers from their borders over the past several decades. With the exception of direct participation in Cold War conflicts in Angola and the Middle East, Moscow's wars have been fought in its near-abroad. Meanwhile, *each and every* interstate battle fought by the PRC (and India) have occurred either along contested frontiers, or in countries directly adjacent to their borders.

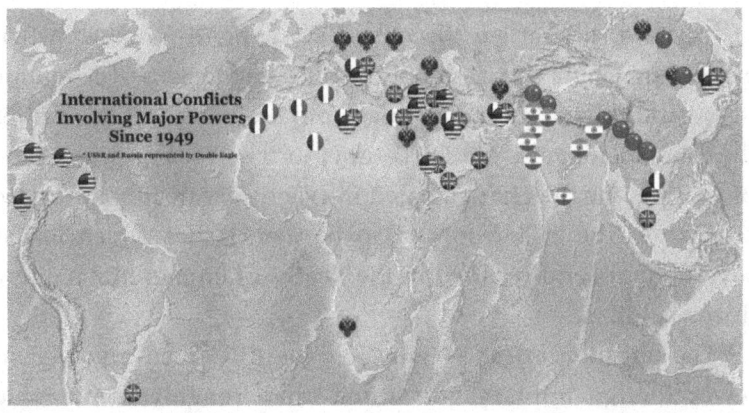

Putting aside philosophical and ethical concerns about various recent conflicts, which are essentially impossible to objectively resolve, an observer may reasonably contend that launching obviously premeditated wars on continents far removed from one's own frontier is generally more indicative of aggressive militarism than fighting in or around one's home territory. Perhaps this trend is driven, at least in part, by China and India's relatively lower per capita GDPs. Waging war on another continent is extremely expensive, and therefore global military adventurism is easier for richer countries. However, regardless of the cause of its trend, the Asian giants have clearly confined their recent conflicts to their immediate periphery.

When considering the factors of frequency, deadliness, duration, and location, the PRC has been relatively *less* militaristic than other relevant global powers. Among other major countries on the global stage in the post-World War Two era, only the UK and India could possibly be responsible for fewer direct deaths from instate military conflict, although, again, the relevant figures are disputed by government officials, historians, and demographers. Even if the UK has been responsible for somewhat fewer combat deaths than the PRC since 1949, the fact that China has had between eleven to 20 times the UK's population seems relevant. A comparison of relative militarism becomes even more notable when examining China's foreign policy following the era of economic liberalization and globalization. From the period of the end of the Sino-Vietnamese border conflict in the 1980s until the time of writing, the PLA has engaged in exactly *one* deadly interstate conflict — the 2020 Sino-Indian border clashes which lasted several hours and resulted in the deaths of no more than a few dozen soldiers.

The question arises — why has the PRC been involved in fewer foreign military adventures than roughly comparable global powers? Is the Chinese government inherently peaceful and benevolent? Probably not. While the CPC has generally been less *internationally combative* than other governments of major global powers, it has still engaged in serious *domestic* deployments of brute force. Immediately before and after seizing power, the CPC targeted landlords in rural areas, killing at least hundreds of thousands and as many as several million. The "Great Leap Forward" was one of the deadliest policy moves in world history, killing between twenty and fifty million Chinese, although most deaths during the period could reasonably be classified as mass negligent homicide rather than premeditated murder. Mao's Cultural Revolution also killed at least hundreds of thousands (and possibly a few million) throughout China. The CPC was perfectly willing to resort to brute force to ensure its monopoly on political power during the 1989 protest movement that swept Beijing and other major cities. Beijing is at least as willing as the leaders of other major global powers to use violence to further its perceived interests; it just happens that, for the entirety of the PRC's existence, such violence has been directed mostly inward.

More recently, critics (most notably US government officials) have cited CPC policies aimed at curtailing individual rights and cracking down on organized dissent, or even *potential* organized dissent, in Hong Kong and Xinjiang as evidence of Chinese aggression. However, it is reasonable to make a distinction between *aggression* and *suppression*. No government on earth, barring the Taiwan-based ROC, officially refutes Beijing's sovereignty over Hong Kong and Xinjiang. While Chinese government policies in the territories may be entirely worthy of criticism and even condemnation from a perspective of idealistic liberalism, they cannot reasonably be construed as evidence of *international* aggression. Various controversial policies by other major governments in various locations within their own territory, be it Chechnya, northeast India, Puerto Rico, or the slums of Paris, may be described to various degrees as illiberal or discriminatory, but they can hardly be cited as proof of interstate aggression against other states.

The essential reason why the Chinese government has been less internationally militaristic than Washington, Moscow, and Paris in recent decades must stem from self-interest rather than any inherent benevolence. Recall that China has more neighbors along its borders than any other country. Although China is, for the time being, more populous and economically powerful than any of its neighboring states, several of these countries, namely Russia, India, and Japan, also wield significant geopolitical and economic leverage. Even some smaller states, such as Vietnam, do not easily yield to direct threats or pressure from global powers. If China acts with excessive overt aggression, other countries can and will cooperate against it. Indeed, this has occurred in recent history. The USSR and India increased cooperation in the 1960s and 70s due to the perceived mutual threat of China. Similarly, Moscow and Hanoi coordinated to counter Beijing. Currently, India and Japan have close ties driven largely by wariness over China's growing power.

Contemporary China is also the world's largest trading power. It is currently economically enmeshed with the global economy in such a way as to incentivize it to avoid direct international conflict which could disrupt flows of investment and trade. Since China intensified its process of relative economic liberalization and increased international trade and investment from the early 1980s, it has fought in exactly *one* international conflict — the 2020 border clash with India. Again, the clash killed no more than a few dozen soldiers and led to no significant changes in territorial control. However, it did result in India imposing restrictions on Chinese commerce and investment in the country, and it prompted Indian leaders to take a tougher stance on China and increase outreach to the US. These outcomes are obviously detrimental to China's long-term interests.

The outcomes of the 2020 Sino-Indian border clash present an illustrative example — broadly, Beijing has avoided initiating international military conflicts because the majority of such conflicts have not advanced the perceived interests of the Chinese government. The one notable exception may be Chinese intervention in the Korean War. The Chinese campaign in that conflict established that Chinese forces were capable of sustaining a ground war against better-equipped opponents, thereby illustrating that any invasion of Chinese territory would, at the minimum, be extremely difficult and costly. Since the Korean War, no foreign power has tried to occupy Chinese territory; this is a significant outcome, when compared to a hundred years prior to the conflict, which saw Britain, France, Japan, and the international coalition of the Eight Power Alliance wage significant wars within China.

Nevertheless, the Korean War was also enormously costly for China in terms of material resources, finances, political capital, and human life. Subsequent international conflicts have not been as costly to the PRC, but neither have they obviously benefited China's geopolitical position. China fared well in the 1962 border conflict with India, but at the cost of its relations with both India and the USSR. The 1969 border war with the Soviet Union was essentially a draw, but it further poisoned relations between Moscow and Beijing, and marginally increased the threat of an inter-communist nuclear war. The 1979 war with Vietnam was not only costly, but it also failed to achieve its objectives. Crucially, it is in the aftermath of the 1979 conflict that the CPC dramatically shifted its strategic focus from raw military power to instead concentrate on developing its economic capabilities. China's rapid economic expansion, and consequent increase in overall power, has coincided with the decades of its (relatively) peaceful foreign policy. So long as this formula works to ensure the CPC's political monopoly and its expansion of relative global power, Beijing is likely to avoid major interstate conflicts.

Many US leaders believe that other powers view Beijing as aggressive. Certainly Japan, India, Vietnam, the Philippines, and (especially) the ROC view PRC claims on territory under their administration as aggressive. However, even these various governments also have significant areas of mutual interests with the PRC, especially in the economic sphere. In addition to military shows of force, Beijing and its rival territorial claimants have enormous trade and investment ties; indeed, mainland China is the largest trade partner for most of them.

Many national governments and populations that don't have active territorial disputes with Beijing tend to view the PRC as not especially militarily aggressive on the international stage. This perception is generally backed up by recent history. At the time of writing, the median age of the human population is about 30. Within the last 30 years, the PLA has killed 20 foreign nationals in direct armed conflict, a figure far lower than comparable numbers of Russia, India, France, the UK, and, especially, the US. In 2013, Worldwide Independent Network and Gallup International asked 66,000 people across 65 countries which nation they consider to be the greatest threat to world peace; 24% of respondents chose the US, while 6% cited China.

There are crucial implications arising from Washington's misperception of an inherently and obviously aggressive China. Most US policymakers view US-China contention through the lenses of the US-USSR Cold War. Washington still sees itself as the defender of smaller countries against a larger and aggressive bully. However, there are enormous and relevant differences between contemporary China and the circa-1950 Soviet Union. Before, during, and after World War Two, the Soviet Union had forcibly incorporated the entirety of the formerly independent countries of Lithuania, Estonia, and Latvia into its territory. Soviet troops occupied a broad swath of territory from the Balkans to Eastern Germany. Leveraging its military presence, the Soviet Union set up governments reasonably described as clients at best and puppets at worst in Bulgaria, Romania, Hungary, Czechoslovakia, Poland, and Eastern Germany. Although such actions were strategically defensive from Moscow's perspective, they were also, quite understandably, viewed as dangerous aggression by many regional states. Their governments openly rallied to the US as a balancing power and ally. Furthermore, the USSR was publicly committed to the cause of global communism, and openly sought to export its domestic system to other countries.

Despite various territorial disputes and shows of force, *China has done nothing remotely comparable to circa-1950 Soviet expansionism for at least several decades.* There is no blatant international Chinese aggression against populated areas anywhere near the scale of the early Cold War-era Soviet Union. While Washington will continue to make efforts, with varying degrees of success, at painting the PRC as an aggressor state, third countries will base their policy on their perceived interests and contemporary conditions, not propaganda campaigns. Additionally, Beijing has an inherent propaganda *advantage* in many parts of the world that have firsthand experience of recent military adventurism by the US and its French and British allies, especially in and around the greater Middle East, and to a lesser extent, Africa and Latin America. Playing up fears of an aggressive China may play well to domestic audiences, and in some of Beijing's immediate neighbors, but they largely fall flat in other parts of the globe.

Fallacy Number Six

The PLA Is Weak

Analysis of the military dimension of competition between the US and China is undermined by the widespread perception that the PLA is weak. Some pundits believe that US forces would be highly likely to emerge clearly victorious from any hypothetical conventional conflict between Washington and Beijing. To be perfectly clear, this is a misconception that will likely never be conclusively proven wrong, since there is only a remote possibility of Beijing and Washington going to war against each other. Nevertheless, US military overconfidence with regards to China is dangerous. Underestimating Chinese military capabilities not only increases the chances of a war occurring, but also could put US forces at greater peril in the event of a conflict breaking out. Historical precedents and a sober evaluation of the contemporary situation indicate that Chinese forces would likely be a roughly even match for their US counterparts during any plausible scenario of conventional conflict over the next two decades. Additionally, if, as is highly likely, Chinese economic output continues to expand more rapidly than that of the US, Beijing will probably have a slight edge in a conflict at some point in the not-too-distant future.

The PLA has performed generally competently in the relatively few direct, interstate conflicts it has engaged in. Recall from the previous chapter, the PLA has fought significant conflicts against the US and its allies during the Korean War (1950–1953), the ROC in the Taiwan Strait and along the Myanmar border (1954–1961), India (1962, 1974, and 2020), the USSR (1968), and Vietnam (1979). Overall, only one of these conflicts — the border war with Vietnam — resulted in an outright PLA failure to achieve its main objectives. In the other contests, PRC forces either achieved their overall goals, or were at least able to deny their opponents an outright victory. Basic analysis of PLA objectives, strategy, and overall performance in these conflicts shows a record of a fighting force with, at worst, decent capabilities. Interestingly, the PLA has historically performed especially well against major global powers, while facing greater struggles against smaller regional states.

The PLA's historic combat effectiveness was most clearly displayed during the conflict in Korea, which, as mentioned in the previous chapter, was by far the largest of the PRC's international wars. For the sake of simplicity, there are three basic metrics that can be used to assess the performance of Chinese forces during the conflict. These factors are casualty ratios, territorial control, and political outcomes.

Detractors of Chinese military capabilities will likely point to the least important of these metrics — the casualty ratio. Chinese authorities have reported about 183,000 military deaths during the Korean War. Meanwhile, official statistics from other combatant states show around 138,000 South Korean, 33,500 US, and 3700 casualties among other allied forces from other countries. Estimates for North Korean military casualties range from around 200,000 to 400,000. Some Western historians and officials dispute the official Chinese casualty figures as an undercount, with estimates as high as 400,000. At any rate, Chinese and North Korean military deaths were significantly higher than those of their adversaries in Korea. This lopsided ratio was driven, in large part, by nearly unchallenged US and allied air and naval dominance during the course of the conflict.

Control over territory is generally a more useful and objective metric for comparing the relative effectiveness of military forces in an open, conventional conflict. Although North Korean forces and their allies did utilize guerrilla operations during the war, the vast majority of fighting in the Korean Peninsula took place along relatively clear fronts of opposing control. The patterns of these fronts clearly demonstrated the overall effectiveness of Chinese units.

Korea had been ruled as a Japanese colony from 1910–1945. Following Japan's defeat, areas north of the 38th parallel were occupied by Soviet forces, while areas to the south were occupied by the US. Leaders friendly to the two Cold War rivals set up rival governments in Pyongyang and Seoul, both of which claimed sovereignty to the entire peninsula. Following a series of significant frontier clashes and deadly political crackdowns on both sides, North Korean forces crossed the 38th parallel in a full-blown attack in late June 1950. They quickly overwhelmed most organized military resistance and took Seoul. By late summer South Korean forces only controlled the southeast corner of the peninsula. In response, the United Nations Security Council passed a resolution authorizing member states to come to South Korea's aid, and the US military (along with other countries, chiefly US allies) deployed forces to the region. US-led militaries quickly turned the tide of war.

The USSR, as a permanent member of the UN Security Council, could have vetoed the resolution that authorized US/UN military intervention in Korea. However, Moscow was boycotting the Security Council at the time, in protest of the fact that China's seat on the council was occupied by the Taiwan-based ROC. In 1949 most leaders of the ROC government fled to Taiwan, though there was some degree of localized ROC guerrilla resistance against the PLA in certain areas, most notably southwest China. The PRC was experiencing international isolation and limited diplomatic recognition, and Beijing was — unfairly from Moscow's viewpoint — excluded from the United Nations.

By early October 1950, US-led forces had pushed beyond the 38th parallel and entered North Korea. Beijing sent messages through neutral countries warning the US that it could directly intervene in the conflict. Mao Zedong and other top CPC leaders were worried that the US military would not stop at the Yalu River separating North Korea from China, but would instead force their way into northeast China, and attempt to forcibly overthrow the PRC with the aim of reinstalling Chiang Kai-shek's ROC government in mainland China. As US-led forces continued their northward drive, the CPC leadership decided to intervene in Korea, and began positioning some 300,000 Chinese soldiers near the North Korean frontier. In an effort at creating political cover and seeking to prevent a wider war which could spill into Chinese territory, the Chinese forces were known as the People's Volunteer Army (PVA), although they were effectively reorganized PLA units.

When the PVA crossed the Yalu River into North Korea in late October 1950, US, South Korean, and other allied forces had already seized Pyongyang and nearly all other major population centers throughout North Korea. Most surviving North Korean units were hiding in the mountainous countryside. In terms of territorial gains, the initial Chinese offensive against their overstretched adversaries was extremely successful; by late December US-led forces had retreated south of the 38th parallel, in what is the longest retreat by the US military in the country's modern history. On January 7, 1951, Chinese forces seized Seoul. Over the course of about eleven weeks of brutal, full-scale warfare against technologically superior adversaries, Chinese forces had fought their way through over 360 kilometers of territory and forced US-led armies to retreat.

Chinese and North Korean forces eventually overextended their lines. The US and its allies retook Seoul in mid-March 1951. The two sides then continued to fight, mostly along the original frontier between North and South, until July 1953. Despite significant various offenses and enormous expenditures in human life and resources, from around mid-1951 the front was mostly static, more or less running along the 38th parallel. When looking at territorial changes during the period of direct

Chinese intervention in the conflict, at first the Chinese and their allies made significant advances, then they pulled back slightly, and finally they maintained a generally stable front line against their opponents. The initial Chinese effort to drive the US away from China's borders and prevent the downfall of the North Korean government succeeded; subsequent Chinese attempts to completely drive out US forces and unify Korea under Pyongyang's rule failed.

Political outcomes are, arguably, the most important metric for determining the overall success or failure of a military campaign. As Carl von Clausewitz wrote in 1834, "War is merely the continuation of policy by other means." The Chinese military achieved the main political objectives sought by Beijing when Mao decided to directly intervene in the Korean War. To be sure, these political accomplishments came at a high cost, and Beijing did not attain an outright victory by expelling US-led forces and uniting Korea under Pyongyang's rule. Before the PVA entered North Korea, the US and its allies had nearly won the conflict against North Korea. Beijing's military campaign ensured the survival of its ally and restored Pyongyang's control over the northern half of the Korean Peninsula. More importantly, the war effectively ensured the survival of the PRC in the international system. The CPC had only taken control of mainland China months prior to the outbreak of the conflict. At the beginning of the war, most national governments still recognized the Taipei-based ROC as the legitimate government of all of China. Many politicians and generals in the US sought to forcibly restore Chiang Kai-shek's government in mainland China. China's ability to launch and maintain full-scale conventional war — the first in which Chinese military forces fought effectively against Western adversaries since Sino-Dutch and Sino-Russian conflicts of the 1600s — clearly demonstrated that any foreign attempt to forcibly restore the KMT was highly likely to end in failure.

Indeed, the highly contested struggle for Chinese sovereignty between the PRC and the ROC was a major factor in the prolongation of the Korean War. Disagreement between the PRC and the US over the fate of PVA personnel captured by US-led forces stalled ceasefire talks. Washington sought to "repatriate" captured PVA soldiers to ROC-controlled Taiwan, while Beijing insisted on their return to mainland China. There were also many captured Korean combatants from the North who wanted to settle in the South, and some from the South who preferred to live in the North. These disagreements were the major factor preventing an armistice after the lines of control between the two sides became largely static from mid-1951.

Looking at their overall performance and outcomes in the Korean War, Chinese forces fought effectively against forces who were generally far better equipped. The PRC had only just emerged from a full-scale civil war, which itself followed decades of Japanese occupation of China's key industrial areas. Japanese occupation was itself preceded by roughly a century of intense civil strife along with predatory, opportunistic colonialism and direct military interventions by Western powers. China's nominal GDP in 1952 was around 31 billion USD, less than 10% of US economic output at the same time. While Soviet military and economic aid was crucial to the Chinese and North Korean War effort, the US also benefited from significant support from its main allies, especially the UK, Canada, and Australia. China's infrastructure, productive capacity, and technological capabilities were far behind those of the US and its allies during the conflict. Despite its adversaries' technological and economic advantages, and the fact that they effectively controlled the sea and sky for the duration of the conflict, the Chinese military was able to push the US and its allies out of North Korea in less than three months, and then hold its adversaries to a stalemate for years. China was able to fight the US to a standstill at a time when Washington's relative power was near its historical peak, and China's near a historical low.

The PRC also fared well in facing peer adversaries during border conflicts with India and the USSR. Over the course of fighting in 1962, India experienced more casualties than China. More importantly, Chinese forces advanced into Indian-controlled territory in both major theaters of fighting along their disputed frontier. After making these gains, Beijing declared a ceasefire and voluntarily withdrew to the pre-conflict fronts. The clash solidified China's control over its claims within disputed Himalayan territory and established Beijing's ability to put military and strategic pressure on India. Following the conflict, the Indian government abandoned its Forward Policy of establishing and maintaining military posts in mountainous frontier areas claimed by China. In terms of immediate political aims, the 1962 Sino-Indian war was an overall Chinese victory. However, there were broadly negative long-term geopolitical consequences for Beijing; the war intensified the Sino-Soviet split and increased sympathy for India in both Moscow and Washington.

Chinese and Soviet forces experienced roughly equivalent casualties during their border clashes in 1969. The sequence of events that sparked the conflict is disputed, and the political aims of the combatants are difficult to discern. Neither side lost any territory that it controlled prior to the conflict. Essentially, the conflict resulted in a stalemate. In terms of longer-range political implications, Moscow experienced some significant setbacks; its Warsaw Pact allies refused to unanimously condemn Beijing for the incidents, effectively weakening the Soviet government's prestige among Communist countries. More importantly, the conflict convinced many in Washington of the feasibility of establishing a *de facto* US-China alliance against the USSR, paving the way for eventual diplomatic and economic ties between the PRC and the US.

To be sure, past performance is not necessarily an indicator of current or future abilities. The PLA has numerous weaknesses that it did not have during its more "active" phase of international conflict from roughly 1950 to 1979. These weaknesses, broadly defined, come down to the essentially internally focused nature of the PLA, its relative lack of relevant real-life combat experience, and corruption within the institution (see **Fallacy Number Seven: The PLA Is a Major Threat to the United States**).

At the same time these weaknesses in the PLA are likely less significant than they may initially seem, especially with regards to the military dimension of contention between Beijing and Washington. Take, for example, the lack of relevant interstate combat experience in the PLA. It is absolutely true that the PLA has little relevant combat experience in its ranks. The deadly frontier clash with Indian forces in 2020 barely counts; neither side fired any guns, and the clashes were highly localized. At the same time, US military forces are also almost completely lacking in combat experience that could be relevant to any plausible scenario of direct, sustained conflict with China. The reader may find this assertion counterintuitive. After all, the US has been involved in a variety of real-world military conflicts nearly continuously since the 1980s. Some of these wars, most notably the US wars in Iraq and Afghanistan, have been fairly large conflicts in which many US units have undergone major and sustained combat.

Nevertheless, experience from these wars would provide little, if any practical advantage to US military leadership in terms of a hypothetical conventional war against China. US forces fighting in Iraq and Afghanistan never had their logistical staging areas, aircraft carriers, or airfields meaningfully threatened by conventional weapons. The US has not fought an adversary with significant conventional capability to strike against US naval assets since World War Two, or in other words, *for the entire career of every single US military officer.* Experience in counterinsurgency operations would be of extremely limited value when facing PLA submarines, missiles, and aircraft in the West Pacific. The US Air Force's extensive experience with bombing targets in Serbia, Iraq, and Afghanistan against essentially no modern air defense or combat aircraft only provides marginal value when contemplating the possibility of bombing runs over the South China Sea or the hills of coastal China. Personnel and officers in various branches of the US military, for all their recent combat experience, have no living memory of facing anything remotely close to a peer competitor with the credible capability to inflict death and destruction on US airfields, ships, combat aircraft, resupply routes, and staging areas.

Furthermore, the PLA's problems with corruption and the fundamentally political nature of the Chinese military may or may not cause serious problems in any remotely plausible scenario of conventional war between China and the US over the next several decades. Corruption that favored the promotion of insufficiently competent officers could undermine the effectiveness of the PLA. At the same time, such issues would be lessened by the raw geographic facts of a US-China war. Any plausible US-China military conflict in the near future would almost certainly occur either primarily or entirely within or near Taiwan, the South China Sea, or the East China Sea. From the perspective of Beijing and the vast majority of PRC citizens, the conflict would therefore be seen as a defensive war fought within Chinese territory, or at least very near to it. Unless corruption leads to outright treason, even corrupt or somewhat incompetent PLA military officers would almost certainly make their best efforts in a war of perceived national defense.

As for the political nature of the PLA, this again is unlikely to be a major challenge in a perceived "defensive" war which would likely arouse popular nationalistic sentiment, at least in the early stages of a major conflict. A prolonged war and resultant economic disruption could drain PLA resources in the event of major social discontent and political instability, but so long as a majority of the Chinese population did not blame their government for initiating or seriously mishandling a war, this scenario is fairly unlikely. At any rate, the CPC would have every plausible motive to promote the effectiveness of the PLA when fighting a foreign adversary.

Granted, Washington's alliances in East Asia could undermine Beijing's efforts during a potential US-China war. The US has a clear overall advantage in this sphere, as Washington has binding mutual-defense arrangements with Japan, South Korea, the Philippines, and Australia. Depending on the specifics of the escalation chain, US forces fighting in the West Pacific could potentially be aided by the ROC military, along with one or two of Beijing's other rival South China Sea claimants. However, it is far from certain that regional governments would be eager to join in a war against the PRC, unless such a conflict was explicitly and clearly initiated by Chinese forces. In the event of the US and China going to war over Taiwan or some escalation of bilateral tensions in the South China Sea, US allies could try to sit the conflict out, especially if the US was seen as initiating the clash, or if the responsibility for the escalatory chain was unclear. There is a plausible scenario in which the US military utilizes its regional bases, especially in Japan, during a conflict with China, while the national governments of Japan, South Korea, the Philippines, and Australia avoid direct engagement with the PLA.

Outside of the West Pacific, aspects of Washington's global alliance system actually create some *disadvantages* in terms of US-China military competition. The US has tens of thousands of personnel deployed in Europe under NATO auspices ready for a direct, conventional war with Russia that will almost certainly never occur. At the same time, NATO's foundational clauses impose strict geographic limits on the alliance's mutual-defense obligations. NATO members are only obliged to come to the aid of other members in response to aggression in Europe, the Atlantic, and North America. Washington's NATO allies would be under no binding duty to help the US in a hypothetical war with China confined to the West Pacific. The US military, while having an overall advantage against China as of the early 2020s, is stretched by its obligations in Europe, not to mention its significant, ongoing deployments in the Middle East. Chinese conventional military deployments, on the other hand, are directed almost exclusively towards the West Pacific. While some Chinese forces are also deployed along the disputed Indian frontier, in the highly unlikely event of a conventional US-China conflict, it would likely be far easier for China to shift its assets within Chinese territory to face US forces than it would be for the US to rapidly transfer troops and equipment from Europe and the greater Middle East to China's direct periphery. Additionally, if the US were to do so, Russia and Iran could take advantage of a reduced US military presence in their regions.

Official reports from various branches of the US military underscore the challenges Washington could face in a war against Beijing. To be sure, such reports should always be taken with a grain of salt (or perhaps, more accurately, enough salt to meet one's entire daily recommended intake of sodium). The authors of these reports have clear institutional motives to hype the capabilities of Washington's most credible global adversary, and thereby justify increased spending on armaments and personnel. Nevertheless, these reports are valuable for providing insight into plausible scenarios in which the US would, at best, struggle tremendously against Chinese military forces.

Since around 2011, multiple war game simulations run by various branches of the US military show the US either struggling enormously or outright losing in a hypothetical conventional military conflict with the PLA over Taiwan. In these simulations, numerous Chinese advantages come into play. First, and most obviously, the mainland of China acts as an effectively unsinkable platform from which missiles and aircraft can be launched. US aircraft carriers and military airfields in the West Pacific would be vulnerable to destruction or incapacitation by land-based missiles fired from China. Chinese forces would need to overwhelm a relatively smaller set of targets, while essentially anywhere on the Chinese landmass within over 5000 km (3100 miles) of potential US target sites could be used to host China's intermediate-range ballistic missile launchers. Such missiles are a key component of China's Anti-access/area denial (A2/AD) military doctrine, which seeks to neutralize US advantages in naval forces, especially aircraft carriers, by either destroying them outright or by dissuading Washington from introducing them into an active conflict theater. While no one can be entirely sure (and it will almost certainly never be proven or disproven anyway), the US strategic reliance on aircraft carriers in a conventional conflict against a capable adversary may be no more useful than battleships were during World War Two. Large global powers, especially the relatively dominant ones, often fall into the trap of preparing for the *last* major war. New technology can disrupt or even entirely negate their apparent advantages in weapon systems which proved crucial during previous rounds of direct great power conflict.

Beyond the specifics of military hardware, tactics, and deployment, China has other, more general advantages that could come into play during a conflict with the US. Remember, China's "real" GDP when adjusted for purchasing power is currently larger than that of the US. China generates more electricity and creates far more steel than the US. In terms of physical productive capabilities, China has an advantage that is likely to only grow. While the US spends more on the military in *nominal* terms than China, this spending gap does not take into account the relative costs of manufacturing in the two countries. Since it has a larger industrial base, China is currently able to produce as many, if not more, conventional war machines than the US.

Additionally, an apparent gap in technological capabilities between the US and China is neither so clear nor so wide as to confer significant advantages to the US in a scenario of conventional war with the PLA. As of the time of writing, the US appears to have an overall advantage in conventional military technology. However, there are areas in which China may have superior capabilities, and in the absence of a direct conflict between the two powers, it is impossible to directly assess which military has superior systems compared to its adversary. In one key field — land-based intermediate-range missiles — China almost certainly has an advantage. The US, under an arms control treaty with the USSR (and then Russia), refrained from developing and deploying missiles with a range of between 500–5500 km (310–3420 miles) for several decades. China never faced such restraints. Although the US withdrew from the relevant treaty in 2019 due to alleged Russian violations, the US faces a conventional missile gap against China in the West Pacific. This gap exists while China's overall productive capabilities are greater than that of the US, so the advantage is likely to continue to grow in Beijing's favor.

The author makes no claims to being expert on specific military systems. There are likely areas in which US missiles, naval assets, and aircraft have some significant technological and operational advantages against their Chinese counterparts. However, recent decades have seen an overall trend of a narrowing US advantage in terms of military technology when compared to China, and this trend is likely to continue. Ultimately, US-China wargaming and speculation on the potential outcomes of a conventional conflict are likely to remain that — speculation. Although it may be interesting and even occasionally useful to make detailed forecasts for exactly how a conflict would play out, it is highly unlikely any such predictions will ever be conclusively proven or refuted.

In any remotely realistic scenario of unrestrained conventional military conflict between the US and China in the coming decades, the war would very likely be extremely costly and difficult for both sides. An analyst who believes either side could avoid massive destruction and thousands of casualties within the first day of full-scale combat is delusional. Even a hypothetical US-Sino conventional conflict that only lasted a week and which resulted in a "victory" for one side or the other would almost certainly prompt economic, financial, and supply-chain disruptions. The mere prolonged blockade of trade between the US and China, even in the absence of a single military casualty, would economically devastate both powers, including the apparent victor, for many years, if not decades. At any rate, even without economic co-interdependence, the US and China both have sufficient military force to credibly deter an intentional attack by their other power. As of the time of writing, the conventional military capabilities of the two countries appear fairly balanced in the West Pacific. In the coming years and decades, Beijing, with its geographic edge and greater economic capabilities, is likely to acquire an overall military advantage in its immediate periphery which, once established, is likely to grow.

Fallacy Number Seven

The PLA Is a Major Threat to the United States

The third common fallacy about the PLA is that it is a strong and threatening military force capable of subjugating China's neighbors and directly challenging US military hegemony. This may seem counterintuitive, given the analysis of the previous chapter. However, while the PLA is likely quite capable in terms of fighting an essentially defensive conflict against a major adversary within or near PRC territory, historical precedent and contemporary realities suggest Chinese forces would probably struggle tremendously in an offensive. The myth of China's conventional military forces presenting an existential threat to the US comes mostly from institutional bias. Washington policymakers have a clear interest in exaggerating the threat of the Chinese military.

US generals and admirals, along with former military commanders who work in the defense industry, have obvious motivations for hyping the Chinese threat to justify US military spending. Additionally, there is a long-standing and intensifying trend of US elected officials and bureaucrats exaggerating the overall threat of China's expanding regional and global power in order to win elections and justify increased federal government influence or control within key domestic spheres, including finance, technological development, and media discourse. Despite rhetoric from Washington, the fundamental reality is that, while China's military is quite capable of defense and deterrent, it would almost certainly struggle enormously in actually attacking and subduing any of its neighbors, or making an unprovoked sneak attack on US forces.

At the outset of this analysis, it must be noted that, based on prevailing domestic and international circumstances, the Chinese government has no plausible motivation to initiate a major interstate war. The PRC remains a prime beneficiary of most major current international trends. Beijing's relative influence when compared to that of Washington has increased during a period in which Chinese forces have largely avoided major interstate conflict, and instead focused the majority of their material, human, and political resources on improving China's economic conditions. Any war launched by the PRC could undermine this trend. Even a brief conflict could destabilize global flows of trade and investment on which the Chinese government depends to grow and maintain the Chinese economy.

This reality was on full display during the deadly border skirmish between Indian and Chinese forces along their disputed frontier in June 2020. The Indian government reacted to the conflict by banning dozens of Chinese smartphone applications from the Indian market and otherwise restricting investment and trade between the two countries. The Indian government imposed retaliatory economic measures in response to a clash in which no guns were fired and in which no more than a few dozen soldiers lost their lives. A broader conflict between the PRC and any other power would almost certainly entail correspondingly greater economic disruptions.

Blatantly attacking a neighboring power without major provocation would almost certainly drive China's neighbors to deepen their cooperation with the US in response to the perception of an increased threat from China. For economic and strategic reasons, overall peace is currently in the overall interest of China's rulers. So long as China's economic growth rate surpasses that of the US, PRC territory is not meaningfully threatened, and the CPC feels secure in its domestic political monopoly, the Chinese government has no apparent motive to initiate a war.

Of course, Beijing's current lack of any clear motive for initiating an armed conflict may not last forever. A variety of scenarios could convince or compel the PRC to initiate or escalate an interstate war. For example, an accident with rival military forces could rapidly escalate and compel Beijing into engaging in a full-scale conventional confrontation. A sudden and prolonged economic crisis in mainland China might prompt Beijing to risk a war in an effort to unite the population. Finally, Beijing could consider launching a conflict if its perceived core interests were sufficiently challenged. For example, an official declaration of Taiwanese independence, which the PRC would see as an outright challenge to its fundamental goal of maintaining Chinese territorial integrity, would almost certainly result in at least some form of military response.

As mentioned briefly in the previous chapter, the PLA has three main weaknesses, namely systematic corruption, lack of relevant experience, and political control, all of which would likely undermine Beijing's efforts in a hypothetical conflict. Notably, these weaknesses would probably be especially noticeable if PRC leadership were to launch a blatantly aggressive conflict. While these weaknesses were concisely addressed in the previous chapter, they deserve a closer examination.

First is the problem of corruption. Serving in the military is highly prestigious in China. It is seen as a guarantor of social standing and economic stability. The government provides individuals who serve in the military with enhanced medical and life insurance, along with other benefits. Ever since the significant downsizing of China's military forces in the 1980s and 90s, it has been difficult for people to apply to join the various branches of the PLA. The situation is extremely dissimilar to that of most Western countries, and certainly any nations with universal military conscription. For decades, families had to pay significant bribes — usually in the range of around two years' average salary in an urban area — just to let their child (almost always a son) join the Chinese military forces. State media in China has also reported on investigations and punishment of formerly high-ranking generals and other officers for corruption in logistics and procurement.

The negative results of corruption within the Chinese military are difficult to accurately assess in the absence of a major sustained armed conflict. Nevertheless, corruption has almost certainty detrimentally impacted the PLA's effectiveness and performance. The practice of bribery being employed by many recruits to enter the military has probably acted as something of a filter, meaning that most military personnel come from the ranks of the relatively wealthy, or at least upper-middle class. The former "one child policy," in effect from the 1980s to 2015, stipulated that most ethnic Han (around 90% of the population) families who officially resided in urban areas (around 50%) were restricted to only having one child. While the population that met both criteria never constituted a majority of the PRC's populace, they were the demographic who made up the vast majority of middle class or higher families. Any prolonged military action resulting in numerous Chinese casualties would disproportionately impact this relatively privileged social group. Although avoiding high-casualty warfare (and warfare in general) is generally in Beijing's interest, the economic demographics of the Chinese military likely make the PLA especially casualty-adverse, potentially in ways that could limit freedom of action in an international crisis. Corruption in recruitment and promotion has also likely had negative impacts on the quality of the officer corps, with more competent leadership potentially losing opportunities for advancement against wealthier or more unscrupulous competitors. Additionally, corruption in the procurement of weapons systems could hinder or disrupt the supply of the most capable and effective military equipment.

There is a long history of military corruption undermining performance during conflicts in China. In the years prior to the first Sino-Japanese War (1894–1895), the Qing Empire had invested heavily in German-made modern warships. However, corruption in the procurement and storage of munitions severely hampered the effectiveness of the fleet; when war broke out, many of the ships couldn't fire their shells. This failure was a significant factor in Japan's crucial naval victories along the Korean and Chinese coastlines. Four decades later, corruption among Chiang Kai-shek's forces contributed to many of the ROC's difficulties fighting Japan during the second Sino-Japanese War, and the subsequent civil war which brought the CPC into power.

Beijing is fully aware of the potentially disastrous impacts of military corruption. Under Xi Jinping, the CPC has made enormous efforts to weed out systemic graft from the various branches of the PLA. While Xi's anti-corruption campaign was likely motivated, in large part, at securing his popularity, undermining potential rivals, and deepening his own influence, it was also aimed at corrupt practices, especially the more blatant ones involving explicit bribery. Thousands of high-ranking officers have been demoted, expelled from the party, or jailed. However, the effectiveness of this campaign within the PLA is difficult to assess. Given the opacity of Chinese governance and tight controls on media, the efforts are nearly entirely driven from the top down, rather than from the grassroots. Some nominally anti-corruption efforts may be aimed more at ensuring political loyalty rather than stamping out corrupt practices.

The second major issue that could undermine Chinese military capabilities is the PLA's lack of relevant combat experience. Following the border conflicts with Vietnam which ended in the 1980s, the Chinese military has had exactly one deadly battle with foreign forces — the clashes with India in 2020 which resulted in a few dozen deaths. Neither side fired guns during the confrontation. In order to secure their claimed positions, Chinese and Indian troops fought with primitive hand weapons. Most of the casualties probably died from exposure after falling into a cold mountain stream at high elevations. There is likely little practical experience gained from such combat which could be used in a full-scale conventional interstate conflict. Although the PLA had gained some combat experience in UN peacekeeping missions, the usefulness of such combat experience is also limited. The same holds true for PLA service members deployed to suppress the protest movement in 1989 and various ethnic riots and clashes during recent decades in Xinjiang and Tibet. Even in terms of the officer class, nearly all personnel who fought or led units during major combat operations against Vietnam in 1979 are either dead or retired.

The final, and perhaps most important, institutional weakness is the essentially political nature of the PLA. The CPC founded the PLA in 1927 to fight against the KMT-controlled National Revolutionary Army (NRA) and its allies after Chiang Kai-shek betrayed the Communists and launched the Shanghai Massacre. Like the PLA itself, the KMT's NRA was formed and directly controlled by a political party instead of the national government. From its very inception, the PLA has been focused primarily on ensuring the CPC's domestic political power. Although it is now, officially, the military force of the Chinese government, the PLA remains in the effective control of the CPC. The successes and shortcomings of the two institutions are tied together. Although this creates a unity of purpose, it also doubtlessly causes bureaucratic inefficiencies. The PLA's main purpose is to ensure the CPC's political monopoly, rather than to defend the Chinese nation. Although this distinction matters little in peacetime, it could create problems in the event of a prolonged and destabilizing conflict.

An overview of the 1979 border war between China and Vietnam provides a useful case study in the PLA's institutional problems. The conflict broke out during the Sino-Soviet Split. A recently reunited Vietnam was close to Moscow and supportive of its efforts to counterbalance China. The Khmer Rouge, which had recently taken power in Cambodia, effectively sided with Beijing in the dispute. Among the many murderous errors the Khmer Rouge made after seizing power in Cambodia was an effort to "liberate" ethnic Khmer areas of southern Vietnam. The Vietnamese government responded in late 1978 with a full-scale effort to topple the Khmer Rouge. Vietnamese forces and their local Cambodian allies quickly seized Phnom Penh, but they faced years of guerrilla resistance (backed by Thailand and a few other US regional allies) in the jungles of western Cambodia.

The PLA invaded northern Vietnam in February 1979. Beijing's war aims were to draw Vietnamese forces out of Cambodia while demonstrating Beijing's ability to undermine Moscow's influence and ward off Soviet adventurism. Chinese forces pressed in as far as about 20 km (12 miles) past Vietnam's northern border, but they faced stiff resistance. Some Vietnamese units redeployed from Cambodia, but not many. Chinese forces began to withdraw from major combat operations in early March, though border clashes continued for another decade. Both sides lost thousands of soldiers. Casualties were likely somewhat higher on the Vietnamese side, but again, in terms of assessing which side (if any) benefits from a war, this is a nearly useless metric.

Although both Beijing and Hanoi claimed victory, China clearly did not meet its goals in the conflict. Vietnamese forces remained in Cambodia for another decade, and the eventual Cambodian peace settlement left their allies in power in Phnom

Penh. China did temporarily seize some border territory, but largely in forested and mountainous areas. Beijing also claimed success because it dissuaded Moscow from directly coming to Vietnam's aid. The war also indirectly solidified the effective anti-Soviet alliance between Beijing and Washington during the 1980s. However, China almost certainly could have shown strength to Moscow and usefulness to the US without initiating a costly and ultimately failed conflict that cost thousands of Chinese lives and soured relations with Hanoi. In the long run, the war helped convince the Vietnamese government (and many Vietnamese people) of China's inherent danger to their nation, though to be fair this perception predated the 1979 conflict by over a thousand years. In the long run, the conflict launched in 1979 ultimately solidified strategic rapprochement, and some degree of mutual cooperation, between Hanoi and Washington following the collapse of the Soviet Union.

The military history of the PRC's major interstate conflicts displays an interesting trend. Chinese forces generally fought well against the US and its allies in Korea — a war that Beijing believed was necessary for securing China's political independence against enemies who sought to forcibly restore the KMT to power. The PLA was also generally effective against India in 1962 and the Soviet Union seven years later. However, they struggled tremendously in what could broadly be seen as an offensive war against their much smaller (if more militarily hardened) Vietnamese neighbor in 1979.

While this chapter may seem to contradict the previous one, stating that the PLA is *neither* weak *nor* a major threat is not a contradiction. The Chinese military almost certainly has the capability to cause extreme harm to an adversary in a prolonged regional conflict. At the same time, it would face extreme struggles in an offensive war against determined local opposition. The PLA is capable of inflicting pain and costs on an adversary, but unlikely to perform well in attacking one of the PRC's immediate neighbors, much less directly attacking the United States. The Chinese military has sufficient weaponry to cause, at the least, immense destruction for a rival military in a conventional sea and air battle near China's shores. At the same time, the PLA, like any modern military, faces nearly insurmountable difficulties in attacking and occupying territory in which a hostile civilian population, motivated by nationalistic fervor, supports armed resistance.

Purposefully initiating an interstate conflict would almost certainly create significant political threats for the Chinese government. The CPC is likely to face little social unrest arising from a war in which Beijing can convince a solid majority of the Chinese population that its military actions are essentially defensive. However, in an offensive war, social discontent could quickly spiral out of control. This is especially true of any conflict that disrupts vital shipping lanes carrying crucial Chinese imports of food and fuel, and the exports that help keep Chinese workers gainfully employed.

Maintaining its domestic political monopoly is the key driver of CPC strategy and policy. War is just another means to this end. The Chinese government has little apparent motive for risking its decades of economic expansion (which is very much reliant on international trade and investment) and consequent growth in relative power. Of course, this trend may change if China faces a pronounced economic crisis, or if Beijing's national authority is directly challenged. The Chinese government is *extremely* unlikely to directly initiate an unprovoked war against any of China's neighboring countries. Such a conflict would almost certainly result in diplomatic disaster, as worried neighbors flock to the US (and likely Delhi) in search of a strategic counterbalance. The PLA would struggle to hold territory inhabited by hostile populations. The Chinese government would face difficulties justifying the inevitable casualties of elite and upper-middle class families who lost their only sons. Any resulting disruptions to sea lanes or investment-curtailing sanctions would undermine the Chinese economy. Nevertheless, the PLA could likely at least hold its own in a conventional conflict arising from an accident, miscalculation, or attack by an adversary — even an adversary with apparent advantages in military strength and technology.

US warnings about the impending danger that conventional PLA forces pose to China's neighbors and the US itself have some basis in reality, but they are also clearly politically motivated. The US government has an obvious interest in justifying its significant military deployments in East Asia to both domestic and international audiences. Even more clearly, the US military and various government agencies seek to justify their budgets by hyping the threat of a rival power.

Diplomatic Fallacies

Significant misconceptions of Chinese foreign policy are frequently repeated in popular discourse. Many common misperceptions of the diplomatic dimensions of US-China confrontation stem from a general lack of understanding of how national governments interact with each other in the international arena. An overly ideological worldview in popular US imagination accounts for much of this ignorance.

To oversimplify a complicated international system, diplomacy is essentially the practice of national governments enticing, pressuring, threatening, or otherwise *convincing* other governments to act in a specific manner. Global and regional powers seek to influence the behavior of others in a way that aligns with their own perceived interests. Diplomacy involves various fronts, but the key drivers are economic, political, and military ties. Additionally, effective diplomatic power can come from a correlation in the general interests between two national governments.

Fallacy Number Eight

Chinese Diplomacy Is Ideologically Driven

Beijing's foreign policy is entirely driven by the perceived interests of the Chinese government. Recall, the fundamental, core goals are perpetuating the CPC's political monopoly, ensuring China's territorial integrity, expanding Beijing's international influence, and maintaining sufficient military force. Beijing is perfectly willing to cooperate with any government that helps promote these goals, and to put pressure on any government that is seen as undermining these core drivers. Chinese foreign policy is *entirely* focused on those four goals. The Chinese government does not care about the political system of other countries, except to the degree to which a country's internal politics can interfere with or aid Beijing's four long-term strategy objectives. China's foreign policy is entirely non-ideological.

Despite Beijing's non-ideological foreign policy, many officials and pundits in the US falsely believe that China seeks to purposefully undermine democracy abroad and export its authoritarian model to other countries. The perception of an ideologically driven Chinese foreign policy hinders Washington's ability to interpret and forecast Beijing's foreign policy moves. Three key factors drive this mistaken belief — historical precedent, instances of Beijing opportunistically using internal political developments in other countries for its own ends, and a psychological projection by US policymakers and members of the public.

With regards to historical precedent, the PRC's foreign policy *was* strongly ideological for several decades after its founding. Mao sought to export Communist revolution throughout the planet with a fervor that made the USSR uncomfortable. In fact, Soviet insistence on maintaining "peaceful coexistence" with capitalist powers was a factor in the Sino-Soviet split. Chinese intervention in the Korean War was primarily driven by the perceived geopolitical need to keep US-led troops from China's border in the immediate aftermath of the PRC victory over the ROC in mainland China. However, support for the global Communist struggle was a contributing factor. From the 1950s until the 1970s, China helped arm and finance various Communist and/or anti-colonial armed struggles in Southeast Asia and Africa.

During its phase of ideological foreign policy under Mao Zedong, the Chinese government didn't only seek to undermine established capitalist powers and their allies. Beijing also justified its hostility towards governments in the USSR and Vietnam as part of an ideological struggle against nominally Communist "revisionism." Tens of thousands of Chinese and Soviet troops engaged in significant clashes along sections of their disputed border in 1969. Later, after the Vietnamese communists drove out US forces and reunified their country, they were seen by Beijing as being too close to the "revisionist" Soviet line.

China's major shift away from an ideological foreign policy came about in the aftermath of the Sino-Vietnamese border war. The conflict, in which Beijing failed to achieve its core objectives, occurred at essentially the exact same time that Beijing established formal diplomatic relations with the US, began reforming its internal economic system, and opened up to outside trade and investment. China's war against Vietnam, while not exactly a disaster, was an overall failure. Thousands of Chinese died over the course of about a month of fighting. Frontier clashes dragged on intermittently for about a decade. While the PLA managed to seize and hold some Vietnamese territory along the border, they failed in their goal to force a withdrawal of Vietnamese troops from Cambodia.

After the failure of aggressive military interventionism in Vietnam, Beijing shifted away from an ideological foreign policy. For most of the 1980s, China acted as a *de facto* ally of the capitalist US against the Communist USSR, though the Chinese government also gradually softened its stance against Soviet "revisionism." In 1981, Deng Xiaoping's government told Asian states that China would stop arming various Communist insurgent groups in the region. Beijing established diplomatic and trade ties with countries that were once seen as implacable ideological enemies, including Israel in 1991 and South Korea in 1994. The Chinese government also established amicable trade and military relations with Russia following the Soviet Collapse.

Now, China has relatively friendly relations with a variety of countries. There is no clear pattern of Beijing specifically favoring authoritarian governments or disavowing democracies.

In terms of economic engagement, China has deep and growing ties with a variety of countries governed under various political systems. China is the largest trading partner of Australia, Japan, Chile, Saudi Arabia, Iran, and Brazil. When considering the European Union as a single economic entity, China is its largest foreign trading partner.

The PRC is even, by a large factor, *Taiwan's* biggest trading partner. Beijing likely sees long-term political advantages from deepening trade ties with Taiwan. However, the benefits are, from Beijing's perspective, in terms of promoting Chinese territorial integrity, rather than advancing the cause of "authoritarianism" or "socialism."

With regards to outbound monetary assistance, Beijing does provide loans and outright aid to a variety of countries that are autocracies or so-called "flawed democracies." Major recipients include Ethiopia, Cuba, Ghana, Cambodia, Sri Lanka, Nigeria, Tanzania, and Zimbabwe. However, this is likely due primarily to the fact that poorer countries, overall, tend to be less democratic than richer ones. Cuba is a notable outlier in terms of receiving a quantity of Chinese aid outside its general economic and demographic importance. While political concerns may come into play in this trend, this could also be explained by Beijing's perceived benefits from counterbalancing US antipathy towards Havana, and efforts to maintain an especially friendly (or dependent) government in the Western Hemisphere. Chinese aid to other nominally Communist powers, such as Laos and North Korea, is minimal when compared to other outflows. Beijing does not render any specific economic assistance to Hanoi.

Western-dominated international financial organizations, like the IMF, similarly tend to provide significant loans to autocracies or "flawed" democracies, including Egypt, Pakistan, Ethiopia, and Honduras. Again, this is likely because, on average, poorer countries tend to be more likely to have less democratic political systems. China's patterns of loans and aid are not especially different from countries and organizations that are not commonly accused of promoting a global authoritarian agenda.

Pakistan has been a key recipient of Chinese economic aid (and a major customer of Chinese military sales) for decades. Beijing's engagement in and commitments to Pakistan have continued their trend of incremental growth over decades and various Pakistani administrations, whether they came into power through elections or coups. The Chinese government sees Pakistan as a key transport node linking far western China with the Middle East. Islamabad also serves as a key counterbalance to India, China's main neighboring rival. Pakistan was also useful as a bulwark against Soviet regional influence until the collapse of the USSR. In recent decades Pakistan has been, at times, a military dictatorship, or a democracy with a deep military influence. Pakistani governments have ranged from outright Islamist to ideologically socialist, but Beijing has continued its support of Islamabad regardless of ideological or governmental changes in the Pakistani state.

To be sure, Beijing also has some tensions with many major democracies. However, these tensions derive from Beijing's perceived need to protect and promote its core interests, rather than any specific antipathy towards foreign democracies in general. For example, Chinese political dissidents tend to be concentrated in prosperous democracies, especially in the US but also in some European countries. Whether for ideological or geopolitical motives, the US and many Western European governments provide a degree of support or at least refuge to Chinese dissident groups, such as various protest moments in Hong Kong, Falun Dafa, and the Uighur World Congress. Beijing sees support for such groups as aimed at undermining, however marginally, the political monopoly of the CPC. The Chinese government therefore responds, usually by putting marginal economic or political pressure on the "offending" government.

Beijing also exploits politically driven ruptures between the US and other countries. The US government sometimes faces criticisms arising from its close relations with authoritarian governments, such as various oil-rich Gulf Arab monarchies. Additionally, there is a provision in US law that restricts aid following a coup against a democratically elected government. Because of this legislation, Washington suspended US military aid to Thailand following the 2014 coup in Bangkok, and political relations between the US and Thailand suffered a degree of strain. Beijing was more than happy to step in and improve ties to the post-coup Thai government. However, this move was not a situation in which the Chinese government sought to purposefully undermine Thai democracy. Rather, Beijing was simply opportunistically exploiting a diplomatic opening that presented itself.

The belief that China has an ideologically authoritarian foreign policy stems largely from misperceptions of the US's own global role, and a degree of psychological projection. Many US leaders, and most of the US public, believe that the US seeks to selflessly promote democracy abroad. This belief is the foundational framework that justifies US engagement in the globe. It is based on the idea that the US government acted selflessly to save democracy during World War Two — despite the fact that the US didn't enter the war until it was attacked, and gladly supported the totalitarian USSR and the imperialist powers of Britain and France (who offered no meaningful democracy to their colonial subjects) in order to win the war. While there are elements of democracy promotion in US foreign policy, the reality of US actions as a global power are far more nuanced.

In many cases the US government's relations with foreign powers are not clearly ideological; rather US policy is a mix of ideology and cynical promotion of perceived US geopolitical interests. The US provides support for a variety of blatantly authoritarian governments, especially in the Middle East. US agencies supported or instigated coups against numerous elected governments during the Cold War. The US provided military support to Beijing itself in the 1980s amid the autocratic Chinese government's tensions with the autocratic Soviet Union. The US similarly was happy to back military regimes in Pakistan against a democratic India during the period of the Cold War when New Delhi leaned towards Moscow. Even after the Cold War, the largest customers of US weapons sales are Gulf Arab monarchies. The US had provided billions in military assistance to Egypt, despite a 2013 military coup during which military forces killed hundreds of protesters. Unlike in the case of Thailand, US military aid continued to flow to Egypt because the US State Department simply said the 2013 coup was not *really* a coup. The US actively undermined the Palestinian general election of 2006 in which the militant group Hamas and its allies won a majority of seats.

Although the various entities that collectively create and implement US government policy sometimes promote democratic governance in foreign countries, this impulse is largely a tactic occasionally used to bring about their more fundamental goals. Elected politicians certainly employ the rhetoric of promoting global democracy, but this is primarily a means to advance their own political power. Presidential administrations may sometimes face some domestic pushback from alliances with authoritarian states or the backing of coups against democratically elected leaders, but this has never been a major deciding factor in national elections. Meanwhile, the professional bureaucracy also occasionally uses the promotion of democracy abroad as a means to enhance the global power of the US government, but they are also perfectly willing to undermine or defy the will of foreign electorates for the same self-interested purposes. US intelligence agencies promote democratic movements in US adversaries, but not in authoritarian states friendly to perceived US interests. The goal of major US-based corporations is to maximize profits, and while they may sometimes be subject to boycotts or other economic disruptions due to especially egregious actions abroad, they are also willing to take profits from economic cooperation with autocratic governments.

Occasionally, the US government has sought to promote (or maintain) democracy in other countries, for ideological reasons and because of the idea of a "democratic peace" — led, of course, in perpetuity, by Washington. All major US treaty allies, including NATO states, Japan, South Korea, and the Philippines, are at least nominally democratic, and most have fairly robust democratic political systems. However, democracy in many of those countries developed decades *after* they became formal military allies of the United States. Washington was perfectly willing to sign and maintain mutual defense pacts with autocratic governments in South Korea, Turkey, and Portugal prior to their transitions to democracy. In practical terms, US promotion of democracy has a spotty record, at best, with Washington willing to work with authoritarian governments or undermine the results of elections when deemed to be in US interests.

Some US politicians and pundits reconcile this contradiction in policy and ideology with the belief that the US is a uniquely and inherently benevolent democratic power, and therefore any action that promotes perceived US interests — even support for a coup against elected leadership, or the arming of an absolute monarchy — *effectively* promoting democracy. They truly believe that any action that promotes the US government's goals ultimately helps global democracy. Other apologists for Washington's antidemocratic foreign policy moves may say they were justified by existential struggles of "democracy" — which they equate, on the global level, with the US government itself — against Communism and terrorism. Perhaps the most deluded think that only *certain* US administrations, or the leaders of the *other major party* have strayed from global democracy promotion, despite consistent instances of antidemocratic foreign policies occurring during every single US administration for at least seven decades. Regardless of any such philosophically creative or politically convenient explanations, many US foreign policy actions are blatantly in contradiction with basic democratic process and ideals.

An individual might believe that Beijing's domestic market liberalization, its cooperation with foreign multinational corporations, and the emergence of billionaires in China have *actually* advanced the cause of global socialism. After all, such policies have benefited the Chinese government, which is the world's strongest nominally Communist power and the standard-bearer of global socialism. Rational analysis would dismiss such a claim as clearly ridiculous — after all, how can capitalist policies promote socialism? Similarly, one must dismiss any claim that Washington's support of coups and autocratic governments have *actually* promoted democracy abroad.

Professed US support for democracy abroad has, at least in many instances, been hypocritical and selectively applied. However, despite the messy specifics, or the extent to which US leadership genuinely believes in its propaganda efforts, promotion of democracy is a core *ideological justification* for active US policy abroad. It also provides a general framework for Washington to justify actions aimed at countering Beijing's expanding power.

Beijing's lack of an ideological underpinning to its foreign policy is both a strength and a weakness in the global diplomatic arena. Most obviously, the Chinese government can largely avoid charges of perceived political hypocrisy. Unlike US leaders, the CPC does not even need to *pretend* to care about the internal political structures of other countries, except to the extent that such systems may benefit or harm Beijing's core interests. This allows Beijing to cooperate freely and flexibly with a variety of governments from a position of straightforward mutual self-interest. The main ideology of China's foreign policy, if it could be said to have one, is an ideology of being non-ideological. Beijing pledges to not interfere in the internal workings of other governments, so long as they do not undermine the CPC's core interests. It is an arrangement that has been generally successful for steadily and incrementally expanding China's relative power on the world stage for roughly four decades.

Furthermore, non-ideological foreign policy has helped Beijing avoid costly commitments and mistakes. Note that China's last major war, which ended in general failure, was against pro-Soviet Communist "revisionists" in Vietnam. Beijing's ideological drive to dominate the global Communist movement was at least a contributing motivation for the conflict. Ideological foreign policy can lead major powers into mistakes. Internalization of the democracy-promoting narrative in the US was a major factor in the US decision to overthrow Saddam Hussein's government in 2003, and failed efforts to create a stable, pro-Washington democracy in Afghanistan. Many US politicians *believed* that the US was an inherently selfless actor seeking to promote much-needed democracy on the global stage. They therefore drastically underestimated the extent of resentment and resistance against their militarized "democracy promotion" efforts in the greater Middle East. Even today, there is a similarly mistaken belief that promoting democracy in China would lessen tensions between Beijing and Washington, as if the fundamental geopolitical issues driving competition between great powers and a strong sense of historic Chinese nationalism would fade in the absence of CPC rule.

Whither Hong Kong and Xinjiang?
US officials and other critics often cite the Chinese government's policies in Xinjiang and Hong Kong as evidence of an ideologically driven, authoritarian bent. Beijing says these criticisms are outside the realm of foreign policy, since they deal with China's "internal affairs." Nevertheless, Chinese actions in Hong Kong and Xinjiang have international implications, at least in terms of influencing Washington's efforts to rally other countries against growing Chinese clout. Objective analysis of the key developments driving Beijing's policies in Hong Kong and Xinjiang is therefore relevant to a discussion about the impacts (or lack thereof) of ideology on US and Chinese policy.

There has been a clear trend in recent years of the Chinese government tightening control and limiting political freedoms in Hong Kong. London and Washington have condemned these moves as violations of the 1984 Sino-British Joint Declaration, which established the framework of transferring sovereignty over Hong Kong from the UK to the PRC in 1997. The Joint Declaration established a "one country, two systems" formula, under which Beijing would have national sovereignty over Hong Kong while the territory would continue to have its own internal systems and related protections for rights for at least 50 years after the 1997 handover.

Beijing notably increased its control over Hong Kong in response to a widespread protest movement launched in 2019 to oppose reforms that would facilitate the extradition of criminal suspects from Hong Kong to mainland China and Taiwan. After several months of massive and disruptive street demonstrations, the pro-Beijing Hong Kong government did withdraw the proposed extradition law. While this decreased the size of the protests, a more hardcore group of demonstrators continued to protest, seeking electoral reforms, increased police accountability, and other political reforms. A vocal minority of protesters openly advocated for establishing the independence of Hong Kong as a sovereign country. In response to these moves, Beijing imposed a National Security Law, which effectively made all campaigning for independence and "collusion" with foreign powers illegal. The US, UK and their allies condemned the National Security Law as a violation of the Joint Declaration; Washington imposed sanctions in response to the move.

Beijing's actions in Hong Kong can fairly be described as authoritarian. However, its authoritarian methods have merely been used as a means to more fundamental goals, namely the perpetuation of Chinese territorial integrity and the CPC political monopoly. Chinese policy in Hong Kong became more authoritarian in response to perceived threats to its core goals. Authoritarian action is a means to an end, rather than an end unto itself.

In stark contrast to Hong Kong, Xinjiang is an enormous, mostly rural, and geographically remote area in which foreign media have little presence and effectively no freedom of movement. The facts of the situation on the ground are more heavily disputed. Nevertheless, there are some commonly accepted realities. Ethnic tensions accompanied by suppressive policies in the region erupted into sporadic riots and separatist attacks targeting civilians and security forces. From around 2017, Chinese officials significantly escalated controls over the multiethnic region and began mass internments of individuals with suspected "extremist" or "separatist" tendencies. Authorities described the facilities where individuals were detained as job-training camps, while critics described them as mass-indoctrination or concentration camps. Detainees in the camps were taught Mandarin and the ideology of the CPC, along with other subjects. Many were apparently coerced into involuntary waged labor at factories or farms. Nearly all the detainees were members of Uighur, Kazakh, and broadly Turkic groups that are overwhelmingly Muslim. While the exact figures of the total numbers of individuals who have ever been detained in such facilities vary widely, estimates range from several hundred thousand to around two million individuals. Mass surveillance preceded the camp system in Xinjiang. The Chinese government also encouraged (or forced) birth control in the region.

Beijing's crackdown on the region was preceded by multiple periods of ethnic unrest in Xinjiang. The region, which was ruled on and off by various Chinese dynasties for roughly two thousand years, has always been strategically vital and multicultural; often it has been wracked by internal violence or major wars. Uighurs and Han Chinese — with societies based on farming and trade — were mostly allies against the primarily nomadic Mongols in the region during the 1600 and 1700s. As with many other parts of the Qing Empire, large-scale rebellions took place in Xinjiang in the 1800s. Following the establishment of the PRC, Beijing adopted an ideology that was nominally in favor of the cultural rights of ethnic minority groups. Some policies were implemented to help correct their historical disadvantages in terms of access to education. However, there were also periods of severe persecution, especially targeting Muslims (and followers of other religions) during the Cultural Revolution.

More recently, the Chinese government has sought to frame its policies in Xinjiang as part of the broader post-9/11 War on Terror. Tensions in the region have, arguably, stemmed more from ethnicity than religion; some Uighurs attacked Hui – who are also a Muslim group, though culturally closer to the Han — during ethnic riots. Nevertheless, a minority of Uighur dissidents have adopted pan-Islamist ideals. Thousands fought alongside the Taliban in Afghanistan in the 1990s and various Islamist rebel groups in Syria during the 2010s. After a deadly clash between Han and Uighur workers at a factory in Guangdong Province in 2009, ethnic riots killed at least 197 people in Urumqi, the regional capital. Several notable terror attacks also occurred in the region, and at least two took place outside of Xinjiang. Most notably, a group of Uighurs armed with knives killed dozens of people at the main train station in southwest China's Kunming in 2014.

It is in this light that Beijing's actions in Xinjiang can be explained — not *excused*, but rather, *understood*. The Chinese government reacted to a perceived security threat with "preventative" measures. It is extremely likely that Chinese officials retroactively examined profiles of Uighurs who had committed violent acts. They found several common characteristics, such as overt religiosity, ties with individuals abroad, unemployment, and lack of Mandarin language capabilities. Then, authorities began mass incarceration/training/indoctrination of individuals with similar "profiles" *before they had done anything violent or otherwise illegal*. One of the often-overlooked consequences of China's mass-surveillance and preventative detention campaign in Xinjiang is its apparent effectiveness. There have been no major incidents of reported ethnic unrest — even from dissident Uighur groups based abroad — or major terrorist attacks in the region since 2017.

Critics have described Chinese government policies towards Uighur in Xinjiang variously as cultural genocide, ethnic suppression, collective punishment, or outright genocide. The US government officially declared the acts as genocide in early 2021. However one defines the policies, they are clearly authoritarian. However, they are also — like the situation in Hong Kong (though far more intense) — clearly authoritarian methods aimed at promoting Beijing's perceived self-interest. Officials intensified suppression in response to escalated violence and apparently growing ties between some Uighur radicals and transnational groups in the greater Middle East.

Although it is tangential to analysis of Beijing's actions in Xinjiang, it is notable to highlight Washington's apparent inconsistencies towards the situation. The US government itself was once somewhat amenable to including Beijing's efforts against radicalized Uighurs as part of its War on Terror. In February 2018, US CENTCOM announced having carried out airstrikes in Afghanistan targeting the East Turkestan Islamic Movement (ETIM), "a terrorist organization with roots in the ethnic Uighur separatist groups in western China." However, in July 2020, the US State Department removed ETIM from its list of designated terror groups because, according to an official, "for more than a decade, there has been no credible evidence that ETIM continues to exist." Apparently either CENTCOM lied about who it was bombing, or the removal of ETIM from the list of terror organizations was a politically motivated move.

It is also notable that US officials have categorized Beijing's actions in Xinjiang a genocide despite the lack of any credible evidence of mass killings in the region. While, at least theoretically, governments could commit genocide without mass killings, assuming their efforts are aimed specifically at destroying members of a group through other means, at no other point in human history has one government accused another of committing genocide in the absence of systematic and widespread targeted deaths of members of the impacted population. Notably, the US government did not declare the mass killings of Rwandan Tutsis in 1994 as a genocide per se, but only publicly noted "acts of genocide" — phrasing apparently aimed at avoiding responsibility to act to stop the massacres.

Recent Chinese policies in Xinjiang constitute, at the least, a historically unique form of preventative, authoritarian rule aimed at controlling the actions and expressions of a targeted group. They likely constitute a form of collective punishment. Reasonable organizations and individuals may, depending on their interpretation of events, aims, and definitions, classify the policies as an apparently novel form of genocide. Nevertheless, the US government has a clear motive in highlighting the issue and making it appear as horrific as it can possibly be. Fundamentally, there are two possibilities regarding US claims of genocide in Xinjiang. If one does not consider Beijing's actions in Xinjiang to be genocide, then Washington is stretching the term with potentially disastrous consequences. The dangers inherent to a story entitled "The Boy Who Cried Genocide" should be self-evident. On the other hand, if one does believe that the actions of the Chinese government constitute genocide, then Washington is even more morally culpable. In this scenario, the US has massive trade ties with a genocidal power, and Washington helps finance its government debt by willingly selling it to a genocidal regime.

Fallacy Number Nine

Beijing Has Foreign Enemies

The Chinese government does not have consistent enemies on the international stage. Beijing broadly considers the US and India as rivals, and it sees the Taipei-based ROC government as a usurper. However, even in those three scenarios the leadership of the PRC neither regards, nor acts towards, the other powers as outright *enemies*. Beijing does not seek to purposefully and consistently damage other national governments for the sake of pure antagonism. Instead, when faced with a perceived challenge to its core interests from another power, the Chinese government engages in focused, and usually time-bound, measures to pressure the targeted government.

A lack of official enemies does not mean that Chinese diplomacy is inherently passive or benign. Beijing has serious areas of contention with other governments, most notably in the realm of territorial disputes. The Chinese government also positions itself to have *capabilities* to counter and limit overall US global dominance. However, at the time of writing, these capabilities are primarily preparatory, and most likely aimed at dissuading the US from making moves to stall or reverse China's growth in relative power.

The Chinese government has more active territorial disputes than any other country. Beijing assets its right to sovereignty over territory that is also claimed by India and Bhutan along their Himalayan frontiers, and Japan in the East China Sea. The Chinese government also claims most islands, reefs, and maritime territory in the South China Sea — a claim that is disputed, at least in part, by Vietnam, the Philippines, Brunei, and Malaysia.

While the number of territorial disputes maintained by Beijing is high, they must be viewed in the context of China's geography. China has more international frontiers than any other country. Fourteen neighboring states share borders with the Middle Kingdom. Those are "just" the land borders; if one considers Japan, the Philippines, Malaysia, and Brunei as near maritime neighbors of China (as Beijing does), then China has eighteen immediate neighbors, and it contests territory with seven of them. The dispute between Beijing and Taipei is, arguably, less explicitly about territory than it is about the legitimacy of the ROC as a government. Nevertheless, if it is included, then Beijing has active territorial disputes with eight of nineteen neighboring states.

The extent of overlapping territorial claims between Beijing and its neighbors is undeniably notable. However, it is also fair to recognize that, while the raw number of disputes are higher, territorial contests are not China's unique purview in the region. Indeed, some of Beijing's neighbors have a *higher* incidence of territorial disputes with their immediate neighbors. India disputes territory with three of the six countries with which it effectively shares land borders. Seoul and Pyongyang both claim sovereignty over the entirety of the Korean Peninsula, and both contest Tokyo's claims over the Liancourt Rocks. Japan, despite having no land borders whatsoever, has territorial disputes with *each* of its nearest neighbors, namely Russia, China, and both Koreas. Even the little Taipei-based ROC disputes sovereignty with all six foreign powers that Beijing currently maintains territorial disputes with, along with Russia. Taipei doesn't recognize the 2004 treaty that settled the border dispute between Moscow and Beijing. In fact, the ROC officially maintains all circa-1911 Qing Empire territorial claims, and has only recently and begrudgingly acknowledged the independence of Mongolia, which was controlled by the Qing Empire prior to its collapse.

Beijing's motivation in maintaining its various territorial disputes stems, to varying degrees, from each of its overarching goals. Perpetuation of the CPC's political monopoly, the cohesion of the Chinese state, ensuring economic growth, and enhancing military capabilities drive Chinese actions in each of these disputes. Note that Beijing is *maintaining* these disputes, since most of these various territorial disagreements arose prior to the foundation of the PRC in 1949. These standoffs help the Chinese government burnish its nationalistic credentials and unify the domestic population against external targets. When Beijing seeks a distraction from domestic political issues, it can ratchet up tensions with a particular power; when Beijing wants to improve diplomatic and economic ties, it can downplay the disputes. Among other motives, the Chinese government maintains these claims because they are useful both for unifying the domestic population and threatening neighboring powers when necessary.

Beijing currently has active territorial disputes with Tokyo, New Delhi, Hanoi, Manila, Kuala Lumpur, Thimphu, and Brunei. The PRC, of course, claims sovereignty over the entirety of ROC-controlled territory in Taiwan. However, these situations of contested geographic sovereignty do not mean that Beijing views its rival claimants as enemies, and neither does it consistently treat them as such.

The case of Sino-Japanese relations is illustrative. Japan is the main target of nationalistic and historical ire in China (and, incidentally, South Korea). Opinion polls consistently rank Japan as the most disliked country in China; China is similarly the most disliked country in Japan. There are long-standing strategic differences between Japan and China. Memories of Japan's brutal invasion and occupation of Chinese territory are a key basis of Chinese nationalism. Beijing is wary of Japan's hosting of a large US military presence. Beijing claims the uninhabited Senkaku/Diaoyu Islands as its rightful territory, and regularly engages in naval patrols in the area, which is effectively controlled by Japan.

At the same time, there are significant economic and cultural ties between the two countries. China is Japan's largest trading partner. During trade tensions between China and the US in 2018, Japan reached out to pledge deepened economic cooperation with China; regarding bilateral relations, Japanese President Shinzo Abe stated, rather hopefully and directly, "We are neighbors; we're partners who will cooperate with each other, rather than be a threat to each other." Japanese companies have major and long-standing investments in China. Prior to the COVID-19 pandemic, China was Japan's largest source of international tourists. Crucially, despite their geopolitical, historical, and territorial tensions, and regular assertive shows of military force, there have been exactly zero deadly clashes between Chinese and Japanese military forces since the end of the Second World War.

China's relationship with India is similarly multifaceted. Trade and investment ties continue despite territorial tensions and the deadly 2020 border clashes. China and India have a significant degree of common ground in the international sphere. Both countries bristle at the perceived unfairness of international environmental initiatives that would restrict economic activity in poorer countries. Indian and Chinese leaders have issued joint statements calling on richer nations to lead through example with regards to climate change concerns.

Undoubtedly, there are major areas of strategic contention between the two powers. China has a long-standing dynamic of economic and strategic cooperation with Pakistan. India reaches out to China's neighbors, especially Vietnam and Japan, to counterbalance Chinese influence. Beijing and New Delhi compete for influence in Nepal, Bangladesh, Sri Lanka, and throughout Southeast Asia. Nevertheless, because of the significant areas of mutual understanding, and in some cases, cooperation, it would be more apt to describe China and India as "rivals" instead of "enemies."

Even Beijing's stance towards Vietnam — the last country that the PRC fought a major war with — is not entirely, nor even primarily, confrontational. The countries ceased their border clashes and reestablished formal diplomatic ties in 1990. China is Vietnam's top trading partner, and an important source of investment in the country. Hanoi is probably the most active of all claimant states in disputing and responding to Chinese deployments in the South China Sea, and Vietnam continues to reach out to India and the US to counterbalance China's regional power. The overall dynamic is one of simultaneous strategic competition and increasing economic entanglement, rather than direct, sustained, and multifaceted animosity.

Similarly, relations between Beijing and Manila have elements of confrontation and cooperation. After Vietnam, the Philippines is probably the second most active South China Sea claimant in terms of disputing Chinese claims over the maritime region. The Philippines has disputed Chinese claims in international courts, most notably at the Permanent Court of Arbitration in the Hague, which ruled in Manila's favor in 2016. Philippine and Chinese vessels occasionally make shows of force near their rival's assets. Additionally, China is wary of Philippine hosting of a US military presence, and the fact that the US and the Philippines have had a mutual defense agreement since 1951. Chinese and Philippine vessels occasionally engage in confrontations near the disputed maritime territory. Nevertheless, there are generally cordial political ties between Manila and Beijing. Some leaders in the Philippines, most notably the controversial, populist, and nationalistic former President Rodrigo Duterte, have courted Beijing as a counterbalance against the perceived high-handedness of Washington, and the US government perceived political interference in governmental and human rights issues. There is also a significant degree of economic cooperation between China and the Philippines, aided in part by the overall relative prosperity and social influence of Filipinos with Chinese ancestry.

Beijing's relations with Malaysia and Brunei are generally cordial. The various branches of the PLA have never had any deadly confrontations with military forces of Malaysia or Brunei, despite some overlap in South China Sea claims. As with the Philippines, both countries have economically imported ethnic Chinese minorities. Investment from China is significant in both countries, and China is Malaysia's number one trading partner. Malaysia and Brunei are also home to large and economically influential ethnic Chinese populations.

As for its rival government in the ROC/Taiwan, Beijing's policies vary between pressure and enticement, with elements of both often being simultaneously exerted. The PRC does not recognize the legitimacy of the ROC. However, in practical terms the relationship has roughly as many elements of cooperation as it does confrontation. PLA aircraft often patrol near Taiwan to put pressure on ROC forces and test their response times. However, no deadly confrontations between the two sides have occurred since 1958. Economic ties began to develop from the 1980s, as Taiwan was a crucial source of "foreign" investment during the early stages of mainland China's export-driven economic boom.

Beijing's stance towards Taiwan can be thought of as a "carrot and stick" approach. The PRC tends to react strongly against any moves seen as promoting formal Taiwanese independence through shows of military force and constraining the ROC's participation in international forums. Beijing also consistently "poaches" countries that previously had formal diplomatic ties with the ROC. Since the PRC and ROC are technically rival governments, no country officially recognizes both governments; embassies are either located in Taipei or Beijing. However, most regional governments and major world powers, including the US and Japan, have *de facto* "informal" diplomatic relations with both the PRC and ROC.

In general, Beijing seeks to establish closer ties with Taiwan when it is under KMT administration. Beijing then changes course to "punish" ROC voters after the election of a Democratic Progressive Party (DPP) government. Despite various marginal policy changes, Beijing consistently attempts to woo the Taiwanese population through economic integration. Mainland China is by far the largest trading partner of Taiwan.

In 2019, Beijing offered to establish a "one country, two systems" formula for relations with Taiwan that would see the ROC maintain its own administration, currency, and even military forces. The proposal was not very popular in Taiwan, coming amid the height of the Hong Kong protest movement and tensions over Beijing's expanding overt political control in the territory. Taiwanese President Tsai Ing-wen rejected the proposal outright. Such a rejection was essentially a foregone conclusion. Nevertheless, the proposal — regardless of implementation specifics and the extent to which Beijing could be trusted to maintain it if and when it managed to achieve a stronger degree of political influence within Taiwan — shows that Beijing does not specifically regard the ROC as an enemy state, so long as Taipei does not officially declare the independence which it already effectively exercises.

To reiterate, Beijing has more territorial disputes with other states than any other country on earth. However, the PRC does not consistently treat its rival territorial claimants, or any other states, as implacable enemies. In recent years mainland China has been the largest trading partner for most of the countries with which it contests territory, including Japan, India, and Vietnam. For the most part, the disputes are limited to the realms of nationalistic flag waving and military shows of force. Beijing's four core interests, rather than consistent antipathy for any rival government, motivate the CPC to maintain these inherited claims.

As for the US, Chinese foreign policy moves meant to marginally undermine or push back against US influence have been *reactive* rather than *antagonistic*. Note that currently the main areas of open strategic contention between the US and the PRC, in which both sides frequently engage in military shows of force, are the South China Sea, the Taiwan Strait, and the East China Sea. Regardless of the extent to which Beijing's territorial claims may be considered excessive in these areas, they are clearly magnitudes of degrees closer to the Chinese mainland than they are to the United States. It would be difficult to reasonably define the US as the main aggressor state if Chinese aircraft carriers were making shows of force near Hawaii, much less the Gulf of Mexico. In the economic sphere, since around 2015 the US has frequently imposed sanctions on major Chinese firms, especially the telecom giant Huawei. Washington has openly sought to marginally curtail Chinese political and economic influence in third countries, usually through targeted sanctions and export restrictions. Washington also imposed significant tariffs on Chinese exports in 2018. The Chinese government has *reacted* to these US policies, generally with smaller countermoves, but it has not significantly *initiated* any policies specifically aimed at undermining US core interests. China's gains in relative world power have come about largely because of the organic growth of its internal economy and consequent increase in trading and financial leverage, rather than any Beijing-led efforts to directly decrease US power.

Beijing's lack of clear, consistent enemies is a key and often misunderstood factor in US-China geopolitical contention. Undoubtedly, Beijing's rival territorial claimants are happy to cooperate with each other, and the US, to stave off growing Chinese power. However, they are also largely entwined with the Chinese economy, and therefore highly unlikely to support any US efforts to undermine China's economic growth. The economic sphere is the area in which Cold War comparisons fall flat — the USSR was never a major trading partner of any US treaty ally. As for raw military dynamics, the USSR effectively conquered multiple states and set up a system of satellite governments throughout Eastern Europe during World War Two. Moscow's clear geopolitical expansionism in the 1940s contrasts sharply with contemporary Beijing, which has not conquered any inhabited foreign territory in recent decades. Washington has serious difficulties in attempting to overtly unite countries against a PRC that does not have clear enemies. Even with regards to the US, Beijing does not view the country as an enemy so much as a rival with a significant degree of common interests. So long as its core interests are not undermined, the Chinese leadership is largely tolerant of US global influence. In only one crucial area — that of *relative* international power — is the current dynamic between Washington and Beijing one of outright contention.

Fallacy Number Ten

Beijing Seeks to Undermine the Global Order

Washington sees itself as the establisher, defender, and overall champion of the post-World War Two global order. Consequently, as Chinese influence has expanded, US officials have increasingly denounced Beijing as purposefully undermining this global system. Antony Blinken, Secretary of State in the Biden Administration, stated directly to Chinese leadership that the US has "... deep concerns with actions by China, including in Xinjiang, Hong Kong, Taiwan, cyber attacks on the United States, and economic coercion toward our allies. Each of these actions threaten the rules-based order that maintains global stability." This language was echoed a few months later when NATO issued a collective statement reading, in part, "China's stated ambitions and assertive behavior present systemic challenges to the rules-based international order and to areas relevant to Alliance security."

Such pronouncements stem from a consistent messaging campaign aimed at domestic and international audiences in recent years, from US leadership, and the leaders of some US-aligned countries. However, to the extent that a post-World War Two global order can be objectively defined, the PRC is a major *stakeholder* in these trends, and generally supports them out of self-interest. Washington's assertions that Beijing seeks to undermine the international order are self-delusion at best and deliberate and politically convenient falsehoods at worst.

Three key developments and trends — relative peace between major global powers, increased international trade and investment, and the sway of multilateral global institutions — define the post-World War Two global order. Key multilateral institutions established in the post-war era to promote peace, cooperation, and economic interdependence include the United Nations Security Council (UNSC), the International Monetary Fund (established in 1945), and the World Trade Organization (founded in 1995 as a successor to the General Agreement on Tariffs and Trade which came into force in 1948). These organizations, and the trends of relative peace and increased economic interdependence they promote, are the essential foundation for defining any post-war "rules-based order."

There has been a clear shift towards relative peace and global economic interdependence since the middle of the twentieth century. From 1960 to 2020, international merchandise trade increased from 16.6% to 41.6% of global GDP; over the same period, global economic output expanded roughly 7.5-fold. Meanwhile, the frequency of major armed conflicts — especially interstate conflicts — has generally declined. During the 1950s, each year an average of approximately 45,000 people died battle-related deaths; in the 2010s, annual totals averaged less than 10,000. This decline is all the more notable since it occurred over a period when the overall human population more than doubled.

The trends of relative global peace and deepened international economic exchange have benefited Beijing more than any other major global power. Recall from **Fallacy Number Five: China Is Uniquely Aggressive** that China has generally engaged in fewer and shorter international conflicts than other roughly comparable global powers in the post-World War Two era. This trend has arisen largely from the perceived self-interest of the Chinese government. China, with more immediate neighbors than any other country, is especially vulnerable to the potentially destabilizing impacts of interstate warfare.

Furthermore, China's rapid economic growth has coincided with its period of avoidance of direct interstate conflict, with both trends especially evident from the late 1970s. China has been the country with the greatest volume of international trade since 2013. Major interstate conflict could disrupt the global supply lines on which the Chinese economy relies. Even in areas far away from China's most key trade routes, the Chinese government has a clear interest in the continuation of the general trend of reduced armed conflict. War generally tends to increase economic hardship, and poor people make poor customers. Peace in far-off regions facilitates Chinese trade and investment.

Beijing also largely benefits from participation in and support to multilateral international organizations. The PRC has been a veto-wielding permanent member of the United Nations Security Council (UNSC) since 1971, when it took over the China-designated seat previously occupied by the ROC government in Taipei. Beijing's position in this elite club of five global powers gives it the right to unilaterally veto any binding resolution within the organization. This is a privilege that only the governments of the US, UK, France, and Russia also possess. According to the UN Charter, the UNSC is the *only* organization with the right to impose international blockades or approve military action (except in clear instances of national self-defense). Theoretically, though not so much in practice, permanent UNSC members have the ability to unilaterally veto any binding international sanctions, instances of non-defensive warfare, and cross-border armed stabilization efforts by any and all other global powers.

The PRC has also benefited from its position within the IMF (since 1980) and the WTO (from 2001), the two most influential multilateral institutions aimed at promoting economic stability and international interdependence. The IMF provides loans to national governments and monitors global economic conditions, among other activities. The WTO provides a framework in which member governments can challenge the allegedly unfair international trade and investment policies of other countries.

Both Washington and Beijing (along with other relevant governments) can and do at least somewhat challenge the three pillars of the post-war order when they deem such policies to be necessary. However, an impartial examination of the historical relationship the two national governments have with these three global trends reveals that Beijing has been, at the very worst, no more of a threat to their continuation than Washington. This is most clearly the case when looking at the military record of the two powers in the post-WW2 era. Since the mid-20th century, the United States has engaged in more frequent, longer, deadlier and far more geographically dispersed international conflicts than the People's Republic of China.

In terms of open international access and global trade, the picture is less clearly in Beijing's favor. While China has the largest volume of global trade, the Chinese government also engages in practices that can reasonably be said to exploit or "game" the systems that govern international trade and investment. Most obviously, China's economic system of mixed state-directed and market activity provides Beijing with enormous means to directly shape the flows of trade and investment to its own perceived advantages. The Chinese government has restricted multinational companies from access to its vast markets based on political concerns. Beijing also maintains currency controls, only allowing the RMB to move within a narrow band every day against the US dollar. Making the RMB artificially "cheaper" boosts Chinese exports, although the controls have and can work both ways, with the Chinese government apparently facilitating upward movement on the value of the RMB when needed. Of course, essentially all national governments with the means to do so influence currency exchange rates to promote their economic goals, but the controls are especially tight within China when compared to other large economies. The Chinese government also strictly controls investment outflows from China. It is extremely difficult for Chinese citizens and companies to directly invest their capital abroad unless they are physically located in another country. Most major overseas investments effectively require the approval of the Chinese government, which may approve or deny such outflows based on its own perceived interests and goals.

A reasonable observer could state, at the time of writing, that the Chinese government currently exploits the post-World War Two trend of increased economic interdependence more than Washington. However, the US government itself also games the system in many ways, and apparently with increasing frequency. Most blatantly, US leadership exploits the current position of the US dollar as global reserve currency in pursuit of its political goals. Washington imposes unilateral sanctions on a variety of national governments and other organizations outside the framework of the UN. In most cases these sanctions extend beyond direct US jurisdiction; Washington not only prevents its own citizens and companies from providing material or economic support to sanctions targets, but also *effectively cuts off all global financial institutions* from directly engaging with the targeted governments, groups, or companies. The list of sanctioned entities includes government entities, individuals, armed groups, and corporations. Nearly all targets are in Washington's list of perceived adversaries or rivals, including Iran, Russia, and China itself. The US justifies such measures on national security or humanitarian grounds. Many critics — including the Chinese government — say these unilateral, though effectively global, sanctions are technically illegal under the UN Charter. In addition to sanctions, the US has also increasingly restricted market access to the US and investment from the US to specific companies — mostly Chinese. There has been a very clear trend of the US government increasingly limiting open international trade and investment as China's economic influence has grown.

Finally, in the realm of their relations with the multilateral institutions that, at least in theory, shape any "rules-based order," a hypothetically objective observer would likely condemn Washington more than Beijing for undermining or subverting these forums. Critics often accuse permanent UNSC members of "abusing" their veto privilege rights to defend their geopolitical allies from censure following apparent violations of international law. Since the PRC has occupied the Chinese seat at the UNSC, it has vetoed seventeen resolutions, compared to 82 US vetoes during the same timeframe. In terms of participation in the IMF and the WTO, neither country has an especially obvious record of either exploiting or ignoring its position within the institutions. Both the US and China have successfully challenged the trade policies of the other power at the WTO, and both governments generally adjust their policies in reaction to the rulings.

Many scholars and politicians may claim that the advancement of democracy is another key feature of the international order. Some further say that the promotion of democracy is an area in which the Chinese play an obviously harmful role when compared to the reigning global hegemon. However, both claims may be reasonably disputed. Generally democratic forms of government have proliferated since World War Two, but some organizations tracking the extent to which governments are democratic say the trend reversed from around 2015, depending on which index is used.

Even assuming that the propagation of democracy is a key feature of the post-World War Two order, the historical record neither condemns Beijing nor condones Washington in terms of actively promoting this dynamic. With regards to internal governance, the US has a stronger claim to being a democracy than China. However, in terms of promoting democracy abroad, the US record is deeply flawed. US intelligence agencies actively supported several coups against democratically elected governments during the Cold War, including in Guatemala, Iran, Bolivia, and Chile. The US government has also actively supported or undermined candidates in numerous foreign elections when candidates opposed the perceived interests of the US government. Although Beijing does promote its interests within foreign governments through various means, including clandestine interference, for the entirety of the PRC's existence there are few, if any, clear historical incidents of the Chinese government using military support or subterfuge to attempt to install a chosen government within a foreign country. Unlike their US counterparts, there is no documented evidence of PRC intelligence agencies planning or supporting a successful coup which overthrew the government of a foreign country.

Blaming Beijing for wanton electronic spying and cyberattacks is another rhetorical point used by US officials to castigate the Chinese government as a destabilizing power. However, the key reality is that *all major global powers* use any means at their disposal to gather as much information on their perceived friends and foes alike. US intelligence agencies are no different in this regard, having, for example, tapped the personal communications of paramount German leaders for years and placed spying devices on a Boeing aircraft used by China's top leadership. US officials often report incidents in which Chinese intelligence operatives have engaged in industrial espionage aimed at acquiring key technologies or trade secrets. However, even in the specific field of economic espionage there is evidence of US agencies targeting, for example, Europe's Airbus. The NSA even launched a largely successful intelligence operation in 2007 to steal customer information and source code from Huawei. The Chinese telecom giant is therefore not only a target of US spying accusations, but also of US spying.

To be absolutely clear, Washington's hypocrisy does not absolve Beijing of any of its suboptimal policies, including some activities that may, at the very least marginally, undermine the post-World War Two trends of relative global peace, strengthened economic interconnection, and rules-based multilateral organizations. Nevertheless, it is interesting to note that three of the four geographic areas in which Secretary Blinken specifically accused Beijing of undermining the rules-based international order — Xinjiang, Hong Kong, and Taiwan — are officially recognized by essentially every government on earth, including the US itself, as Chinese territory.

Beijing's actions, policies, and rhetoric in these three areas may be reasonably defined as oppressive or disruptive, but it is hard to see how they could constitute threats to individuals and organizations outside the immediate area in which they occur, much less decades-old global trends. Of course, the Chinese government also claims sovereignty over the South China Sea. Given the disputed legal basis of Beijing's (and, incidentally, Taipei's) extensive claims over the region, and the fact that the overlapping national claims have historically resulted in military clashes and bloodshed, this is one area in which criticism of the Chinese government's potentially destabilizing actions are likely the most reasonable.

While some official US criticisms of specific Chinese policies are generally valid, if often hypocritical, the idea that Beijing is trying to purposefully undermine an overall global order that has enormously advanced its core interests is patently illogical. Such accusations are motivated primarily by Washington's fears over China's rise at the expense of US relative power. It also stems from the US self-perception as the international "good guy" who won World War Two and subsequently ensured the relative peace and prosperity of recent decades. These positive trends have existed at the same time as the US has been the clearly dominant global power. While the USSR did meaningfully challenge US dominance for several decades of the Cold War, the overall trend of US military, political, and (especially) economic supremacy was consistent. There has been a clear *correlation* between Washington's historically high degree of global influence and an era of relative global peace, prosperity, and cooperation. However, this does not necessarily mean that such trends were primarily *caused* by US power and influence.

Numerous global trends are likely responsible for our current era of relative peace and prosperity. Most obviously, technological advancements, especially in terms of production, communication, and transport, have helped bring about an era of relatively high prosperity, trade, and investment. Technological propagation is also likely the main reason for recent rarity of major interstate war. Most obviously, countries armed with nuclear weapons avoid direct conflict due to their own, and their rivals', fears of mutual destruction. A Third World War between competing Cold War camps would probably have broken out were it not for the nuclear arsenals possessed by both sides. As nuclear weapon technology has spread to other powers, such as India and Pakistan, their national governments are also incentivized to avoid further rounds of direct and unrestrained conflict. Perhaps Washington's greatest contribution to promoting global peace is not its massive naval and aerial firepower and its global network of military bases, but rather its successes in the Manhattan Project and the horrific devastation unleashed on Hiroshima and Nagasaki.

The proliferation of effective small arms, especially relatively cheap and effective assault rifles, and the spread of literacy and nationalism, also deserve credit for the reduced frequency of aggressive wars by stronger powers against weaker adversaries. In the late 1800s and early 1900s, imperial powers could generally crush native resistance due to their superiority of their organization, transport, and weaponry. In many cases, locals did not especially resent the outsiders more than their own rulers. Now, however, blatantly offensive warfare against a population that is willing and capable of sustaining resistance against foreign invaders is nearly impossible to sustain. Despite their enormous advantages in conventional and nuclear weapons systems, neither the US nor the USSR could ensure the political survival of their local allies in Afghanistan. Both the US and China also suffered serious setbacks against determined local resistance in Vietnam. Simply put, interstate warfare is now relatively rare because it is rarely an effective tool for advancing a national government's long-term interests.

It is possible that relative peace, economic interdependence, and the influence of international institutions will decline when the US is supplanted as the globally dominant power. However, such a development is highly unlikely, as any government that surpasses the US in total international influence is almost certainly going to benefit from and seek to continue such trends. The national government of any dominant power is highly likely to generally continue to benefit from international economic interdependence, especially if it dominates the flows of trade and investment. Indeed, it is probable that recent US moves to, at least marginally, limit global economic exchange through sanctions and limiting exports of sensitive technology are motivated precisely by a perception in Washington that the US is losing its relative advantage. Additionally, given the reality, which will almost certainly persist, of major interstate conflict being generally ineffective at promoting the interests of national governments, the trend of relative peace will also probably continue. The rulers of an established power have every motive to try to convince its population and other countries that a rising challenger poses an existential threat to their interests, but such claims are naturally self-interested and suspect, and worthy of an attempt at objective comparative analysis.

A Brief Synopsis of Current Trends and Likely Future Developments

The previous chapters outlined several key fallacies that hinder generalized understanding of Sino-US relations. Where does reality lie? The following is a reiteration of the core goals of the US and Chinese political systems, and a comparison of the relative advantages and disadvantages of the two powers in terms of global military, diplomatic, and economic influence. A brief, overall forecast in terms of the projected course of these relative advantages is also included.

Key Aims of Institutions Shaping the US Political System

1. Elected representatives seek to maintain or expand their political power through winning elections.
2. Government bureaucracies want to ensure the political power of the US Federal Government, both domestically and internationally.
3. Corporations seek to maximize their profits.

Key Aims of the Chinese Government

4. Maintain domestic monopoly on political power.
5. Ensure sustained economic growth.

6. Protect Chinese territorial integrity.
7. Develop and deploy a military force sufficient to withstand outside pressure and with the ability to pressure other powers.

Relative US Military Advantages

8. An overall quantitative and qualitative edge in terms of conventional and nuclear equipment. The ongoing trend of Beijing rapidly undermining this advantage is likely to continue.
9. A network of global military bases and formalized cooperation with other powers, including several influential countries. Washington will probably maintain this advantage for the foreseeable future.
10. Officers and personnel with combat experience. The US will likely maintain this relative advantage.

Relative Chinese Military Advantages

11. A "home field" advantage in which any plausible scenarios of conventional conflict with the US take place near China's borders. Beijing's military forces are concentrated within or near PRC territory, whereas those of the US are dispersed throughout various around the globe locations. This trend is likely to continue until at least mid-century.
12. The numerical edge in terms of human resources and industrial capability. China will almost certainly continue to enjoy this relative advantage over the US for the foreseeable future, though demographic decline will likely eventually erode its degree. By the end of the century, China's population will probably "only" be

around twice or three times that of the US, instead of its current fourfold advantage.

Relative US Diplomatic Advantages

13. A network of formalized alliances. Washington is highly likely to maintain this advantage.
14. Effective correlation of key interests with multiple Asian states (especially India, Japan, and Vietnam) concerned about expanding Chinese influence. Again, Washington is highly likely to maintain this advantage.
15. Superior media influence to shape public opinion in third countries. Overall, the US will probably maintain this advantage, though it will likely be undermined, at least in some key regions, by concerted Chinese efforts and economic influence.

Relative Chinese Diplomatic Advantages

16. The avoidance of direct entanglement in armed disputes between or within outside powers. This advantage is highly likely to continue.
17. Effective correlation of key interests with Russia. Beijing is highly likely to maintain this advantage.
18. The appearance of being an "alternative" to populations and governments resentful of US (or broadly defined "Western") domination. This advantage is likely to continue, unless Beijing itself becomes globally dominant and overtly hegemonic.
19. Numerical superiority in terms of Chinese-born and ethnic Chinese individuals living abroad. This advantage is almost certain to continue.

Relative US Economic Advantages

20. Superior technological capabilities in certain industries. The Chinese government is currently making concerted efforts to undermine this relative US advantage; overall, Washington is extremely likely to lose its edge in most key fields no later than mid-century.
21. The position of the US dollar as the global reserve currency. The RMB will probably not replace the US dollar in this position. Nevertheless, the US dollar will likely be replaced by some form of multilateral medium for international exchange, and the current US advantage over Beijing is likely to end no later than 2040.
22. Ability to attract inbound immigration, thus securing international talent and delaying a demographic shift to a rapidly aging population. The US will probably maintain this advantage, though it is likely to slowly ease as a gap in living standards between the US and most other countries narrows.

Relative Chinese Economic Advantages

23. The numerical edge in terms of human resources and industrial capability. China will almost certainly continue to enjoy this relative advantage over the US for the foreseeable future, though demographic decline will likely lessen its degree. As previously mentioned, by the end of the century, China's population will probably be "only" around twice or three times that of the US, instead of its current fourfold advantage.
24. Remaining economic growth potential, especially in the poorer regions of China. This advantage is likely to continue until at least mid-century, though it will probably slow as relative geographic economic disparities ease.

25. Trade ties with third countries. China's relative advantage here is extremely likely to continue and grow.
26. Ability for the government to plan and implement consistent policy over multiple decades. Barring a major change in governmental structure in either country, this advantage will continue.

Section Two

Predictions

Analysis of the present situation may be intellectually stimulating and useful for understanding current and near-term developments. However, the true measure of the utility of geopolitical analysis is its ability to predict future events and dynamics. Here this work makes nine key predictions. If the following forecasts are proven broadly accurate over the course of the coming decades, then the basic analytical framework in this book has been sound. If, on the other hand, relevant developments occur that counter these predictions, then the analysis has serious flaws. These predictions are based on a broadly defined business-as-usual model for interstate relations over the coming decades. "Unexpected" (though still quite plausible) developments that could knock the trajectory of Sino-US relations off their forecasted path are discussed in the Grey Swans section near the end of this work.

First Prediction
Controlled Competition Continues

Washington and Beijing will continue their dynamic of overall geopolitical contention for at least as a long as they govern the two most powerful countries on Earth. This trend is likely to continue through at least mid-century, and assuming no system-disrupting disaster occurs in either country, quite possibly well beyond the 2050s. While both governments will continue policies aimed at expanding their own relative power at the expense of their main competitor, they will also seek to ensure that the competition does not escalate into a crisis that threatens their other core imperatives, or the global system as a whole. Given the immense military power and economic capabilities possessed by both sides, neither government is at all likely to be able or even willing to entirely knock the other from the field of overall global competition. Meanwhile, strong and enduring motives for continuing engagement, and even cooperation, in certain fields will further drive a dynamic of controlled competition.

Only one key aspect of Sino-US relations is effectively a zero-sum game, in which the advantage of one side always comes at the cost of the other. This is the field of *relative* power. While the relative power of various governments is composed of various complex forces, in this book they are broadly categorized into economic, military, and diplomatic realms. So long as the US and China are the world's two most powerful countries, there will be an irreconcilable competition for overall relative dominance.

However, it is vital to note that *only in the area of overall relative global power* do the goals of Washington and Beijing directly contradict one another. Within the US, this field of relative power is most important to the unelected bureaucracy in Washington

DC. Both the CPC and the US government also have other key interests, which in many cases are actually complementary. Most obviously, they want to ensure their own survival, both in terms of overall governance system (more important in China) and in terms of their political party or administration (key in the US, especially for elected politicians). Leaders in China and the US use economic stability and nationalism to strengthen their political positions. Meanwhile, economic growth is essentially the *only* goal of large corporations, one of the three "branches" that effectively form the US political structure.

While the overall dynamic of US-Sino contention is likely to continue until at least mid-century, it may begin to shift in later decades, depending on the development path of other powers. Historically, Chinese and US leaders have cooperated against perceived mutual threats, from Imperial Japan in the 1940s to the USSR in the 1980s. Although this geopolitical dynamic is unlikely to reoccur in this century, such a scenario cannot be entirely ruled out at some future date. Barring some sort of major and currently unforeseen development, the only potential contenders to become global powers that appear at all likely to directly challenge US and Chinese economic, military, and diplomatic clout are India and some sort of geopolitically united European state.

Broadly, there are two questions to consider when examining current and likely future dynamics of the US-China competition for position as the world's overall strongest government. Which center of power has the overall power advantage? Which government is expanding its relative power faster than the other?

As of the time of writing, Washington has an overall advantage over Beijing in terms of its military capabilities, and diplomatic ties with third countries. The US also has a larger nominal GDP, though China has larger "real" economic output when measured in terms of PPP GDP. However, China's relative power, especially when measured in economic terms, is growing faster than that of the US. Because of the high likelihood that major global powers will avoid direct military conflict (see **Fourth Prediction: China and the US Will Never Purposefully Go to War**), and the fact that diplomatic power is generally "softer" and largely dependent on military and economic strength, economic power is the single most important facet of US-China contention.

The current dynamic of a dominant Washington challenged by an ascendent Beijing explains the basic contours of Sino-US rivalry. The US government wants to maintain its dominant position, and therefore enacts policies meant to thwart or limit Chinese power and influence. The Chinese government slowly pushes back, but for the most part does not directly initiate confrontations, because it (likely correctly) believes that time and momentum are working to its overall advantage. Overall antagonism between the two powers is likely to grow as the overall power gap between them narrows.

The trends arising from this dynamic of bilateral contention — broadly defined by a dominant US attempting to slow (or even reverse) an ascendent China's expansion in relative power — are likely to noticeably change when, as is highly likely, the Chinese government occupies the generally dominant position. Of course, it will be difficult for both governments, and other relevant powers, to define exactly when and how this shift occurs. Different fields of power will likely shift at different times. For example, China will almost certainly have a clear overall advantage in the economic sphere when its nominal GDP surpasses that of the US, likely sometime before 2030 (**Third Prediction: China Overtakes the US Nominal GDP by 2030 and Maintains Higher GDP for the Rest of the Century**). Relative dominance in terms of military capabilities will likely never be conclusively defined, since the two countries will almost certainly continue to avoid fighting a direct, sustained conflict. Nevertheless, the overall advantage in military strength will likely belong to Beijing sometime in the 2040s or 2050s, as the Chinese government harnesses some of its superior productive capabilities to out-build and out-research the US in key military fields. As for influence over third powers, it is possible that Beijing will face Washington from a slightly disadvantaged diplomatic position for at least several decades, and possibly even for the remainder of the 21st century. Although Beijing will have more international economic leverage to utilize in pursuit of foreign policy goals, the US will probably continue to have strong military alliances in East Asia, as growing Chinese strength drives neighboring powers to seek an outside counterbalance. US military alliances in Europe may be undermined if tensions between Washington and Moscow eventually ease, or if major European states form a truly united military and foreign policy front. Nevertheless, barring any major unforeseen developments, an overall US diplomatic advantage is likely to persist long after its relative economic and military power are overtaken by Beijing.

If China becomes noticeably stronger than the US, and Beijing continues to expand its power at a rate surpassing that of Washington DC, then overall antagonism between the two powers is likely to gradually decrease. In a scenario of an overall ascendent and increasingly powerful Beijing, Washington would have less leverage with which to limit or stunt additional Chinese growth. However, the US government would almost certainly remain sufficiently capable of fending off any Chinese efforts to directly antagonize the US, undermine Washington's core perceived interests, or severely limit US global influence. India will also increasingly come into play in this dynamic, which is most likely to be a clear global trend from around 2035–2050. Beijing's geopolitical power balancing efforts may be focused primarily on a relatively ascendent India, instead of a US facing an overall decline in its relative global power and prestige (see **Ninth Prediction: India-China Contention Supplants US-China Rivalry**).

While a scenario of Beijing occupying the position as the strongest global power and continuing to expand its relative influence is the most likely dynamic from around 2040, it is by no means an inevitable outcome. If some internal condition, such as a combination of economic, political, and environmental crisis, prevents China from attaining an overall power advantage against the US *and also* majorly disrupts China's relative growth, US-China contention is likely to generally ease. In general, dominant powers who are reasonably confident in their ability to maintain their relative dominance do not tend to engage in potentially dangerous antagonism against weaker, and increasingly relatively weaker, states. Even when China's relative power *was* clearly growing from around 1990–2010, the US government did not react especially antagonistically towards Beijing until it was clear that the Chinese government was a legitimate threat to overall US dominance.

However, US-China contention is only likely to ease in a scenario of continued and strengthened relative US dominance if the cause of China's relative weakening is essentially internal, as opposed to the result of some sort of effective gambit by Washington to check Beijing's power. If the US government openly, deliberately, and "successfully" enacts policies that result in a halt or reversal of China's growing relative power, then Beijing would likely retaliate in unpredictable and potentially combustive ways. A Chinese government that no longer had confidence in expanding its relative power largely through internal development due to a US move would be incentivized, instead, to expand its relative power by directly weakening Washington's position. While this scenario is unlikely because of the enormous risks and disruptions to both countries that it would entail, such a possibility cannot be entirely ruled out. At any rate, whether it could occur "naturally" or deliberately, a dynamic of a dominant Washington expanding its relative global power faster than Beijing is unlikely over the coming decades.

An interesting possibility that could develop around the mid- to-late 21st century is one in which China has an overall power advantage, but it is challenged by a newly ascendant United States. This scenario is also generally unlikely, but certainly not impossible. China will face significant demographic challenges from its aging population — a systematic threat to continued economic growth that is mostly countered in the US by robust inbound immigration. China is almost certainty going to have a significantly higher population than the US through the end of the century, and the existing trend of globalization "flattening" the earth and smoothing out economic disparities between historically wealthier and poorer countries will probably continue. Nevertheless, various other internal calamities could also upset China's trajectory to the relative advantage of the US government. In a scenario of an overall dominant China being challenged by a resurgent, "upstart" US, the current global dynamic will likely be essentially flipped on its head. A dominant Beijing would probably seek to incrementally disrupt the upward trajectory of the US by putting economic pressure on its technological and economic development. The Chinese government could even attempt to project military force near the US mainland, and out to powers in Latin America concerned about a rising and increasingly assertive US.

A far more likely scenario near the end of the century is India rising in relative power against a dominant China. In this scenario, Washington may act essentially as a junior partner to Delhi as the Indian government seeks to counter a dominant Beijing. Such a dynamic would probably also result in strengthened Chinese commitments to Pakistan and intensified outreach to Nepal, Bangladesh, Sri Lanka, and Myanmar.

Regardless of its specific dynamics regarding overall dominance and power expansion, US-China contention for relative power will persist. At the same time, the two governments will continue to share many broadly common interests. Most noticeably, Beijing and Washington have a clear, overriding goal of avoiding nuclear annihilation or environmental collapse. Both governments also want to maintain national economic growth, which in both countries is heavily influenced by conditions in the other. Beijing and Washington benefit from safe oceanic trade, and, as evidenced by recent history in the western reaches of the Indian Ocean, they will probably maintain a united front against non-state piracy. They will also likely have broad cooperation against mutual threats such as cooperation against transnational radicalism and terrorism, the emergency of novel diseases, and the spread of nuclear weaponry (so long as both governments view such threats as roughly equivalent challenges). The US and China may even, someday, again cooperate against a perceived mutual geopolitical threat. There are numerous areas in which the two powers have common interests. These shared imperatives, especially a basic commitment to combating or preventing threats to human survival, are apparently far more important than their contention for relative global power. The various facets of interactions, tensions, and dependencies between Beijing and Washington will almost certainly never devolve into an entirely zero-sum game in which one side's progress always results in a negative impact for the other. Nevertheless, in the area of relative power contention is inevitable, and the two countries will shape their strategies and policies accordingly.

China and the United States will probably maintain a significant degree of economic and financial engagement over the coming decades, despite their geopolitical tensions. The political elite in both countries benefit from bilateral trade and investment, and will therefore seek its continuation. While there will likely be incremental changes to the terms of the economic ties, they are likely to continue, barring some sort of uncontrollable escalation into outright conflict, a general collapse in the global economic system, or some radical technological transformation.

Bilateral trade and investments arise largely from the relative advantages each country has in terms of production. Currently, China has an overall advantage in a broad range of manufacturing due to its relatively lower costs of labor, cheaper electricity, good physical infrastructure, the concentration of industry, and some direct government support. These advantages facilitate China's exports of vast quantities of manufactured goods to other countries, including the United States. Meanwhile, the US, due in part to its far lower population density and its historic technological dominance, has overall advantages in grain production, many professional services, and some advanced manufacturing. While less substantial than its imports, the US also exports numerous goods to China, especially foodstuffs, but also energy, and some relatively high-technology products such as commercial airplanes. US firms also provide various services to Chinese clients. Barring some sort of unforeseen technological development or generalized global catastrophe, the US and China will likely continue to have some form of respective relative advantage in economic specialization when compared to the other country. Bilateral tourism and educational ties will likely also continue. US-China trade generally encourages economic activity and benefits the governments of both countries, despite various trade and investment grievances.

Overall, Washington has been more willing to disrupt US-Chinese economic ties in recent years. Under the Trump and Biden administrations, the US government has imposed tariffs on Chinese imports. Washington has also implemented (and maintained) technology and export controls on Chinese telecom giants Huawei and ZTE, nominally for violations of the US government's unilateral sanctions on Iran. While these actions, and other similar policies, have marginally disrupted bilateral trade and between the US and China investment, they have not significantly reduced them.

Official US efforts to *marginally* disrupt direct economic ties with China — and in some cases, China's economic engagements with other countries — may have slightly slowed China's overall rapid economic expansion and increased interlinking with other countries. However, if they were aimed at actually *reducing* China's international economic engagement, then they have spectacularly failed. During the period when Washington made apparent efforts to reduce global economic engagement with China, Chinese exports to the US continued to grow, and China became the largest trading partner of the EU and ASEAN.

Washington's various sanctions and other economic policies targeting China actions are probably aimed primarily at signaling Washington's willingness for further punitive actions, and attempting to discourage third powers from deepening their economic engagement with China. Domestic political concerns are also motivating factors, as various administrations perceive a benefit from appearing "tough on China." However, if Washington's goal has been to significantly disrupt China's economic assertion and derail it from its apparent trajectory of overtaking the US as the world's largest economy, then it has failed abysmally.

With sufficient political will, Washington *could*, at least theoretically, impose broad-reaching financial sanctions and trade embargoes on the Chinese government. Such efforts may then spark an overall economic crisis that disrupts China's expanding global influence. However, such a move would almost inevitably prompt a generalized global financial and economic catastrophe which would also impact the United States causing immense problems for the ruling administration and possibly generalized social and political instability. Therefore, such a move to decisively and forcibly disrupt China's global economic engagement is extremely unlikely. The US government was unable or unwilling to blatantly seek to stop or reverse China's economic growth and consequent increase in global influence when the US economy was five or even three times larger than China's in nominal terms. Washington is therefore extremely unlikely to attempt such a gambit when the Chinese economy is worth over seven-tenths of that of the US.

The US government is likely to seek to marginally disrupt China's global economic ties and technological development for as long as the US government believes it has an overall advantage in terms of financial leverage. However, a total break in relations is not a realistic scenario. If, as is highly likely, the overall advantage continues to shift in Beijing's favor over the coming years and decades, then any US moves to seek to economically hobble China become increasingly dangerous. While US-China contention will almost certainly continue, at some point before mid-century China will probably be in the overall leading position, with the US behind it.

Second Prediction

Both Governments Overstate the Extent of Bilateral Contention

Citing the threat of a foreign adversary to help unite the domestic population and justify expanded government power is one of humanity's oldest and most effective political strategies. Leaders in Washington and Beijing have a clear interest in exaggerating the threat of their main geopolitical rival in order to cement their own positions and ensure government control over their populations. Throughout the coming decades, politicians in the US and China will continue to employ public rhetoric that grossly exaggerates the extent to which the fundamental interests of the two powers are actually in contention. So long as they administer the world's two most influential countries, officials are highly likely to overstate the extent to which the actions of their foreign rival pose an imminent threat to common citizens. Furthermore, both governments will use the bilateral contention to expand their power within society, restrict the scope of politically acceptable rhetoric regarding the appropriate approach to the foreign rival, and justify controls on information. Since the US currently has greater liberty with regards to speech and overt government control than the PRC, US society and politics are consequently highly likely to experience a more pronounced shift to authoritarianism driven by the increasingly obvious struggle for overall global influence.

The trend of leaders in the US and China escalating their rhetorical condemnation of the rival geopolitical power is already clear, especially in the United States. In recent years, official US statements have progressed from calling the Chinese government a "competitor" to a "rival" and a "threat." The rhetoric has generally escalated regardless of which political party controls the presidency. China is now portrayed not only as a challenger to overall global dominance, but a threat to the prosperity of individual Americans and even the domestic political system of the United States. In December 2020, the intelligence chief of the outgoing Trump administration described the Chinese government as "the greatest threat to America today, and the greatest threat to democracy and freedom worldwide since World War Two." In March 2021, President Biden, referring to China, said, "they have an overall goal to become the leading country in the world, the wealthiest country in the world, and the most powerful country in the world. That's not going to happen on my watch because the United States are going to continue to grow and expand."

The Chinese government has also increasingly played up the perceived threat of the US to justify its own domestic political controls. Beijing frequently blames instances of regional civil unrest — most notably in Xinjiang and Hong Kong — on "foreign interference." In February 2021 Xi Jinping stated directly that "the United States is the greatest threat to our country's development and security." On both sides of the Pacific, the government pronouncements are notably dire and antagonistic for two countries who engage in enormous volumes of trade and investment, and who have not engaged in direct conflict for over 70 years.

Official rhetoric has had a clear impact on popular perceptions in the two countries. According to Gallup, the share of Americans with overall unfavorable views of China increased from 45% in early 2018 to 79% in early 2021. The increase in popular antipathy was almost certainly driven by various factors, such as the protests in Hong Kong and the COVID-19 pandemic. The rapid increase in negative views is nevertheless remarkable. While polling is generally less robust and reliable in China, surveys also show markedly increased negative feelings towards the US among China's population in recent years. However, the degree to which negative sentiment towards the US has increased is significantly less than the increase in anti-China feeling in the US.

The US government exercises far fewer overt government restrictions on the spread of information and political activity than Beijing. The current trend of a shift in global power dynamics in Beijing's favor is also threatening to Washington's perceived interests. The combination of these two factors means that the United States faces a much higher probability of having its political system effectively changed by the trends of intensified bilateral confrontation. Indeed, a trend of marginally increased illiberalism, rhetorically justified by the need to combat foreign authoritarian powers, is already evident in the United States. Multiple US administrations, going back to at least the Obama years, have incrementally restricted US investment in certain Chinese firms, mostly technology companies. Under the Trump Administration, federal authorities began restricting visas for Chinese nationals studying certain high-tech subjects in US universities.

The US Federal Government has cited perceived external political threats from China and other powers to justify its own apparently illiberal actions and policies. For example, in 2020 and again in 2021 the US government seized multiple news websites operated by the Iranian government, based on alleged violations of unilateral US economic sanctions. Working in concert with social media conglomerates, the US government has increased its efforts to combat what it classifies as "misinformation" campaigns from Russia, Iran, and China. US officials have also moved to force the sale of TikTok over fears of Chinese influence and data collection. While these moves have so far been fairly marginal, they display a clear trend towards greater informational and political control justified by the supposed threat of foreign adversaries. Such moves are highly likely to increase in scope and frequency if, as is highly likely, the relative global power of the Chinese government continues to grow at the expense of Washington.

Heightened US-China rhetorical tensions may also be a factor in the Chinese government's expansion of its already extensive political and social controls. Beijing will continue to criticize any major localized protest movement or political campaign for increased personal freedoms as part of a foreign plot. Additionally, any major economic setback in China will almost certainly be condemned — fairly or otherwise — as a consequence of Washington's efforts to curtail China's internal development. In this sense, the higher profile of US-Chinese political contention in recent years may be a godsend for the CPC. The US government *has* imposed some measures to restrict China's international economic engagement and technological capabilities. Although the moves have been (and will likely continue to be) mostly incremental, Beijing can still blame such moves if China, for whatever reason, faces an internal economic crisis. The Chinese government has a clear interest in deflecting any discontent arising from widespread or prolonged economic malaise from its own policies to the actions of its main foreign rival. US rhetoric about China's threat and countermeasures provide the CPC with ample "evidence" to prove that any crisis is, ultimately, Washington's fault. Of course, as always, various US politicians will also continue to blame China for various kinds of economic hardship experienced in the US.

Beyond increased political controls and scapegoating, both Beijing and Washington will continue to leverage their rivalry to justify other central government goals. For example, when pushing for increased infrastructure spending in the US in early 2021, the Biden Administration specifically cited the need to compete with China. The Chinese government will likely also frame its various internal initiatives, outreach efforts to third countries, and research spending on the need to enhance China's position in competition with the US.

The fact that the US is formally an electoral democracy will further drive extended rhetorical contention. Neither party in our effectively two-party system desires the appearance of being "soft on China." When in opposition, they will criticize the ruling administration for actions or policies seen as insufficiently harsh. The party in opposition will also denounce, and may seek to block, any initiatives aimed at bolstering ties or bilateral cooperation. Such rhetoric does not necessarily mean that, once in power, a new administration will actually implement major policies to meaningfully upend or restrict the terms of bilateral US-Sino engagement. Rather, it merely means that it will be extremely difficult for any high-level politician on the national stage to openly and honestly advocate for reduced US-Sino tensions.

Both the US and Chinese governments face dangers from hyping the threat of the other power. The United States has a large and growing East Asian community of mostly US-born citizens, along with millions of Asian immigrants. Washington's hyping of China's threat is, of course, not aimed at creating dangers or difficulties for this population. Increasingly shrill rhetoric will nevertheless, at least marginally, increase the threat of racist attacks on random East Asian individuals in the US. Much of the population of any country throughout history fails at understanding any clear distinction between a "threatening" foreign government and ethnic groups who share visible features with the leaders of the rival nation. High-profile US messaging decrying espionage, technology theft, and internal political subversion arising from China inevitably create at least some difficulties for Asian-Americans in general and Chinese Americans in particular. If sufficiently intense, such hardships may undermine US advantages in terms of attracting and retaining human talent from parts of Asia. At the same time, the Chinese government also has a key interest in encouraging foreign nationals, including Americans and other broadly defined "Westerners," to visit, work, and do business in China. Any heightened anti-US sentiment that undermines the safety of foreign nationals in China could also undermine this long-standing imperative.

So long as Sino-US competition continues a trend of general intensification, entrenched interests in the US and Chinese governments will use this dynamic to justify or expand their own domestic power. The rhetoric regarding their competition will almost certainly continue to increase in both countries, as officials use the excuse of an outside threat to justify social control and government initiatives. However, escalations in rhetoric will not necessarily indicate relevant changes in fundamental policies. As Beijing and Washington denounce each other and warn their citizens of the foreign threat in increasingly shrill tones, the basic realities of bilateral engagement will likely remain in place. So long as the dynamics of Sino-US mutually assured military and economic destruction continue, beneficial engagement will likely coexist alongside their competition for overall relative power.

Third Prediction

China Overtakes the US Nominal GDP by 2030 and Maintains Higher GDP for the Rest of the Century

By 2030, China will have a greater volume of economic output than the US, and, barring either unforeseen catastrophe or a major technological revolution, China will remain the world's largest national economy for the rest of this century. China's nominal GDP eventually surpassing that of the US is not an especially bold or controversial prediction. In late 2020 the Centre for Economics and Business Research, a consultancy based in the UK, estimated that China's GDP would surpass that of the US in 2028, a prediction that has also been cited by other organizations. Recall from previous chapters that when measured in PPP terms, which account for the overall lower prices of comparable goods and services in China, the Chinese economy is already larger than that of the US and has been since around 2016.

Improved Chinese productivity has largely driven the trend of China's rising nominal GDP. As China has urbanized and its workforce has shifted from agriculture to industry and services, productivity has increased rapidly. Advances in education, infrastructure, and technology have also helped boost average productivity. Productivity is the main factor for China's rapid increase in GDP, in both PPP and nominal terms.

Another factor that impacts *nominal* GDP but not PPP GDP — the relative value of the national currencies of the US and China — has also played a role in China's relative economic expansion. The Chinese government shapes the rate of exchange of renminbi (RMB) to US dollars (USD), only allowing its national currency to weaken or strengthen a maximum of 2%

against the USD each day. Previously, controls were even more strict. From 1997 to 2005, the RMB was pegged to the USD at a rate of 8.27 to one. The Chinese government also uses other means, such as outbound exchange controls, to influence the exchange rate of its national currency.

Recent decades have generally seen a slow appreciation in the RMB when compared to the USD. After the People's Bank of China lifted the direct peg between China's national currency and the US dollar, the RMB has generally appreciated. At the time of writing, it has strengthened by about 14% compared to the dollar since 2005. Given the high and rapidly increasing degree of US government debt, and the strengthening importance of China in the global economic and financial system, a general trend of RMB appreciation against the USD is likely to continue. While Beijing could try to keep the RMB artificially cheap to boost its exports, the Chinese government may also eventually seek to effectively lessen the costs of imported energy, food, and minerals by allowing the RMB to appreciate against other major currencies. This scenario is especially likely if the USD depreciates rapidly against third currencies, perhaps as a result of an eventual challenge to the dollar's status as the main international currency of choice for facilitating international trade.

The second part of this prediction — that China will maintain its advantage in nominal economic output after it overtakes the US — depends on long-term economic, technological, and demographic trends. While it is true that China is facing increasing financial pressure from an aging population, this is unlikely to majorly divert its course to becoming the world's largest economy in nominal terms. Both the US and China, along with many other major countries, will face economic and social problems from an aging population. These issues are highly likely to be somewhat less pronounced in the US, due to immigration of relatively young people into the country.

However, barring a major local or global catastrophe, a China that is slightly greyer than the US will still have an enormous advantage in terms of overall population well into the next century, with well over double the population of the United States. At that point, differences in nominal GDP per capita between the two countries will probably be minimal. Even if overall disparities do continue, it is extremely unlikely that by the end of the century the average worker in the US would be twice as productive as their Chinese counterpart.

As the trend of relative Chinese economic ascension becomes increasingly clear from roughly the late 2020s to the early 2030s, the US government could attempt dramatic moves to perpetuate its dominance by enacting policies meant to stall or even reverse China's economic development. As discussed in previous chapters, there have been some marginal efforts on this front, with Washington imposing tariffs on Chinese imports, targeting major Chinese technology companies with sanctions, and enforcing other economic or financial controls on Chinese individuals and organizations accused of human rights violations in Xinjiang and Hong Kong. Again, any US efforts to truly economically or financially cripple China would invariably cause extreme uncertainty and tremendous disruptions throughout the world, including in the US, and are therefore highly unlikely. Such policies could even backfire, increasing Chinese technological self-reliance, incentivizing Beijing to purposefully target the USD's reserve status, and could cause more long-term economic disruptions within the US itself than in China.

That China's nominal GDP will almost certainly remain higher than that of the US through the end of the century does not necessarily mean that China will have overwhelming economic dominance on the global scale. Unless China both develops and successfully monopolizes a major technological advancement, or an unexpected disaster leaves most other countries in ruins, China is highly unlikely to experience the type of relative global economic dominance that the US experienced after World War Two. Directly after the war, the US accounted for nearly half of global economic output, as many of the other main industrialized areas were destroyed, damaged, or seriously disrupted.

The trend of more equalized global growth and productive capabilities is likely to eventually chip away at China's overall economic lead. India will almost certainly overtake China as the most populous country by 2030. Eventually, as its infrastructure and access to technology improves, and as China harvests the remaining branches of low-hanging development fruit, India will likely experience faster economic growth than China.

Although its dominance will exist in a more multipolar global economic dynamic, China, once it achieves the top position, is highly likely to remain the largest national economy through the end of the century. China's leading economic position will give its government further leverage to invest in technological development and military hardware. It will also strengthen China's financial leverage over other countries, which will in turn enhance Beijing's overall diplomatic position. While the US is very likely to remain an important global economy, it will almost certainly be forced by the nearly inescapable realities of demographics, globalization, and improved productive capabilities to cede its position at the world's overall largest economy. Once lost, the position will probably never be regained. The extent to which this transition is painful for the US political elite and population remains to be seen.

Fourth Prediction

China and the US Will Never Purposefully Go to War

This prediction regarding the future of Sino-US competition is perhaps the most sweeping and arguably the most important: the leaders of neither country will ever intentionally launch a war against the other. Direct bilateral contention will remain confined almost exclusively to economic, diplomatic, and technological arenas. Although Washington and China will continue to position themselves in preparation for a bilateral war that will never come, military competition will remain limited to strategic deployments, mutual shows of force, and deterrent-driven buildups. While an essentially accidental clash could occur, both sides would either rapidly de-escalate the situation, or risk a conflict that could destroy the survival of their governments in any recognizable form.

The basic logic behind this prediction is simple — no matter how much relations deteriorate, neither government will be willing to risk the inevitably dire consequences of a direct, sustained, and full-scale Sino-US military conflict. No potential benefit from initiating such a war could be worth the entailed risks of self-destruction. Outside a scenario of a very limited and localized clash, nuclear exchange would be extremely difficult to avoid. Even if nobody launched nuclear weapons, a war would prompt simultaneous and severe economic collapse in both countries.

During the initial minutes and hours of a hypothetical full-scale Sino-American war, a lack of perfect information would create enormous difficulties for both sides. Even if Beijing and Washington desperately *wanted* to keep the conflict limited to purely conventional weapons, neither side could feel entirely confident that their competitor would maintain the same self-restraint. Commanders seeing incoming enemy missiles and strategic bombers could not immediately know if they face conventional or nuclear attack. Leaders would therefore be incentivized to launch their own nuclear arsenals in response to any major strategic attack. Both sides are aware of the likelihood of this scenario, and are therefore extremely unlikely to purposefully initiate either a large-scale nuclear or conventional attack, as a first strike would invite strategic nuclear retaliation.

The horrific results inevitably arising from essentially any plausible scenario of Sino-US nuclear war are difficult to overstate. However, despite the natural unpleasantness of the task, they are worthy of consideration, since they demonstrate exactly how insanely self-destructive either government would be to purposefully risk such an outcome. Obviously, nobody knows the *exact* scale of destruction a major nuclear war would bring out, but various studies indicate it would be utterly and globally disastrous. A country or countries hit by nuclear weapons would experience mass devastation, panic, and infrastructure collapse, possibly triggering social breakdown. In addition, radioactive fallout could kill millions both within the target country and its neighbors. A large-scale US nuclear strike on mainland China could result in widespread death and panic in parts of the Korean Peninsula, Taiwan, Japan, Vietnam, India, and Russia, likely causing significant social upheaval and causing deep, and lasting, anger and hatred against Washington DC. Even a limited detonation of "only" 250 or so nuclear devices in urban areas would probably produce massive ash clouds, reducing sunlight and disrupting the global climate. According to a 2019 model published in *Atmospheric Science*, such an exchange could lower global temperatures by up to five degrees Celsius (nine degrees Fahrenheit) for multiple years, and average rainfall would decrease 15–30%, possibly triggering widespread famine *even in countries not directly impacted by nuclear weapons.*

China has an estimated five hundred or so nuclear warheads. Beijing is not party to any binding arms control treaties, and it is likely quietly expanding its nuclear arsenal. The US reports having a stockpile of around 3000 nuclear weapons, with roughly 1000 actively deployed in various silos and submarines. This numerical disparity gives the US some apparent strategic advantage, but its practical utility is questionable at best. First, even the results of "only" a dozen or so Chinese nuclear warheads detonating over key targets in the US would likely trigger generalized social and governmental collapse. Given China's possession of advanced hypersonic weapons, it is extremely likely that Beijing would be able to hit at least some key targets in the US in the event of a bilateral nuclear war.

Even supposing the US military could somehow launch an entirely successful first nuclear strike on China, miraculously destroying all of China's strategic nuclear counterforce and successfully intercepting all inbound Chinese nuclear weapons, the result would be a disaster for the US government. Such a war would invariably involve the detonation of hundreds of US nuclear warheads in Chinese territory. These detonations would then likely trigger a nuclear winter that would cause global famine, from which the US itself would not be immune, probably leading to an overall social breakdown within the United States itself. As mentioned previously, deadly radiation from China could impact other neighboring nuclear-armed states, such as India, Pakistan, Russia, and North Korea, who might seek to retaliate against the US for causing widespread death in their countries. The US government would, at the very least, find itself a global pariah, hated and resented by the world to a historically unprecedented degree. Resentment and panic from starving and impoverished American citizens could lead to an overall collapse in society that would be difficult to overcome.

These are the consequences that would almost invariably arise from a "successful" nuclear war. If Beijing eventually achieves an overall strategic nuclear edge over Washington in the coming decades, through sheer quantity of warheads, better delivery systems, and/or effective missile defense, it will face the same constraints. Even the costs of "victory" in a nuclear war far outweigh any conceivable benefits, except in a scenario in which a national government truly believed its own destruction was imminent.

All national governments have a clear, enduring, and shared interest in avoiding nuclear warfare. This means that the central prediction that no intentional war will be fought between the US and China also applies to other nuclear-armed states. China and India will not engage in full-scale war; neither will the US and Russia, nor will any other nuclear power intentionally initiate a war with another. However, this prediction does not preclude accidents or serious strategic miscalculations leading to *unintentional* conventional or nuclear conflict between relevant powers.

Even in the extremely unlikely scenario of either Beijing, Washington, or both somehow being able to guarantee that nuclear weapons would not be used in a hypothetical military conflict, the consequences of a US-China war would, at the very least, result in the utter destruction of the global economic and financial system as it currently exists. Hundreds of billions of dollars' worth of bilateral trade would instantly erase, and trillions in foreign investment would essentially evaporate within the first day of a war. Any conflict extending beyond a simple, accidental clash would trigger mass financial panic and market crashes. A conflict persisting for more than a few days would disrupt global supply chains. The material conditions of common citizens in both the US and China would rapidly deteriorate, with likely dire implications for social and political stability. Jobless, hungry, and angry masses could in turn pose a threat to either or both national governments.

There is a solid case study that demonstrates the historical, and highly likely perpetual, policy imperative for both Beijing and Washington to avoid direct armed conflict. On April 1, 2001, a US Navy signal intelligence craft collided with a PLA fighter in the South China Sea near far southern China's Hainan Island. The Chinese pilot died, while the US craft was forced to crash-land on a nearby Chinese military airfield. Some geopolitical observers feared that a more drawn-out conflict could ensue. At the time, the US was not engaged in any major military conflicts, and China, though still overall quite poor, was the most obvious candidate for an eventual rival to US global hegemony. When compared to all other relevant global powers in early 2001, China was the only clear contender for eventually emerging as a serious rival to Washington's global economic, military, and political dominance.

Furthermore, the power discrepancy between the two countries was far greater at the time than it is today — China's nominal GDP was less than a seventh that of the United States at the time of the Hainan Incident. Some recent developments had increased US-China geopolitical tensions in the previous years. The PLA had made a major show of force near Taiwan in 1996, which prompted the US to deploy two aircraft carrier groups to the region. During the 1999 NATO air campaign against Yugoslavia, US forces (ostensibly accidentally) bombed the Chinese Embassy in Belgrade, killing three Chinese journalists and prompting a series of intense anti-US protests and calls for revenge. Nevertheless, during the 2001 Hainan Incident Washington and Beijing quickly reached a mutually acceptable negotiated settlement. Following several days of tense negotiations, the two sides came to an agreement wherein the US expressed regret for the death of the Chinese pilot, while the Chinese government repatriated the US crew and eventually returned the damaged US aircraft (though they disassembled the craft and probably reverse-engineered much of its relevant technology). In the years immediately following the incident, US military surveillance flights near the Chinese coast were generally less assertive, though more intense patrols resumed roughly a decade later.

Beijing and Washington were willing to make concessions to avoid direct, sustained military conflict during and after the Hainan Incident. Neither power perceived strategic benefit from challenging the other through direct military action or even major shows of force during the period of heightened tension. The threat, however remote, of a confrontation accidentally escalating into nuclear warfare was a powerful deterrent; concerns over the state of the global economy and general regional stability also likely inclined the governments toward a peaceful resolution.

None of these imperatives have meaningfully changed, and in fact, if anything, they remain *truer* now than they did two decades previously. Crucially, the balance of economic and conventional military power was *overwhelmingly* in Washington's favor during the Hainan Incident. China's nominal GDP was worth only around 13% that of the US, instead of roughly 70%. Even in PPP terms, China's economic output at the time was less than half that of the US. Additionally, in early 2001, the US had not yet strained its military resources, diplomatic leverage, and general international prestige in the post 9/11 wars in Afghanistan and Iraq. If, somehow, the two powers could have guaranteed that nuclear weapons would not be used, in 2001 the US would likely have more or less "won" a conventional naval and aerial conflict against China. And yet, near the very peak of post-Cold War US economic, diplomatic, and military dominance, Washington was not willing to risk a war against a

China that was far less militarily and economically capable than it is today.

The motives for Beijing avoiding a direct conflict with the US are even more apparent and enduring. A direct war with the US, even one that was somehow guaranteed to remain purely conventional, would undermine the CPC's core interests. China's economy is hugely dependent on international trade, including on exports to the US and other major countries. Any sustained war with another major power would instantly plunge China's economy into a crisis. China is also the world's largest energy importer, and while it has significant oil and gas pipelines running overland from Russia and Central Asia, the vast majority of China's imported fossil fuels arrive via tankers in China's Pacific ports. Although Chinese naval and land-based forces have the capability to cause direct and significant damage to the US Navy, Beijing still has an apparent overall disadvantage in terms of total military strength. Any sustained conflict would almost certainty, at the very least, drastically reduce China's ability to engage in oceanic trade.

More importantly, China's economic and military capabilities, when compared to the US, have been on a sustained upward trajectory for decades. Why would Beijing seek to initiate a war now, when the balance of power is constantly shifting in its favor? China would likely fare far better in a (hypothetical and unlikely) conventional war with the US now than it would ten years ago; in ten years' time, its relative advantage is likely to grow. Even if bilateral war were inevitable — and it isn't — it would be highly illogical for Beijing to initiate a conflict, unless or until somehow the trajectory of relative power growth shifted in favor of the US.

Many otherwise reasonable historical and strategic analysts believe that the contention between US and China creates a dynamic of nearly inevitable warfare, known as a Thucydides Trap. The term refers to a situation in which military conflict between a dominant power and an ascendent rival is impossible to avoid, largely because of the fear of the more powerful nation and the ambitions of its upstart challenger. Besides ancient Greece and Sparta, other parallels have been found in history, most notably the relationship between Britain and Germany in the lead-up to the First World War.

While some parallels exist, historical antecedents do not necessarily apply to forecasts for future dynamics of the US-Sino relationship. Most notably, the economies of contemporary China and the US are far more mutually dependent than any other historic rising and ascendent powers who, with the power of retrospect, were "destined" for conflict. True, there was significant trade and investment between Germany and Britain prior to their first round of direct warfare, but it was still far less than currently existing between the US and China. Secondly, and far more importantly, a direct, unrestrained war between Athens and Sparta, or between the UK and Germany circa 1914, would not and could not result in the destruction of the capital cities of both warring powers within the first day of conflict. Nuclear weapons make the concept of "inevitable" warfare between major powers either outdated or suicidally illogical. Without nuclear weaponry, direct warfare between the USSR and USA would have been, if not inevitable, at least highly likely, given the intensity of their global geopolitical and ideological contention. However, in a world with nuclear weapons, the war never occurred, despite decades of sustained and intense mutual hostility, and the absence of significant economic ties between the two powers. If Moscow and Washington could avoid going to war with each other for decades, so can Washington and Beijing. Indeed, they have no reasonable alternative but peaceful coexistence.

Geographic Areas of Military Contention

There are essentially three areas in which direct military confrontation between US and Chinese forces is remotely possible over the next several decades — Taiwan, the South China Sea, and Japanese-controlled islands in the East China Sea. However, in each of the theaters, which are scenes of active military posturing between the two powers, both sides still have clear and overriding interests in preventing tensions from spiraling out of control into open conflict. As always, this common, and likely enduring, interest in preventing purposeful conflict does not rule out the possibility of accidental escalation, but from the examples seen below, it becomes clear that direct warfare, even in regions with significant disagreements, is extremely unlikely. While there are certainly significant trends driving Sino-US military competition in these various regions, the tremendous risks inherent to open warfare far outweigh any plausible motives either power might have to initiate an attack against rival forces.

Long-standing tensions over the political status of Taiwan frequently prompt verbal sparring and military shows of force by both the PLA and US military forces. Beijing, of course, would prefer to bring Taiwan "back" under its rule. Such an outcome would boost the CPC's nationalist credentials and significantly improve the PRC's geopolitical position, economy, and technological prowess. In 2019, Xi Jinping offered a "one country, two systems" formula for PRC-ROC unification, in which Taiwan would be allowed to keep its military and government system. Taiwanese officials rejected the offer, but it shows the extent of concessions Beijing is willing to make in order to bring about reunification with Taiwan.

Although Beijing would obviously prefer to bring Taiwan under its rule, any direct and unrestrained military effort by the PLA to forcibly incorporate Taiwan into the PRC would entail enormous challenges and risks that could undermine the core interests of the CPC. Even if the US refrained from direct intervention in such a conflict, invading hostile coastlines against determined resistance is a difficult prospect in even the best of circumstances. While the ROC does not have the economic, geographic, or human resources to directly counter PLA capabilities, it does have fairly sophisticated weapons systems and a military posture oriented almost exclusively towards making any mainland Chinese attack as difficult and costly as possible. Even were the PLA to eventually "win" such a conflict, the outcome would be a military occupation of a largely hostile and mountainous territory. A scenario in which PLA forces faced determined guerrilla resistance in the mountains of Taiwan would undermine the PRC's nationalist credentials, as mainland Chinese would wonder why so many of their Taiwanese compatriots forcibly reject unification. Furthermore, the conflict would be economically disruptive, as enormous volumes of trade and investment link the PRC and Taiwan.

Even in the "best-case" scenario of a rapid victory and the avoidance or quick suppression of guerrilla resistance, the outcome would strike fear into surrounding countries. Despite Beijing's assurances that the conflict was an internal matter between two Chinese factions, the PRC's carefully maintained image of an ascendent power committed to "peaceful rise" would be destroyed for decades. A full-scale PLA assault on Taiwan would almost certainly result in neighboring states enhancing their cooperation with each other, and likely outside states such as the US and possibly India, against perceived Chinese aggression.

Beijing is extremely unlikely to initiate an unprovoked, full-scale war against Taiwan. However, there is one development which would almost certainly prompt the PRC to attack Taiwan — an official Taiwanese declaration of independence.

The Taiwanese government is still "The Republic of China," with at least theoretical claims on the Chinese mainland. So long as it maintains this status, Beijing is unlikely to risk a war against it. Taipei is well aware of this dynamic, and therefore refrains from declaring Taiwanese independence, as such a declaration would, somewhat ironically, invite a PRC attack and threaten the *de facto* independence Taipei currently enjoys. The continuation of the status quo means Beijing misses out on the economic, geopolitical, and technological benefits of controlling Taiwan, but initiating a conflict to forcibly integrate Taiwan in the PRC would entail enormous risks far beyond the apparent benefits of such a move. Maintenance of the dispute helps to bolster the CPC's nationalistic credentials. The status quo has some diplomatic costs for Taipei, but ultimately it is far better than the alternative of risking a direct war with Beijing. The leaders of the ROC know that Beijing is somewhat politically constrained by its territorial claim on Taiwan, and would essentially be "forced" to respond militarily in the event of a Taiwanese declaration of independence. They are therefore highly unlikely to directly test the resolve of their giant, nuclear-armed neighbor and largest trading partner.

Washington has a key interest in preventing Beijing from incorporating Taiwan into the PRC, because such an outcome would significantly shift the balance of overall global power in China's favor. US policy towards Taiwan is intentionally ambiguous. As a precursor to establishing diplomatic ties with Beijing, the US representatives in 1972 signed a bilateral agreement reading, in part, "The United States acknowledges that all Chinese on either side of the Taiwan Strait maintain there is but one China and that Taiwan is a part of China." This "One China" policy officially remains in place. At the same time, the US has continued "informal" ties with Taipei and maintains weapons sales to the ROC government.

The US officially opposes "unilateral changes" to the PRC-ROC status quo. Essentially, Washington's commitment to maintaining Taiwan's *de facto* independence is predicated on Taipei refraining from legally declaring its existence as a Taiwanese, rather than a "Chinese," state. As noted above, such a development is extremely unlikely. If Taipei were to upset the delicate political balance and declare independence, it is highly unlikely that Washington would risk direct conflict with Beijing. The US might provide some incremental support to try to drag out the conflict and tie PLA forces down in Taiwan. However, Washington is highly unlikely to risk an either horrifically prolonged or suicidally brief war with the PRC in defense of a Taiwanese government that made the foolhardy choice to dramatically upset an otherwise broadly acceptable, if somewhat legally farcical, status quo. At any rate, such a scenario is extremely unlikely, since all relevant sides — Beijing, Taipei, and Washington — know the stakes involved in escalating the dispute into open warfare.

In the extremely unlikely event of the PRC and ROC going to war over the coming decades, the most realistic scenario of such a conflict would be brief, limited in geographic scope, and not directly involve US military forces. Recall that the ROC controls not only Taiwan, but also some islands in the South China Sea and, more crucially, some minor islands situated extremely close to the Chinese mainland. The PLA would almost certainly be able to seize these islands before a major US military intervention could be organized and dispatched to the area. Kinmen, Matsu, and other nearby islands are small, with a combined population of around 140,000. Kinmen's main island is about 8 km (5 miles) from the Chinese mainland; Matsu lies 16 km (10 miles) from the coast. The island of Taiwan, on the other hand, has about 23 million people and is at its closest point about 129 km (80 miles) from mainland China.

Seizing the ROC's outlying islands would also be far less costly and risky than mounting a full-scale invasion of Taiwan. If the PRC faces a stability-threatening internal political crisis, or if Taipei makes a significant move towards independence, a PLA invasion of these minor islands is far more likely than an invasion of Taiwan. Beijing could even try to justify the move by organizing some locals, who tend to have a somewhat different political and cultural outlook than ROC citizens on the island of Taiwan, into "inviting" the PLA presence. Occupying the outlying islands would benefit Beijing by displaying military prowess and nationalistic determination, while also marginally improving the PRC's geopolitical position, with far less costs and risks than a full-scale invasion of Taiwan.

China avoiding direct warfare with the US also effectively means that the PLA must avoid open military aggression against US treaty allies. This precludes China from directly waging war against Japan and the Philippines, despite China's active territorial disputes with both countries. It also means that the Chinese government will not directly attack South Korea.

Nevertheless, the Sino-Japanese territorial dispute over the Senkaku/Diaoyu Islands in the East China Sea is a major front in which military contention between the US and China could potentially escalate into open warfare. At the same time, as with the other areas of direct contention, none of the powers who could initiate a war are at all likely to purposefully do so. First, and most obviously, because of the 1960 US-Japanese Security Treaty, a Chinese attack on the Japanese-controlled islands would result in a war with the United States. The US government has made this explicitly clear, warning that, although it does not specifically side with Tokyo in the territorial dispute, the islands are covered under the terms of its security pact with Japan. Beijing likes to keep the dispute on a low boil, ratcheting up tensions when politically convenient. Japan is China's main historic nemesis and regional enemy. Of course, the dispute is also politically useful for the Japanese government; some Japanese politicians play up the cause of nationalism and the threat of China's expanding power.

Despite the historical tensions and rhetoric, an open war between China and Japan is extremely unlikely. Even if a conflict somehow did not involve other powers, and even if it were extremely brief and limited in geographic scope, it would, at the least, trigger a horrific economic depression in both countries, if not globally. Sino-Japanese economic ties are massive; China is Japan's largest trading partner. Both countries are also highly dependent on oceanic trade. Crucial sea lanes would be majorly disrupted in any direct war. Although Beijing would like to control the Senkaku/Diaoyu Islands for nationalistic reasons and to gain access to potential nearby energy reserves, the costs entailed by going to war with Tokyo — and probably Washington — over the small and uninhabited features far outweigh any conceivable benefits. Meanwhile, because the islands are effectively controlled by Japan, it is unclear how either Washington or Tokyo could use the dispute to initiate an attack on Chinese targets, assuming for whatever reason that was their goal.

The South China Sea is another key area in which Chinese and US military deploy key military assets and engage in displays of force. For decades, China has been building up artificial islands and airstrips on atolls and other features under its control in the region. The US, and some US allies, conduct "freedom of navigation patrols" near Chinese-controlled areas. Beijing decries such moves as violations of its sovereignty. The Philippines and the US share mutual-defense obligations; Manila is also a rival claimant to China in parts of the South China Sea. Vietnam similarly disputes most of China's claim, along with claims of the Philippines and Malaysia over the region. The Taipei-based ROC maintains essentially the same territorial claim in the South

China Sea as Beijing. PRC, Vietnamese, ROC, and Philippine vessels routinely make shows of force near the military assets and features controlled by rival claimants. The underlying threat of a military clash in the region cannot be entirely ruled out.

Beijing is almost certainly never going to give up its expansive claims in the region, but it is equally unlikely to go to war to enforce them. Note that, although the PLA claims all territories within the Nine-Dash Line as its own, it has not used deadly military forces against the assets of other rival claimants in recent decades. The PLA has the largest military presence in the South China Sea, though many islands are also effectively held by Vietnamese, Philippine, Malaysian and ROC outposts. Beijing's claims on the disputed South China Sea give the PLA a reason to turn parts of the territory into a "forward base" for Chinese military influence. This is likely aimed less at planning an attack on, say, Malaysia or the Philippines, and more on securing Chinese trade routes in the (unlikely) event of a war with the US. Essentially all of China's oceanic trade with Europe, Africa, the Middle East, and Southeast Asia passes through the South China Sea. As the rulers of the country with the largest volume of exports and imports traversing the South China Sea, the Chinese government has the least apparent motivation of any power to risk an actual war in the region.

In addition to serving as a justification for regional military deployments, Beijing's extensive claims over the South China Sea provide an essentially perpetually unsolvable territorial dispute that can be used to ratchet up nationalism when necessary. The Chinese government is not alone in this regard — both Manila and, especially, Hanoi also dial tensions in the region upward when politically convenient. It is important to note that this is a multilateral dispute — the various claimant states have overlapping disputes with each other, as well as China. However, all of the claimant states are reliant on oceanic trade passing through the maritime region. While they will likely continue shows of force, intentional, direct, deadly, and sustained military conflict would be against the common interests of all the disputant powers.

Washington generally benefits from increased tensions between the PRC and other claimant states in the South China Sea, though US leadership is extremely unlikely to directly and intentionally start an open conflict with the Chinese military in the area. Such a war could quickly escalate into a general war against China, which would at the least seriously disrupt the US economy and at worst effectively end human civilization. If Washington was unwilling to escalate a conflict against China in the South China Sea during the 2001 Hainan Incident, when, as mentioned previously, the US had immense economic, diplomatic, and military advantages, Washington is even less likely to do so now, given the obvious shifts in the balance of retaliatory power. Accidental naval or aerial incidents could occur in the region but purposeful war is extremely unlikely. Nevertheless, Washington will continue shows of force in the South China Sea as a means of displaying power and testing Beijing's responses. Naval and air patrols also serve to bolster Washington's profile to other countries in the region who are wary of Beijing's expanding military capabilities.

Although the likelihood of direct warfare remains low, of all the areas where the US and Chinese militaries come into contact, the South China Sea is the front in which the threat of direct, tactile conflict is the highest. Sovereignty in the region is obviously disputed. Rules of engagement may be intentionally unclear. A show of force could result in a deadly accident, similar to the events of 2001. However, as in the 2001 Hainan Incident, both countries would have a common and overriding interest in negotiated de-escalation.

Whether in the South China Sea, the East China Sea, or near Taiwan, Washington is somewhat more likely to risk a limited military clash with Beijing, so long as the US government believes it has an advantage over China in overall military force. The fact that Beijing continues to expand its overall global power — especially its economic capabilities — could incentivize the US into attempting to provoke a military crisis and Chinese overreaction. Some US actions, such as patrolling near PLA assets in the South China Sea, or marginally increasing engagement with Taipei, may be motivated by a desire to see Beijing overreact, with the hope that Beijing's overreaction would incentivize third powers to support US anti-China geopolitical containment efforts. However, given the enormous and unpredictable consequences of even a limited and entirely conventional war, the overall threat of direct, sustained, and intentional conflict remains low. US and Chinese militaries will almost certainly continue to keep lines of communication open and attempt to de-escalate any accidental clash. Washington would also likely lose significant diplomatic support if third parties believed the US intentionally launched an unprovoked attack on Chinese assets.

The core prediction that there will be no direct, intentional military conflict between the US and Washington creates enormous implications for all fields of bilateral contention. So long as neither side develops and deploys technology to significantly undermine the long-standing dynamics of Mutually Assured Destruction, one can remain confident that threatening rhetoric and shows of force by either or both powers will remain primarily symbolic and aspirational. Furthermore, as both governments are dependent on the overall stability of a global economic system involving significant inputs from the other country, any accidental or localized incidents are highly unlikely to spread into a wider conflict.

The forecasted lack of direct warfare does not mean that Sino-US competition will be less intense in other fields. In fact, the obvious constraints faced by both sides in directly attacking the other with military assets likely contributes to the intensification of competition through other means, especially within the realms of economics, diplomacy, technology. In previous eras, great powers who faced upstart rivals could attempt to disrupt their competitor's ascendent trajectory through direct military conflict on the land and seas. Growing powers could similarly use their increased military strength to directly attack more dominant rivals, and stake a claim to areas of control or influence. The grim realities of nuclear counterforce have largely rendered such strategies obsolete, at least among nuclear powers. Instead, both Washington and Beijing must rely primarily on economic development, alliance systems, and technological advances to secure their relative position against the rival power.

Despite the near-certain lack of direct conflict, US and Chinese leaders will have a common and enduring interest in continuing preparations for a bilateral war they know must never occur. Beijing and Washington's varying interests in third powers help motivate such preparations. Citing the perceived threat of the US military gives Beijing a reason to build up its own capabilities, including weapons systems that can be used to enhance China's hard power against its neighbors. Washington benefits from keeping tensions in the West Pacific on a low boil, as contention in the region helps the US justify its regional presence to countries concerned about Beijing's increasing capabilities. Entrenched bureaucratic interests within the US government and influential corporations also benefit from military spending in general, and China provides a useful justification for spending on expensive systems and equipment. Furthermore, the old adage "to ensure peace, prepare for war" still holds much relevance. As the world's two most powerful global powers, both Beijing and Washington are highly motivated to maintain sufficient conventional military forces to match the other, even if they are fully aware they will never be used in direct conflict with their main rival.

Fifth Prediction

US Alliance Systems Continue; China Does Not Form NATO-Style Partnerships

Even though China will overtake the United States in terms of being the globally dominant economic and military power, Beijing will likely continue to lag behind Washington in terms of institutionalized diplomatic influence for at least several decades. The Chinese government will not seek to cement its superpower position with binding mutual defense agreements, as the US has in the North Atlantic and West Pacific. Beijing and its partners will likely never form a "Chinese NATO" or "Chinese Warsaw Pact"; such partnerships are essentially unnecessary for promoting the contemporary interests of the Chinese government, and the costs of such initiatives would likely outweigh any potential benefits. Meanwhile, the US government is highly likely to maintain its formal mutual-defense agreements with its key partners in NATO and the West Pacific for the foreseeable future. Washington currently has, and will likely continue to have for at least several decades, an apparent diplomatic advantage over China in terms of formalized mutual self-defense agreements with third countries.

In order to examine and compare the contemporary alliance systems of the PRC and the US, it is first necessary to define what an "ally" means in a geopolitical sense. While many countries can, and do, have fairly sustained economic and political cooperation, a formal alliance is established through binding and clearly defined mutual responsibilities. For the purposes of this work, allies are countries that have clear obligations to defend each other in case of armed attack.

Currently, the US has five active mutual defense treaties. The first and most expansive is the North Atlantic Treaty

Organization (NATO), a multilateral agreement which was formed in 1949. Under Article 5 of the North Atlantic Treaty, NATO member states — currently including the US, Canada, Turkey, and most European countries — are obliged to defend each other in case of an attack. However, the geographic scope of NATO's mutual-defense obligations is limited to Turkey, Europe, North America, and the Atlantic Ocean North of the Tropic of Cancer. Washington could not cite Article 5 and oblige other NATO states to go to war after an attack on, say, Hawaii, or US forces in the West Pacific. The clause limiting the range of NATO's mutual-defense obligations meant that Portugal was unable to call the treaty into force when the Indian government forcibly seized (or liberated) Lisbon's colonial possessions along the Indian coast in the 1950s. The only time a member state has successfully invoked Article 5 was following the September 11, 2001 attacks on the US. Washington activated Article 5 following the attacks and obliged NATO member states to support subsequent US military operations in Afghanistan.

During the early stages of the Cold War, the US also established several mutual-defense pacts with countries in the West Pacific. Washington signed bilateral defense pacts with the Philippines (1951), Japan (1960), and South Korea (1963). The US, Australia, and New Zealand also signed a mutual security pact in 1951. However, The Australia, New Zealand, United States Security Treaty does not have any explicit mutual-defense obligations, and regardless, New Zealand's membership in the treaty was partially suspended in the 1980s after Wellington banned nuclear-capable weapons systems from its territory. Nevertheless, Australia can reasonably be defined as a US military and diplomatic ally. While the same designation may also apply to New Zealand, the relationship is decidedly more ambiguous.

Geographic realities have helped to create the system of alliances between Washington and its NATO and West Pacific allies. These essential factors also mean that the US-led alliance system is likely to endure for at least most of this century, if not beyond. While the exact origin of the quote "geography is destiny" remains disputed, the statement's accuracy has ensured its relevance and popularity.

The United States completely dominates its immediate periphery in terms of overall geopolitical influence. The US also has access to both the Atlantic and Pacific, facilitating Washington's power projection in both Europe and the Pacific. Canada, Turkey, and the various European NATO member states look to the US (more so historically but to at least some degree contemporarily) as an outside balancing power to Russian ambitions. Similar dynamics exist in the West Pacific, where the US provided strategic balance against the Soviet Union and its allies and, subsequently, against an increasingly powerful Beijing. Alliances with the US are specifically attractive for national governments that have obvious power imbalances when compared to Russia and China. At the same time, they provide Washington with enormous influence and leverage over the more junior members. Washington's alliances provide the US military with staging grounds in which to project power against Russia and China.

Of course, domestic political concerns also help sustain the US-led alliances. Mutual defense treaties with Washington grant governments of smaller states direct benefits in terms of economic assistance, political support, and access to advanced military technology. Some degree of political duress may also come in to play. Historically, Washington has backed leaders of political parties that are in favor of their alliances with the US, including with covert support. Simultaneously, the long-standing existence of NATO and US treaty obligations in the West Pacific mean that entrenched political interests in Washington DC take such arrangements for granted. Any effort to potentially reconsider them is likely to remain outside the range of accepted political discourse, and will be widely condemned by mainstream voices as appeasement or the results of malign interference from Moscow or Beijing.

Although they will likely endure, Washington's various alliances are unlikely to offer the US government *decisive* advantages in terms of its global competition with Beijing. With regards to the military aspects of contention, US alliances that involve mutual-defense obligations have limited direct utility if — as is highly likely — the United States and China never go to war. Even in the extremely unlikely case of a direct, sustained Sino-US conflict, the militaries of either the Philippines, South Korea, or Australia would likely make little material difference in the overall balance of pure military power. Even in the case of Japan, there would currently be somewhat limited conventional force contributions. In 2023, Japanese military expenditures in nominal terms were less than a fifth of China's, which were in turn about a third those of the US. A hypothetical adjustment for purchasing power would make Beijing's spending worth over eight times that of Japan, though it would still leave Chinese military spending less than half that of the US.

The US does have significant military bases in South Korea and Japan that could help with forward deployment during a hypothetical US-China conflict. However, Chinese forces would almost certainly target such bases within the first hours of any conventional war. All remotely likely scenarios of Sino-US military conflict over the coming decades would likely see a significant Chinese home-field advantage, in which Chinese military planners need to destroy or incapacitate a relatively small number of US airfields and naval assets in the West Pacific, while being able to deploy, conceal, and transport their own long-range weapons systems in various locations throughout the Chinese mainland. With regards to NATO, Washington couldn't automatically trigger its mutual-defense obligations in response to a clash with Chinese forces in the Pacific. The

UK and France have some assets that could be deployed to aid US efforts in the region, but they would be under no explicit obligation to do so.

While US-led alliance systems are likely to remain in place, it is highly unlikely that Washington and other governments will form *new* and explicitly anti-Beijing mutual-defense pacts in the coming decades. Existing bilateral security agreements between the US and other powers were created in a global environment vastly different from the current international dynamics. Following the Second World War, the US was by far the most powerful country on earth by all reasonable military and economic metrics. The US — and its allies in Europe and Asia — also faced an ideologically driven enemy openly intent on spreading its preferred vision of an ideal political and economic system around the world.

During the Second World War, Moscow directly absorbed three formerly independent states (Lithuania, Latvia, and Estonia) into its territory. The leaders of the USSR also utilized their military presence in Eastern Europe to set up aligned governments in Poland, Romania, Bulgaria, Czechoslovakia, and Eastern Germany. Despite China's various contemporary territorial disputes, there is no remotely comparable analogy between Beijing's current regional stance and that of circa-1950 Moscow. Uninhabited atolls in the South China Sea are not comparable to Baltic states with populations in the millions. Furthermore, China has far greater and deeper international economic engagement than the USSR ever had — engagement that includes enormous volumes of trade and significant international investment with major US treaty allies. The Chinese government is also keenly aware that any move it could make to blatantly expand its territory through interstate war would drive its neighbors to increase cooperation with each other and with the US to counter Chinese expansionism.

Recent years have seen the emergence of an apparent anti-China grouping that is more signal than substance. Leaders of the "Quad" formed by the US, India, Japan, and Australia have engaged in some multilateral political and economic initiatives clearly meant — despite public claims to the contrary — to signal a united front against growing Chinese influence. However, this grouping is highly likely to remain informal; simple cost-benefit analysis demonstrates why a potential evolution of the Quad into a binding mutual-defense agreement is extremely unlikely. Outside of current US-Japan and US-Australia bilateral pacts, the various Quad powers would not be willing to risk a war with China in defense of the others' interests. Beijing has active territorial disputes with both India and Japan. Tokyo is extremely unlikely to put itself in a position in which it would be forced to go to war against China, risking at the very least nearly inevitable economic catastrophe, in defense of India's contested borders along the Himalayas. Delhi, for its part, has no conceivable interest to wage war on behalf of a handful of disputed uninhabited rocks in the East China Sea.

Furthermore, a formal Quad alliance would force the US, Japan, and Australia to consider war against a nuclear-armed Pakistan in the event of another war breaking out between South Asia's fraternal rivals. India has no conceivable motivation to risk its decades of friendly ties with Moscow, much less open war with Russia, in defense of Japan's claims over the Kuril Islands. More broadly, governments that form formal alliances with the US effectively must contend with the possibility of being targeted by Chinese and Russian military planners in the event of a nuclear exchange between the major global powers.

Economic risks compound the military and political threats. China is by far the largest trading partner of South Korea, Japan, and Australia. Despite their contested frontier and general geopolitical rivalry, China is also India's largest trading partner. The various Quad governments do have a common interest in cooperating to limit the expansion of Chinese military and political power. However, they are likely to continue informal cooperation with each other instead of creating a formal alliance system, which would formalize overt confrontation with Beijing, with all the attendant political, military, and economic risks.

All current US alliances in the West Pacific are bilateral, and will almost certainly remain so for the foreseeable future. South Korea has no formal obligation to go to war on behalf of either Japan or the Philippines. While all three powers do broadly benefit from their alliances with the US, and have varying degrees of concern about expanding Chinese influence, they are not keen on formally allying with each other. Indeed, there are significant underlying *tensions* between US partners in the region, especially South Korea and Japan. Washington would be unable to corral Seoul, Tokyo, and Manila into a binding mutual-defense pact with each other. The US government would face even greater difficulties in roping India, with its own power projection capabilities, strategic imperatives, and historical outlook, into a formal treaty system.

Unlike Washington, Beijing will likely continue to prefer more flexible and less formalized partnerships over binding defense pacts. Beijing currently has three relations that may reasonably be defined as *effective* alliances. North Korea, Russia, and, especially, Pakistan, are either officially or semi-officially allies of Beijing, with varying degrees of mutual obligations with the Chinese government. While its alliances are not as close and formalized as those of the US, they do provide Beijing with a significant degree of strategic space in China's near abroad, allowing Beijing to focus on potential security challenges to its south and east. Whether by design, the accidents of history, or (as is most likely) some combination of those two aforementioned factors, China's alliances are located along its potentially vulnerable land frontiers, while those of the US are focused primarily on projecting power across the Pacific and

Atlantic Oceans. The more informal and loose nature of Beijing's alliances grants the PRC, and its allies, greater flexibility with regards to interpretation and implementation of their duties. In some ways, this is a disadvantage as compared to Washington's formalized and integrated alliance systems, though ambiguity also provides distinct advantages.

China currently has only one explicit mutual-defense treaty. According to the Sino-North Korean Mutual Aid and Cooperation Friendship Treaty, Beijing and Pyongyang are obliged to "immediately render military and other assistance" if the other party is attacked. While this mutual-defense obligation is explicit, the specific enforcement mechanisms of the treaty are unclear. Beijing did not cite the treaty during its border clashes with the Soviet Union in the 1960s; such a move would've put Pyongyang in an extremely awkward position, since it maintained friendly ties with both sides during the Sino-Soviet split.

North Korea's nuclear weapons program has strained the alliance. Beijing, as an established nuclear power, fears the spread of nuclear weaponry, as any trend of additional countries acquiring nuclear weapons effectively undermines the strategic power of the Chinese arsenal. The Chinese government is especially wary of the possibility of Pyongyang's nuclear weapons incentivizing Seoul and Tokyo to develop their own nuclear weapons systems. Since 2017, Beijing has generally cooperated with UN efforts to persuade Pyongyang to give up its nuclear weapons by imposing economic sanctions on North Korea. Despite these tensions and contradictions, the formal Sino-North Korean alliance remains in place, at least on paper. Although the Chinese government is less enthusiastic about North Korea than in previous decades, Beijing is unlikely to give up the relationship, so long as it continues to perceive a US-led threat along the Western Pacific.

US Alliance Systems Continue; China Does Not Form NATO-Style Partnerships

There are two key areas in which the Chinese government will probably strengthen its *de facto* alliances over the coming decades. Most importantly, Beijing and Moscow will maintain their cooperation — which falls just short of an actual formalized alliance — for at least as long as the United States maintains its own system of formalized defense treaties with other countries. Additionally, Sino-Pakistani cooperation will also continue for so long as the two powers perceive a mutual challenge from Delhi. Since such a dynamic is almost geographically and politically inevitable, the partnership between Beijing and Islamabad is almost guaranteed to continue for the foreseeable future.

Perhaps the closest relationship to an active, fruitful, and long-standing alliance that Beijing maintains is the mutual cooperations between China and Pakistan. The two countries have been effective allies since the 1960s. Both powers are wary of Indian regional influence. In previous decades their cooperation was further cemented by shared concerns about the Soviet Union, especially during Moscow's 1979–1989 war in Afghanistan.

Pakistan provides China with direct overland links to the resource-rich Middle East, while China is a key military, economic, and political patron of Pakistan. While there is no formal, publicly acknowledged treaty system in place between the two countries, both sides qualify the relationship as an "iron brotherhood." Chinese officials have reportedly described Pakistan as "our Israel." The comparison is meaningful on multiple levels. Decades of support for Pakistan — a nuclear armed country founded in the late 1940s as a homeland for people with a specific religious national identity — provides China with access to and influence in the Greater Middle East. At the same time, it intensifies resentment and fear of China in India, Pakistan's fraternal adversary. At any rate, for as long as Indo-Pakistani disputes remain active and as long as Sino-Indian contention continues, the *de facto* alliance between Beijing and Islamabad will remain generally stable.

While Pakistan has been a consistent strategic ally of China for decades, it is the Beijing-Moscow alliance that is perhaps the most important to Beijing's current international strategic position. Of course, the Russian and Chinese governments have not always been allies — indeed, they have been competitors or even enemies for most of their shared bilateral history. The Russian and Qing Empires fought over territory in Siberia on several occasions. Even while the USSR was generally supportive of both the KMT and the CPC in their struggles against Japan, Moscow sought to expand its influence from its Central Asian territories into Xinjiang. Around a decade of alliance following the founding of the PRC devolved into ideological and geopolitical rivalry from the 1960s.

The collapse of ideological-driven foreign policy in Russia (due to the collapse of the USSR) and China (driven by post-Mao reforms) paved the way for the current *de facto* Sino-Russian alliance. Instead of arguing over philosophical and political differences, the two countries decided on cooperation to advance shared self-interests. Economic relations play a key role in the relationship — Russia's abundant natural resources and China's insatiable demand for fossil fuels, timber, and metals create an obvious mutual interest. Additionally, Russian technological expertise and China's productive capabilities have created mutually beneficial synergies.

However, geopolitical realities are the main drivers of Sino-Russian partnership. Beijing and Moscow are *de facto* allies largely because of their common perception of US pressure. Such pressure comes from, among other factors, the maintenance (or in the case of Russia, expansion) of US-led military defense pacts along their strategic frontiers. Therefore, for as long as Washington maintains NATO and its West Pacific alliances — and it likely will in the coming decades — Sino-Russian strategic cooperation will continue. Unless the US withdraws from NATO, or China begins a campaign of blatant territorial aggression in Eurasia, any efforts by Washington to wean Moscow from its partnership with Beijing are doomed to failure. While Beijing and Moscow do have areas of contention — for example, China's growing influence in Central Asia and Moscow's continued friendship with India — these are minor issues when compared to their shared perception of US threats along their frontiers and spheres of influence. Additionally, both Russia and China see the US as an ideologically aggressive power intent on spreading its political system to other countries and undermining internal stability within its main rivals. US support for Russian and Chinese dissident groups, and overall US efforts to undermine various rival regimes, further contribute to Russian-Chinese cooperation.

China and Russia's alliance is grounded in mutual interest, but it goes deeper than being a relationship of mere convenience. In 2021, China's Foreign Minister Wang Li described bilateral dynamics as "Not an alliance, but better than allies." Nevertheless, their partnership is somewhat formalized by the 2001 Sino-Russian Treaty of Friendship, which calls for economic and political cooperation. Article 9 of the Treaty is a (perhaps purposefully) ambiguous call for mutual defense cooperation: "When a situation arises in which one of the contracting parties deems that peace is being threatened and undermined or its security interests are involved or when it is confronted with the threat of aggression, the contracting parties shall immediately hold contacts and consultations in order to eliminate such threats."

China is overall likely to continue its *de facto* alliances with Russia and Pakistan, and potentially other powers, instead of formalizing them with binding mutual-defense treaties. There are several reasons for Beijing's current, and probably long-term, preference for informal geopolitical partnerships. First, formal alliances can complicate or damage bilateral relations with the traditional or contemporary rivals of one's allies. A formal alliance with Moscow would hurt China relations with Ukraine and other European countries. Russia's relations with India and Vietnam would similarly suffer were Moscow to form a binding mutual-defense pact with Beijing.

Formalized security agreements also entail significant costs and risks, especially for the dominant power in the arrangement. For example, a mutual-defense pact with Pakistan would oblige Beijing to go to war based on developments occurring during the fraught and unstable Indo-Pakistani rivalry. Potential clashes between Pakistan and Afghan or Iranian forces could similarly compel Beijing to fight a war that it would otherwise seek to avoid. Formalized alliances can make interstate wars generally less likely, but they also decrease the strategic flexibility of alliance members, sometimes forcing them into costly, large-scale, and potentially disastrous conflicts with other powers. Historical precedents — especially the events leading up to the First World War in Europe — demonstrate the dangers inherent to inflexible alliance systems.

In Southeast Asia and the Middle East, Beijing prefers overall friendly ties and deepened economic engagement instead of exposing itself to risks arising from local rivalries by favoring specific sides in various disputes. Although it does have overall closer ties with some powers, China's "principled" (and self-interested) doctrine of domestic noninterference limits exposure to internal threats and regional conflicts. For example, while Beijing has close ties with Cambodia, it is unlikely to damage relations with countries that have historical rivalry with Phnom Penh, such as Vietnam and Thailand, by overtly allying with Cambodia and backing the Cambodian position in bilateral disputes. Chinese investment in and support for Iran is not so great as to meaningfully threaten Beijing's ties with the

Israeli, Saudi, or Turkish governments. Beijing generally prefers economic and diplomatic engagement with various countries on an individual basis. Bilateral arrangements allow Beijing to more directly leverage its overall advantages in economic power, while avoiding potentially costly and difficult-to-control commitments.

The Shanghai Cooperation Organization (SCO) demonstrates the limited degree to which both Russia and China are currently willing to engage in formalized multilateral arrangements. Formed in 2001 by Russia, China, and most of the former Soviet "Stans," the SCO is narrowly defined as a force to jointly combat the "three evils" of terrorism, separatism, and extremism. While SCO members have coordinated some fairly minor joint military drills, the grouping has limited aims of essentially perpetuating the political status quo in Central Asia and combating transnational Islamists in the region. The fact that both India and Pakistan have joined the SCO clearly demonstrates that the grouping is not a formal alliance aimed at countering the US or any other power. Although it is extremely limited in scope, the SCO does provide a framework for its member states to advance areas of mutual interest — namely, ensuring the continuation of current national borders, cracking down on separatist movements, and minimizing the threat of revolutionary Islamist organizations.

The globally sweeping and formalized alliances of the US create geopolitical problems as well as opportunities for Washington. As mentioned above, Washington's foreign alliances in Europe and Asia incentivize and perpetuate the strong partnership between Moscow and Beijing. Washington's NATO and West Pacific alliances also oblige the US to maintain constant preparations for the potential of simultaneous wars against both Russia and China. While these wars will almost certainly never occur, merely maintaining the credible ability to fight such conflicts thousands of miles from US territory is a significant drain on limited government resources. US military efforts in the Middle East further stretch its capacity. Currently, Moscow only needs to prepare for war against NATO along its western front, and most of China's military focus is along its eastern shoreline. Washington's alliance system and general pursuit of total global military dominance has obliged US forces to maintain a state of readiness of simultaneous war against Moscow, Beijing, and Teheran.

The US could only draw Moscow away from China if Washington abandoned or drastically reformatted its NATO commitments. This outcome is extremely unlikely, due to Washington's global and domestic self-image, along with general political inertia. Even as China undergoes the process of displacing the US as the overall globally dominant power over the coming decades, Moscow and Beijing will likely continue a partnership to stabilize their mutual frontier and concentrate on other challenges. The only alternatives would be dangerous and likely fruitless rivalry or antagonism with a nuclear-armed trading partner.

Geography, along with contemporary economic, political, technological, and strategic realities mean Beijing is highly unlikely to seek to create global alliance systems similar to those employed by the US. China borders more states than any other country. Its overseas power projection is also somewhat limited by the presence of Japan and the US in the Pacific, and India in the Indian Ocean.

There is a possibility, as China's overall global power continues to grow, of Beijing reaching out to countries near the US who perceive a potential threat from US influence. Hypothetically, China would attempt to counterbalance Washington's West Pacific alliances by reaching out to Mexico, or possibly various Caribbean countries. However, cost-benefit analysis shows how such a move is unlikely. Beijing does not

US Alliance Systems Continue; China Does Not Form NATO-Style Partnerships

want to overcomplicate its foreign policy, or risk a nuclear exchange over a potential US-Mexico conflict. China's non-ideological and nakedly self-interested approach to foreign policy, along with the contemporary reality that major interstate conflicts rarely advance a government's long-term interests, mean that NATO-style alliances are not needed for China to ensure its global influence and key goals. Deepened economic engagement and leverage and a general policy of mutual noninterference (i.e., noninterference for governments that also stay out of Beijing's "internal" conflicts with Taipei) have allowed China to vastly expand its military, political, and (especially) economic power in recent decades. So long as the general international system continues, Beijing is highly unlikely to risk a more complicated and unpredictable global stance.

Sixth Prediction

US Allies Support Geopolitical Countering of China but Not Economic Crippling

Over recent decades Washington's treaty allies have maintained their military and political ties with the US while simultaneously deepening economic engagement with China. This overall dynamic will almost certainly continue. Numerous national governments perceive benefits in keeping political and military cooperation with Washington, and also expanding trade and investment ties with China, though the trend has created some tensions and contradictions. Any US efforts to enlist its military allies in a systematic campaign to meaningfully contain, or even roll back, Chinese global economic influence will probably fail. Meanwhile, any attempt by Beijing to pressure many of China's key trading partners into reevaluating, or even abandoning, their alliances with Washington is also highly unlikely to succeed. Beijing may, at some point in the coming decades, experience some degree of success in convincing European states to expand their political ties with China, potentially to the detriment of US government aims.

All US treaty allies in Asia have a clear overall interest in supporting Washington's efforts to counterbalance Beijing's growing military clout while at the same time maintaining or enhancing economic ties with China. China is the largest single trading partner of Japan and South Korea. Beijing's economic entanglement with the Philippines, Washington's other West Pacific defense pact ally, is less robust but still significant. Meanwhile, few economies are more dependent on trade with China than Australia. Washington's strategic allies in the Pacific would experience immense economic disruptions if they supported an effort to cripple China's economy.

Furthermore, the people and leaders of South Korea, Japan, and the Philippines, for better or worse, need to live with and in close proximity to China. Any support by their governments for a strategic effort explicitly aimed at undermining the key interests of the Chinese government would almost inevitably expose them to retaliatory measures. If Beijing cannot expand its power mainly through peaceful methods, or it faces a sudden and acute internal economic and political crisis, then these countries would be forced to contend with unpredictable geopolitical destabilization in their immediate periphery. Keeping Beijing largely content and focused primarily on engaging with its neighbors through mutually beneficial economic ties is likely safer and more predictable than trying to forcibly suppress China's development.

Although their geopolitical imperatives are rather different from Washington's Western Pacific allies, the main NATO powers are also perfectly happy to keep economic ties with China. In 2021, China overtook the US as the European Union's largest trading partner. Although the EU is not NATO, the overlap between the two groupings is also fairly robust. China's economic ties with Canada and Turkey are also extensive. None of the various NATO members would stand to benefit from an economically crippled China.

Indeed, many NATO members — especially major European countries of France, Germany, and the UK — may find their overall geopolitical position *strengthened* by the trend of increasing Chinese global influence. Firstly, Beijing's growing power makes these countries more important to the US. The emergence of an alternative economic and geopolitical power center forces Washington to take the demands and interests of its allies more seriously. The more Washington needs the support of European allies to shore up the US government's preferred global initiatives, the greater leverage these allies have. . European countries can, at least to some extent, play Beijing and

Washington against each other in the economic and diplomatic spheres, while maintaining overall strategic alliances with the US. The fact that China — situated on the opposite end of the massive Eurasian landmass — apparently poses no direct threat to core European security interests helps solidify this dynamic.

In the interest of accuracy, it must be acknowledged that US treaty allies *have* been willing to curtail bilateral economic engagement with China in some marginal areas when sufficiently pressured or enticed by the US government. Notably, Washington has made a concerted effort to discourage its treaty allies from using telecom infrastructure used by Huawei, allegedly due to US concerns about potential intelligence gathering. After years of such efforts, the US has succeeded in convincing the UK, Japan, Australia, and New Zealand to ban Huawei from contributing to their national 5G infrastructure. However, the impact of these restrictions has been minimal when compared to the overall expansion of economic and trade engagement between these countries and China.

The trend of China making further inroads into US treaty allies is highly likely to continue. Since at least the early 1990s, there has been very little contradiction in various countries expanding their economic engagement with China while continuing alliances with the US. Indeed, even the US government itself has followed such a course, as have Beijing's other apparent main rivals — namely Delhi and Taipei. China's economy, along with its international trade and investment ties, will likely continue to grow. The vast majority of national governments have a clear self-interest in continuing to take advantage of opportunities created by this trend.

Although US treaty allies have varying degrees of strategic concern regarding Beijing's growing power and influence, essentially no national government is willing to pay the costs incurred from significantly decreasing their economic engagement with China. These trends and obvious self-interest will likely continue to drive enhanced economic ties between China and US allies. Of course, even the United States government itself is highly unlikely to risk attempting any concerted effort to truly cripple China's economy. Instead, Washington and its allies will likely continue marginal efforts to combat Chinese influence in certain critical technological or strategic sectors, even as China's overall economic engagement with the world grows.

Seventh Prediction

A Traditional Arms Race Is Unlikely; If It Does Occur, Washington Will Lose

Several relevant parallels exist between the current dynamic of US-China global contention and the former US-Soviet Cold War. However, a key feature of that previous struggle — the direct arms race between Washington and Moscow — is unlikely to occur again. An examination of essential strategic interests and capabilities of the Chinese and US governments demonstrates why a "traditional" arms race, in which both powers try to match and exceed the weapon systems deployed by the other, is unlikely. Nevertheless, such a scenario is possible, and the possibility necessitates the second part of this prediction. If a direct arms race does occur over multiple decades, Washington will probably find itself outmatched, outclassed, and outspent, and would consequently lose such a struggle with Beijing.

Direct and open competition with Washington to build and deploy more conventional weaponry and strategic nuclear capabilities is generally against the interests of the Chinese government. Firstly, such a dynamic could destabilize China's periphery. A rapid and blatant buildup of military hardware by the Chinese government would likely inspire India to undertake a similar military expansion, increasing the number of weapons that could target China's cities, military bases, and other key assets. Pakistan would then, in turn, be incentivized to increase its own military deployments, even though it lacks the economic and industrial base to match India on a unit-for-unit level. Similarly, a buildup by both China and the US could cause Russia to invest more resources into its military capabilities. Other countries with historically uneasy relations with China, such as Japan and Vietnam, would likely expand their militaries in a scenario of a prolonged and open arms race between the US and China.

Strategists in Washington may believe that this scenario of an expanding arms race in East Asia would support the US government's core strategic interest of maintaining its position as a globally dominant military power. It would incentivize regional US treaty allies, namely Japan, South Korea, and the Philippines, to welcome additional deployments of US firepower in the region. However, ultimately an arms race would almost certainly weaken Washington's relative overall position against China, because the US would be unable to keep up with China's military expansion.

China's *nominal* GDP is almost certain to surpass that of the United States, and then likely continue its relative dominance for the rest of the century. That prediction is predicated by measuring GDP in US dollar terms; in terms of PPP, which is an overall better indicator of the physical economy, China's GDP has been larger than that of the US since at least 2016. When compared to the United States in 2023, China had over four times the workforce, generated more than twice as much electric power, and produced *over twelve times* the volume of steel. With sufficient political will, China could *easily* surpass the United States in terms of producing both conventional and nuclear weaponry. Barring unforeseen and enormous disruptions to long-standing trends, this gap in potential military production will only grow larger.

If a direct, tit-for-tat US-China arms race develops and continues for multiple decades Washington will lose. China can produce more missiles, more naval vessels, more fighter jets, and more nuclear weapons than the US. While some broad technological and quality comparisons in key weapons systems may currently marginally favor the US, such advances are likely to become increasingly small. In other key technological areas that could determine the overall advantage in a hypothetical conventional or nuclear conflict — such as medium-range missiles and hypersonic weapons — China currently has an apparent advantage over the US. Regardless of quality comparisons (which will likely never be conclusively tested by direct and unrestrained bilateral conflict), China currently has the upper hand in terms of raw productive capacity.

During the Cold War, the US always had an advantage over the Soviet Union in terms of overall productive capacity. While Soviet steel output did surpass that of the US for some time, the size gap was never especially notable. In terms of generating electrical power, the USSR always lagged behind the US. In the 1970s and 80s Washington indirectly helped bring about the collapse of the Soviet economic and political system by compelling Moscow to spend increasingly larger sums on military spending to "keep up" with the US. Similarly, a direct arms race with China would result in intensified inefficiencies and increased risk of systemic economic collapse in the United States. Attempting to outspend and out-produce a more productive and economically dynamic rival is clearly illogical in terms of the long-term interests of a nation, though it may provide short-term benefits to arms producers and other influential lobbies.

Ultimately, because the US and China will almost certainly never intentionally go to war, the economic repercussions of a potential bilateral arms race are more important than the pure military aspects. Once a dynamic of mutually assured destruction is in place — and assuming it can be maintained — the practical implications of military competition between large nuclear powers is restricted largely to the realms of posturing, imposing leverage on third countries, and economic repercussions. Because of China's geographic position, and the fact that the trends in the shift of relative power significantly favor the Chinese government, Beijing's core interests are best served by *quietly* building up its military capabilities. The

Chinese government would prefer to avoid destabilizing its immediate periphery with an explicit buildup of conventional and nuclear weapons. Meanwhile, US vessels can patrol as much as they like near China's coast without upsetting the balance of overall power. As Beijing feels more confident in its relative global position, it may shift its policies to make regular displays of force outside its immediate frontier. If US-China contention continues in the coming decades, Beijing will deploy large flotillas in international waters near Hawaii, or even California, as an effort to bait the US into a spending and production competition that Washington simply cannot win.

Eighth Prediction

The Chinese Government Retains Relative Edge in Domestic Political Effectiveness If It Remains Rational and United

Beijing can implement its desired long-term strategic policies. The Chinese government is nakedly self-interested and is not directly accountable to the public through regular, competitive elections. This dynamic is naturally offensive to mainstream Western political doctrine, which holds that limited government, held directly accountable to its electorate, tends to produce the best and most effective policies. Comparative results of the US and Chinese governing systems over the last four decades show the apparent advantages of the CPC's (largely) non-ideological, authoritarian political monopoly. The Chinese government, with an ability to leverage vast human resources over a significant and strategically located landmass for multi-decade projects, will likely retain its overall relative domestic political advantages against Washington. If Chinese policymaking reverts to a more ideological basis, it may lose its relative advantage. If, on the other hand, China's overall political system remains rational and united, it will retain a superior ability to draft, implement, and, when needed, modify long-term strategic policy.

What is the core basis of the CPC's policy and governance? Clearly, Chinese government actions are not driven primarily by either rigid ideology or appeals to the masses via competitive elections. While there are politicians and bureaucrats within the PRC who are not CPC members, the CPC effectively monopolizes political control and policymaking within China. Political success within the CPC depends largely on two factors — personal patronage ties and quantitative success. As with any bureaucratic and largely autocratic system, personal ties between various leaders and their subordinates play an important role in determining the career course of many individuals within the power structure. Personal patronage plays a key role. Personal or political rivalries may doom a cadre who backs the "wrong" side in an internal dispute. The Party is aware of this trend, and therefore leadership positions are rotated on a regular basis, with successful and ambitious politicians moved from location to location and within various roles to prevent them from amassing an overly powerful localized base of influence and control. For example, Xi Jinping (the son of a prominent CPC leader) first served in the Party as the assistant to a leader in the Central Military Commission, then as secretary for the CPC in a rural county in northern Hebei Province, then at various governance and Party roles in southeastern Fujian Province, then Zhejiang Province, and Shanghai, before returning to Beijing for a role in central Party leadership. This range of geographic postings is broadly typical for CPC members who achieve high positions within the Party.

The politics of personality are mostly important on the level of top national leadership. For the vast majority of CPC members and government officials below the top hundred or so cadres, *performance* is the key to determining political success. The Party uses various metrics to determine effective performance. Economic growth, health outcomes, social conditions (such as the number of protests), crime, environmental readings (for example air and water pollution levels), and other key metrics in the location and/or field where a bureaucrat is posted are used to quantify performance. The better the quantitative record, the better one's career will develop. The CPC is constantly shifting the relative weight of these various metrics in pursuit of adjusted policy goals. For example, the Party may reduce the relative prioritization of income levels and rely more on air quality readings to aid national, provincial, or local initiatives to reduce environmental pollution. For the majority of CPC cadres involved in governance (and government officials who are not Party members), career success is largely dependent on quantifiable outcomes.

Of course, this creates a degree of perverse incentives, as local leaders may want to hide their shortcomings or failures from the higher levels of administration. The CPC therefore employs fairly sophisticated and, in most cases, opaque methods to determine "true" figures for various governance metrics. Government and Party bureaucracy harshly (if usually quietly) punishes officials for intentionally falsified figures or reports. Nevertheless, the PRC's lack of open media and unfiltered mass information exchange does exacerbate challenges for the accurate measurement and confirmation of the all-important datasets; after all, metrics are only truly useful to the extent that they are accurate.

Chinese officials at various levels of government must avoid major scandals or disasters to maintain their political careers. If a particular agency or local government fails to prevent (or adequately respond to) an apparently avoidable disaster, then the Party will punish the leaders deemed to be responsible. Such disasters may include consumer deaths from unsafe products, high-profile corruption scandals, or the failure of key physical infrastructure. In addition to attempting to improve the metrics on which they are judged, officials want to prevent major mishaps in their area of responsibility. Authorities of various ranks — up to and including the former head of internal security for the entire country — may be stripped of their rank, expelled from the Party, sentenced to lengthy prison terms, or even put to death for major corruption scandals. More minor breaches of discipline or policy failures typically result in demotion and a transfer to less-desirable postings.

There is also a limited, but nevertheless important, degree of popular input into the political system. Officials do facilitate some direct elections for some positions in local government;

Party members also cast anonymous ballots to determine leadership positions within the CPC. Furthermore, Chinese citizens can, and do, complain directly to various government departments. Local governments in China operate various feedback lines for issues like transport problems, medical care issues, perceived laxity law enforcement, and other grievances arising from day-to-day governance. Additionally, authorities provide channels to solicit public input when key legislation is being drafted.

Street protests also occur in mainland China. Localized issues, such as land disputes, demands for owed wages, and environmental concerns prompt most demonstrations. Broader social issues occasionally spark broader demonstrations; changes in language policy sparked fairly significant protests in Guangzhou in 2010 and Inner Mongolia in 2020. While officials usually react to sustained protest activity with crackdowns, authoritarians have also adjusted policies in response to organized unrest. For example, authorities scrapped plans for a controversial chemical plant near a residential area of Xiamen in response to significant street demonstrations. Protests specifically denouncing the CPC are effectively banned, but demonstrations based on local issues sometimes proceed without major violent opposition. The frequency and size of protests in a specific area provides the government with another data point on which to judge the performance of local officials. While this system incentives crackdowns, it also motivates officials to prevent major protests through awareness of popular grievances and efforts to address public concerns.

The final, and perhaps most important, manner in which popular sentiment shapes CPC policy is through the possibility of a violent revolution. Peasant rebellions have occurred throughout China's long history. Many of these uprisings "merely" weakened the government and drained its sources; several resulted in the direct overthrow of a ruling dynasty and the violent death of its leaders. These internal conflicts have nearly always arisen in response to a perceived or actual collapse in effective governance.

The Mandate of Heaven is a deeply held philosophical current that has shaped Chinese politics for over two thousand years. According to its basic tenets, various Chinese dynasties justified their rule as divinely ordained *specifically because* they were able to effectively bring general peace and sufficient prosperity to the masses. If and when instability and hardship begin to grow (a dynamic often, but not always, linked with major natural disasters) then rebels might raise their standards against the ruling dynasty, saying that its apparent failures signal the Emperor's loss of the Mandate of Heaven. The top leadership of the CPC knows full well that if they lose power, the Party is extremely unlikely to become a form of loyal opposition within a new governance system. The most likely outcome instead is that rebels would kill the top CPC leadership, or, at the very least, strip them of their wealth and force them into exile. Political power in China comes with enormous risk and responsibility. So long as they can govern effectively and generally improve the material conditions of the majority of people, the CPC's reign is essentially secure. Most Chinese people who are politically aware realize the basic formula of the governance system, which uses force, the threat of force, mass surveillance, but most of all persuasion, to secure its perpetuation.

The effective motivations for Chinese officials have created a fairly efficient governance system in the post-Mao era. It has facilitated a rapid expansion in economic output and undertaken apparently successful mass infrastructure projects while maintaining overall social and political stability. By measuring and adjusting quantitative inputs based on observed outcomes, the Chinese system also has the ability to modify policies in an incremental fashion. However, to say that the system is *rational and effective* is not to say it is necessarily humane or benign.

Using data to draft policy can also justify repression — as with the data-driven preemptive security apparatus in Xinjiang.

In contrast, direct accountability within the US political system is based largely on mass appeal. Political leaders are held accountable through election cycles. Obviously, a major policy failure can cause an individual candidate or the reigning party to lose its position. However, policy failures do not necessarily mean defeat, if an incumbent or party can convince the electorate that they remain the best choice when compared to their rival. The key point in US political accountability is therefore not necessarily objective, quantifiable outcomes, but rather the mass *perception* of these outcomes. There is therefore a major incentive for elected US politicians to focus more on messaging and communication than effective governance or rational, long-term policy. While in China it is merely sufficient for the population to obey government directives, in the US politicians seek to implant their ideas within the voting population. This is often done through appeals to group identity and a castigation of political rivals.

Elected politicians in the US are subject to cyclical electoral accountability. Bureaucrats are also somewhat exposed to election cycles, if they have an obvious party loyalty. Nonpartisan bureaucrats have fewer clear lines of accountability, outside of avoiding major scandals and maintaining ties with powerful partners within various US government bureaucracies. Meanwhile, the third pillar of US political power — large corporations — are effectively only directly accountable to their customers and shareholders. Their main imperative, as always, is to secure market share and grow their profits.

The current Chinese political system is obviously more united than that of the US. Instead of having competing interests among various elected officials, bureaucrats, and corporate boards, the CPC effectively subsumes all powerful interests in society within itself. Internal Party divisions are well hidden behind closed doors. Instead of being lobbied by large corporations to enact, or refrain from enacting, certain policies, the CPC effectively tells corporations what they must or cannot do. The CPC bureaucracy controls major state-owned enterprises; Party leadership can also direct the actions of private firms through various regulations. The Chinese government is not subject to the whims of a fickle electorate or self-serving corporate lobbyists. Beijing can further its long-term policy goals based on its own perceived interests and quantitative inputs. While Beijing's overt control over the domestic population is greater, its stakes are also higher. A high-ranking US politician who loses an election typically retires to a comfortable position either directly within or supported by major corporate patrons. For the top levels of the CPC, losing national political power would likely be a literal death sentence. This ultimate accountability also solidifies a greater degree of internal unity.

However, Beijing's advantage in terms of political unity can also be its downfall. The system works *if and only if* the Chinese government pursues generally rational policy, and adjusts its approach depending on actual conditions. For better or for worse, the Chinese government can essentially enact any policies it wishes to within China. This is an advantage when the policies are fundamentally rational, and a tremendous disadvantage when they are not. The disastrous results of ideological policy are obvious, both in China and in the US. The Great Leap Forward and Cultural Revolution, beyond being human disasters, weakened the government and likely delayed its development path by two or three decades. Meanwhile, Washington's ideologically driven conflicts in Vietnam, Iraq, and Afghanistan also created humanitarian disasters and weakened the US government's relative power. Beijing's advantage in terms of political unity will be lost if it seeks overly ideological aims, instead of continuing to pursue raw self-interest.

Ninth Prediction

India-China Contention Supplants US-China Rivalry

The ties and tensions that define relations between China and India are an increasingly important factor shaping global geopolitics. Towards the end of this century, India is likely to surpass the US as the world's second-largest national economy, while China maintains the top position. India's growing productive capabilities will allow for increased diplomatic heft and military expenditure. While Sino-US competition will remain a key driving feature of global interaction over the coming decades, this long-standing trend will probably be subsumed by Sino-Indian contention as a key geopolitical dynamic towards the end of the 21st century.

There are several key factors that will likely drive India's expansion in overall global influence. First is human potential. India's population growth remains robust, with the country likely to overtake China as the world's most populous country well before 2030. UN forecasts see India's population at around 1.64 billion in 2050, compared to 1.4 billion in China and around 379 million in the US. Globalization has generally led to decreased disparities in per capita output; India will be the main beneficiary if this trend continues. India, with a current per capita nominal GDP of less than a fifth that of China's, has significant "low hanging" development potential. India's demographic structure over the coming decades is also favorable to overall economic expansion — while the working age population in China is set to shrink, it is poised to grow in India.

Purposeful US support may be another major driver of expanding Indian influence. China has over four times the population of the US. So long as a major crisis does not occur within China to hold back its economic potential, then from sheer size alone it has a tremendous advantage that Washington simply cannot directly counter. However, as China grows more powerful, the US government is likely to deepen political, economic, and technological cooperation with India as a counterbalance. India has a massive (and growing) population, along with previously mentioned underdeveloped economic potential. These economic realities, along with its geographic position along China's southwestern frontier, make India by far the strongest candidate for serving as an effective geopolitical counterbalance against an increasingly dominant China.

Assuming Washington maintains an active military presence in Asia and seeks to maintain a goal of checking China's relative power, India is a natural partner. While mistrust and somewhat differing strategic priorities could dampen US-Indian cooperation, the likely overall trend is one of increasing cooperation. Short of purposefully instigating a crisis within China, attempting to openly curtail its economic development or launching a war — gambits that would be extremely dangerous — encouraging India's development is probably Washington's best bet for countering China over the coming decades. This imperative, however, could eventually backfire in terms of Washington's relative global power. US support for China against the Soviet Union in the 1980s helped set the stage for Beijing's growth in overall global influence. A similar dynamic could see Delhi eventually supplanting Washington as the second (or in the event of a Chinese crisis, first) preeminent global power sometime this century. In the long run, such an outcome is probable regardless of explicit US support to India.

The basic drive to become or remain the world's preeminent power, which currently shapes China-US relations, is highly likely to become a defining feature of Sino-Indian ties as the 21st

century progresses. In the absence of a sufficiently disruptive disaster in any of the three countries, or the emergence of a new power, China, India, and the US are highly likely to clearly occupy the positions of the world's top three globally influential countries from around 2050. In terms of total influence, the ranking in mid-century will probably be China, followed by the US and then India. Towards the end of the century, India will supplant the US in the second position. There is also a possibility of India being able to directly challenge or even upend Beijing's overall dominance towards the end of this century.

Naturally, there are also many factors that may conspire to hinder India's economic development and associated rise in global importance over the coming decades. India is far more linguistically, culturally, and politically diverse than China. This greater diversity has helped contribute to internal conflict in some parts of India, as in the Kashmir Valley, minority areas of far northeastern India, and in tribal-dominated regions of the east and southeast. The PRC's various internal divisions, while at times locally destabilizing, have not resulted in any unresolved, multi-decade armed insurgencies within mainland China. India is also exposed to religious tensions between Hindus and Muslims that can (and have) resulted in riots impacting multiple parts of the country simultaneously. Additionally, the continued influence of the caste system has greatly exacerbated internal social divisions and hampered potential growth. Some contemporary high-caste landlords in rural India, and other powerful interests who seek to perpetuate their advantages within the caste system, have purposefully sought to keep members of lower castes poor and illiterate. Despite the various historical and contemporary excesses and abuses within the PRC, at no point in China's recent history have its leaders sought to purposefully prevent a population under their control from achieving basic literacy.

Furthermore, India's federal structure and diversity of political parties often prevents the central government — which faces regular and contentious elections — from enacting its long-term policy goals. In some instances, this has been to India's apparent advantage when compared to the PRC. An independent India has never experienced a nationwide famine brought about by stubbornly irrational government policy. Various facets of Indian culture and arts remain vibrant, having never been purposefully curtailed by an attempted Cultural Revolution or by especially stringent government censorship. Nevertheless, the lack of consistent internal political unity may hamper the Indian government's ability to impose effective long-term policies and strategies. Any major attempts to centralize control or institute effective one-party rule — under the guise of the "Hindu nationalist" vision of the currently dominant Bharatiya Janata Party (BJP), for example — would almost inevitably invite major resistance from powerful interests at the state level and various opposition parties. There are systemic advantages and disadvantages inherent to India's democracy and plurality.

Despite its various challenges and internal contradictions, the most likely trend in the coming decades, but especially from around 2050, is one of increased relative Indian power and influence. For all their internal divisions, India's major political and economic institutions do share a common interest in broadly strengthening the country and its overall global position. The likely continuation of improvements in education, infrastructure, and overall economic conditions generally bode well for strengthened social and political stability. While political and social contention will continue, if the material conditions of India's people improve, the masses will have greater stake in the overall continuation of the system in which they live.

Geography, in addition to overall global power dynamics, will continue to shape Sino-Indian ties and contention. Like China itself, India finds itself in an extremely strategic location, for better and for worse. India shares land borders with two significant, nuclear-armed geopolitical rivals (Pakistan and China), along with Bangladesh, Myanmar, Nepal, and Bhutan (and Afghanistan, if one recognizes Indian claims over Pakistani-controlled territory in northwestern Kashmir). India geographically dominates the northern reaches of the Indian Ocean, allowing the Indian government to exert influence on vital oceanic trading routes linking the Middle East, East Africa, Southeast Asia, and East Asia. These routes, of course, are also of vital importance to the Asian and European countries that also trade extensively in the Indian Ocean, including China.

In many ways, the basic geopolitical stances of both Beijing and Delhi are surprisingly similar. Both governments feel geographically constrained by neighboring rivals (or potential rivals). Both countries occupy globally crucial areas with significant opportunities for international trade and investment. China has superior overland access to energy markets via Pakistan, Central Asia, and Russia. However, India, at least for the time being, faces fewer potential constraints on maritime trade. Unlike China, Delhi does not need to contend with powers who have the ability and potential motives to disrupt its trade routes in its immediate oceanic periphery.

Beijing and Delhi have contemporary and historical tensions with smaller countries in their immediate neighborhood, some of whom reach out to outside powers as a counterbalance. Just as, say, Vietnam enhances cooperation with the US and India while generally avoiding any move that would completely alienate it against Beijing, countries such as Sri Lanka and Bangladesh have deepened their engagement with China while attempting to avoid the wrath of the Indian government. As for their mutual neighbors, India is allied with Bhutan (which has no formal ties with China), China is effectively allied with Pakistan, and both countries vie for influence over Nepal and Myanmar. For their part, Nepal and Myanmar, like Sri Lanka and many Southeast Asian states, generally try to play Sino-Indian rivalry to their own relative advantage.

The most crucial factor of geography that will help define Sino-Indian relations is the disputed border between the two powers. India and China must live with each other. This can, and does, drive rivalry. Unlike the US, which could potentially draw down its global political and military commitments, India cannot physically distance itself from China. At the same time, this proximity also creates some significant common interests. While both Delhi and Beijing seek regional (and eventual global) preeminence, they also want to ensure overall geopolitical stability and economic growth. Beijing has sought to entice India with increased economic and infrastructure ties through proposed overland rail routes through the Himalayas. So far Delhi has rejected direct participation in such a scheme. However, regardless of the ebb and flow of their tensions and ties, both powers will seek cooperation in areas of obvious mutual interest, such as seeking to avoid or mitigate major disruptions arising from climate change and interstate nuclear war.

If, as is likely, India overtakes the US as the overall second most powerful country in overall terms, then Sino-Indian rivalry will become the most geopolitically important bilateral trend in the world. Broadly speaking, the power dynamics between China and India may mirror those that currently shape contention between the US and China. The two countries will seek to entice and pressure third governments to support their interests against the rival power. A relatively dominant China may one day attempt to curtail or even disrupt India's development through economic or diplomatic moves. Delhi may seek to broaden and deepen its economic ties with third countries, and with China itself, in order to make itself indispensable in the global economic system. As with current Sino-US contention, both sides will seek to keep their rivalry limited to certain spheres while perpetuating economic ties and avoiding accidental military conflict. Lessons learned — or ignored — from previous cycles of great power rivalry will continue to shape their competition.

Section Three

Grey Swans

China and the US will remain the two most powerful countries on earth for at least several decades. Washington and Beijing's struggle for overall relative global dominance will shape their relations with each other and other national governments. Nevertheless, common interests, and the dangers inherent in open confrontation, will prevent other powers from purposefully engaging in direct military conflict. By around 2040 China will occupy the overall dominant global position. These four core predictions form the foundation of this book's other forecasts for likely future developments. However, there are plausible scenarios that could prevent or reverse this overall forecast.

Grey Swans are the foreseeable events or developments that could disrupt the core predictions made in this book. They are not "Black Swan" events, because analysts can foresee the potential for Grey Swan scenarios in advance of their occurrence. While these Grey Swans remain generally unlikely, they are sufficiently plausible and sufficiently disruptive as to warrant consideration and discussion. The predictions in this book are based essentially on the continuation of preexisting long-standing geopolitical, social, and economic trends. Such trends may be knocked off their course by a Grey Swan event, or a combination of such scenarios.

Grey Swan Number One

Nuclear War

An interstate nuclear war — any interstate nuclear war — would act as an enormous disrupter to nearly every major military, economic, and diplomatic dynamic in the world, including the key trends driving Sino-US relations. Such a conflict would almost certainly be contrary to the overall economic and political interests of essentially every global government. However, depending on the specifics of the parties of the nuclear exchange, it could *conceivably* work to the advantage of the *relative* power of either Beijing or Washington. It could also effectively destroy both governments (and quite possibly most other countries as well). An essential point to remember when examining the likely results of a nuclear war is that the only *possible* "winner" of a nuclear exchange is the country that does not participate in the conflict.

While forecasted scenarios vary significantly, most experts agree that a nuclear war would be an unprecedented human disaster. In a scenario of "only" around 250 nuclear weapons being used in urban areas, even countries on the other side of the world would likely experience years of reduced temperatures and sunlight, resulting in crop failures and famine. Sustained interstate nuclear warfare is an inherently self-destructive proposition. Therefore, a purposeful nuclear exchange between two powers, both armed with nuclear weapons, is extremely unlikely.

However, forecasted devastation and the clear interest all governments have in avoiding such a scenario do not render nuclear war impossible. There are numerous historically documented nuclear "close calls" in which the military forces of a nuclear-armed country have *almost* ordered a nuclear strike.

Most of these incidents were due to communication lapses or errors. Many of the best-known cases come from the former Soviet Union — possibly because of greater international access to military archives following the collapse of the USSR.

Officers aboard the B-59, a Soviet submarine armed with nuclear torpedoes, almost fired a payload at US targets during the 1962 Cuban Missile Crisis. US naval craft were targeting the B-59 with low-explosive depth charges to try to force the vessel to surface; however, the B-59 crew thought they were under direct attack by powerful weapons. They were cut off from radio communication and believed a war had already broken out. Unanimous agreement among the three main officers aboard the sub was needed to fire a nuclear torpedo at a US ship. One of the three main officers aboard vetoed the decision to launch the weapon. The decision of *one individual* who stood in opposition to his peers was the only factor that prevented a tactical Soviet nuclear weapon from destroying US vessels in the Caribbean during the Cuban Missile Crisis. Similar near-misses came close to triggering nuclear exchanges at multiple other points during the Cold War.

At least nine countries currently have nuclear weapons. Total nuclear stockpiles of these various countries are in the thousands. Even if the odds of a nuclear war breaking out at any given time are extremely low, humanity rolls the dice every single day. Unless nuclear weapons states reach a comprehensive agreement to verifiably destroy their arsenals (and they probably won't), the risk of nuclear warfare will continue.

Specifically, with regards for the implications of potential nuclear warfare on US-China relations, there are four overall scenarios to consider. First is a direct US-China nuclear exchange. The second and third possibilities are scenarios in which either China or the US engage in nuclear war with a third country. Finally, nuclear conflicts that involve neither China nor the US could occur.

A direct US-China nuclear war would almost certainly result in the effective destruction of both national governments. Obviously, neither country has a sufficiently belligerent motive to risk total annihilation by launching a premeditated nuclear first strike against the other. Given current technological constraints (which will probably generally continue), it is extremely unlikely that either country could "safely" attack the other without at least experiencing some degree of a successful nuclear counterstrike. Nevertheless, an essentially accidental nuclear exchange between the US and China cannot be ruled out. Such a scenario would probably effectively destroy both governments, leaving other powers to shape a shattered global system by expanding and protecting their own power within it. Depending on the scale of the nuclear exchange, a near-total breakdown of the state-based global system could occur. At least some human beings, especially those located in regions of the world far from the detonations, would likely survive the fallout and resultant global cooling, crop failures, famine, and political breakdown. However, the economic, political, and military dynamics that eventually emerged would be essentially unrecognizable from their current form.

This overall forecast — effective destruction of the national governments involved in a nuclear war along with, at the least, tremendous hardship and disruptions in noncombatant states — applies to any nuclear exchange between major countries. Nobody "wins" a nuclear war, but the states that participate stand to lose far more than those that do not. Therefore, there would be a *potential relative* benefit (though enormous risk) for either Beijing or Washington if their main rival for overall global influence engaged in a nuclear war with a third country. This is especially true for a theoretical nuclear war that "only" involved the detonation of fewer than a hundred or so nuclear warheads, as such an exchange would result in more limited global cooling and crop failures, giving noncombatant countries and regions a greater chance at recovery.

The US is not the only credible strategic nuclear threat to China; a Sino-Indian nuclear war is also possible. Both China and India have several hundred nuclear weapons, though perhaps neither government could use all the warheads before the war concluded. Radiation from a nuclear exchange would likely devastate nearby countries, including densely populated and economically vital areas of South, Southeast, and East Asia. Despite the massive devastation and global economic disruptions, the US government could *possibly* survive a China-India nuclear war and the resulting upheaval. The main areas of devastation would be located far from American shores. In terms of relative global power, Washington could therefore theoretically benefit from a Sino-Indian nuclear war, as such an exchange would destroy the two countries most likely to surpass the US in overall influence this century. The US government is extremely unlikely to seek to bring about such a scenario, as the disruptions and risk involved would be enormous. However, both Beijing and Delhi would be wise to remain cognizant of the possibility, however remote, of potential US maneuvering to increase the odds of a nuclear exchange between the Asian giants.

By the same standard, China could emerge as the relative "victor" of a nuclear war that only involved the United States and a third power. For example, China would almost certainly emerge as the strongest remaining national government following a US-Russia nuclear exchange. However, Beijing would face a higher possibility of eventual internal collapse due to massive economic disruption and likely crop failures, as both the US and Russia would likely detonate at least several hundred nuclear devices in each other's territory during the course of a war. A more manageable scenario that would also likely leave Beijing as the world's predominant power would be a scenario in which both North Korea and the US detonate a handful or a few dozen nuclear warheads in each other's territory. Depending on the specifics of the conflict, the US government could potentially survive in some form, but it would be greatly weakened. While Beijing would lose an important regional buffer with the effective destruction of the North Korean government, it would stand to lose far less than a US government that survived the detonation of several North Korean nuclear devices within its territory.

Nuclear war could also occur between two countries without direct involvement of either China or the US. For example, India and Pakistan could engage in such a conflict. The result of that exchange would likely be more disruptive for China than for the US, since China borders both countries and, depending on weather conditions, could experience significant radioactive fallout. On the other hand, if the Chinese government was able to survive the literal and figurative fallout of such an exchange, it could also eventually emerge with an improved regional geopolitical position, as the national government of its main counterbalancing rival along its southwestern border would likely be either destroyed or tremendously weakened.

Theoretically, a nuclear war could occur between any two nuclear-armed states. Depending on the contour of future alliance systems, an eventual Franco-Russian exchange is not impossible; neither is nuclear conflict between Israel and another regional state that is able to develop and deploy nuclear weapons. There is even the possibility of a nuclear power using its ultimate weapons on a rival that does not possess nuclear weapons, although such a move is extremely unlikely, unless a national government faced an imminent existential threat.

In the event of a relatively "minor" nuclear war that does not completely destroy humanity's reigning political, diplomatic, and economic systems, other nuclear states may be pressured to give up their own weapons. Some governments could voluntarily disband their nuclear arsenals in order to avoid being targeted in future nuclear conflicts. While larger powers — namely the US, China, Russia, and India — will almost certainly never have sufficient mutual trust to disband their nuclear devices, they may eventually agree to a binding, multilateral treaty that caps their arsenals at, say, around 100 warheads apiece. This number of weapons would be sufficient to deter attack, but (hopefully) not so many as to permanently cripple human civilization in the event of their use. Large countries could also work in concert to put sufficient economic and diplomatic pressure on smaller nuclear powers, such as Israel and North Korea, to disband or at least drastically reduce their own arsenals.

The overall likelihood of a direct, intentional war between two nuclear-armed countries is extremely low. Costs inherent to any such exchange outweigh any conceivable benefit for all national governments. Nevertheless, even an extremely unlikely scenario becomes progressively likelier given the passage of time. Assuming that the odds of a nuclear war breaking out on any given day are only one in a million, the probability of such an exchange occurring increases to roughly one out of 28 over the course of a century. The threat of an interstate nuclear exchange should be taken very seriously — far more seriously than all national governments and most individuals apparently regard the possibility.

As for the implications for US-China competition, essentially all scenarios of interstate nuclear war, even one that did not directly involve Beijing or Washington, could be against the overall interests of both governments. However, in terms of *relative* global power, any government that avoids a nuclear war could conceivably emerge as the "winner" of an exchange between its main rival and another country. There is an inherent risk that either Beijing or Washington could eventually seek to encourage or covertly bring about a scenario in which its challenger for hegemony is crippled or effectively destroyed via nuclear war with a third power. This is a possibility such third powers — primarily India and Russia — have a clear interest in monitoring and preventing.

Grey Swan Number Two

European Countries Form a Geopolitically United Global Power

The formation of a truly geopolitically united European conglomeration, with a unified foreign policy and military command that represents and subsumes the interests and capabilities of its member states, could seriously disrupt the overall forecasted course of Sino-US contention in the 21st century. A United Europe could emerge as a serious contender for the position of the world's secondary, or potentially even primary, global power. Such a development would then bring about a realignment of great power global geopolitics, impacting relations among the US, China, Russia, and possibly India. Although the emergence of a geopolitically united Europe would be a significant development forcing a serious reexamining of this book's core predictions, it is also fairly unlikely. This is chiefly because, as currently structured, many member states of the European Union have significantly divergent domestic and geopolitical priorities, and different strategic goals. For example, several EU states, including Austria, Ireland, Malta, and Cyprus, are not members of NATO. These countries would likely refuse to join any United Europe that obliged them to go to war in response to an attack on the US, UK, Canada, or Turkey.

Even among EU members that *are* a part of NATO there are often significantly divergent geopolitical imperatives. Generally, the closer they are to the Russian frontier, the stronger their motivation to counterbalance Moscow by acting as staunch US allies. True, essentially all European NATO members *generally* share common concerns about balancing against Russian influence and potential aggression, but the national interests of, say, Portugal, Spain, Greece, and Italy with regards to a perceived Russian threat are far removed from those of Poland and Estonia.

Furthermore, some EU and NATO member states have significant cultural, economic, or even military ties with areas outside the region. Most notably, France maintains interests and influence in its former African colonies. There are also French overseas territories, which are officially integral parts of the French Republic, in South America and the Pacific. Paris' possession of overseas territories and extensive interests in parts of Africa create long-standing French geopolitical imperatives that are obviously not shared by, say, Hungary, Norway, or Albania. Hundreds (or in some cases thousands) of years of mutual historical animosity between EU states also hinder the potential of the EU and its ability to coalesce into a united geopolitical force on the international arena.

Even the EU's current structure as a collection of independent states tied into a united market through the free movement of people, goods, and capital, causes a significant degree of national resentment in most member states. Many EU members resent the dominance of large countries, especially Germany, in influencing (some would say effectively dictating) EU monetary policy. Recent decades have seen an overall trend of slow disintegration of the EU, most vividly illustrated by the withdrawal of the UK from the grouping following a 2016 referendum. Additional member states may leave the EU in the coming years and decades, as openly advocated by numerous political parties and movements in various European countries.

Somewhat counterintuitively, the prospect of additional states leaving the EU marginally *increases* the likelihood of the organization, or possibly a separate entity formed within or alongside the EU, emerging as a geopolitically united power. Generally, the more diverse and numerous a political grouping is, the more likely it is to either remain internally divided or to split up entirely. Countries with governments that voluntarily stay within the EU during a process of the organization shrinking are far more likely to seek to deepen and expand its institutional integration. A group of "core" European states, for example Germany, France, the Netherlands, Belgium, Denmark, the Czech Republic, Slovakia, and possibly other adjacent countries, are far more likely to form a geopolitically united front on the global stage if "freed" from the constraints of dealing with members on the European periphery.

How could the hypothetical emergence of a truly United Europe change US-China dynamics? First, such a grouping would possess far greater capacity for effective independent foreign policy on the global stage than its individual members currently have. Although it would probably remain within NATO, a United Europe composed of Germany, France, and other neighboring states could effectively resist or push back against unwanted US (and for that matter, Russian or Chinese) policies, pressures and influence. France's possession of nuclear weaponry and permanent UN Security Council membership currently grants it a degree of independence and initiative on the international stage that Germany currently lacks, while German economic might would give the United Europe sufficient productive and financial heft to effectively influence major global initiatives.

A United Europe of France, Germany, the Netherlands, Belgium, Denmark, the Czech Republic, and Slovakia, would be a nuclear power. If it were to be formed at the time of writing, it would have a population of around 195 million and the world's third-largest nominal GDP. Barring a major catastrophe in either China or the US, and any sudden rapid and sustained economic development in India, it would probably be overall the world's third most powerful geopolitical force. Under a dynamic of continued Sino-US contention, it could tip the scales on important global issues and during times of crisis or change to seek to bring about its desired outcome.

This United Europe would be positioned to the West of Russia and across the Atlantic from the United States. As with current European NATO states, it would *not* share nearly the same degree of concern held by Washington regarding a trend of continued expansion of overall Chinese global influence. In fact, it is possible that, eventually, such a power could seek to *expand* cooperation with China in response to concerns about balancing Russian, or even, potentially, US pressure. Assuming (as is extremely likely) that Britain stayed out of a United Europe, London would likely seek to further deepen its already extensive ties with Washington as a precautionary balancing act. Any enhanced US support for London could in turn deepen geopolitical suspicions within a United Europe. While a major and open rupture in US-European relations would remain unlikely, the mere act of core European states formally uniting on the global stage would invariably cause other powers to alter their stances in potentially unpredictable ways. A United Europe which lacked a frontier with Russia may be less inclined to fear Moscow's influence. If, on the other hand, Poland and other Eastern European countries were a part of the group, policies aimed at securing the frontier with Russia would continue.

Strategic economic concerns could also impact United Europe's relations with other regional and global powers. Like China, nearly all European states are highly dependent on fossil fuel imports. Also, like China, some powerful European states, most notably Germany, are highly dependent on exporting manufactured goods. These dynamics create a degree of different foreign policy imperatives from countries with negative trade balances (the US) and net energy exporters (Russia, and in some recent years, also the US).

Generally, the emergence of a United Europe would likely blunt or at least soften US global diplomatic influence. The emergence of an "alternative" nuclear-armed, democratic, prosperous, and economically influential Western power — even if it remained formally aligned with Washington — would by the very nature of its existence effectively reduce US influence in Europe, and probably other global regions. Due to its geographic position, a United Europe would likely be less of a relative challenge to Beijing's global imperatives, though it could potentially compete with China for economic and political influence in Africa and the Middle East. A United Europe could also potentially provide India with an alternative global partner in Delhi's efforts to counterbalance Chinese influence.

The creation of a truly United Europe on the international stage is a generally unlikely development. Nevertheless, such an occurrence would disrupt global diplomatic, economic, and military trends in ways that would in turn impact Sino-US relations. Unless, for some unforeseen reason, a United Europe overtook either China or the US in terms of overall global power and influence, it would not change the general trend of controlled contention between Beijing and Washington. It could, however, realign global power dynamics.

Grey Swan Number Three

Climate Change Majorly Undermines Global Agriculture

Global climate change will impact Sino-US contention, though the ways and extent to which it will shape the relationship is unclear. A general trend of significant warming will almost certainly continue for the Earth as a whole throughout the 21st century, though specific impacts will vary considerably by location. Rainfall patterns, currents, and winds may shift dramatically. These developments will inevitably impact key agricultural areas throughout the planet. A seasonally ice-free Arctic Ocean will probably facilitate new trade routes between Europe and Asia. Significant change to diplomatic systems, and even military contention, are possible. While the specifics of the exact speed and intensity of climate change remain somewhat unclear, current indicators are that it will be more rapid and more disruptive than most people and organizations, including national governments, care to realize. Some national governments may attempt to ameliorate increasing temperatures through geo-engineering projects. At the same time, many warming trends form positive feedback loops that work to further accelerate overall temperature increases. No matter the exact extent, speed, and localized impacts of global climate change, the trend will help shape Sino-US relations, and if global warming is sufficiently disruptive, major changes to overall bilateral dynamics are possible.

Changes in weather patterns arising from climate change may disproportionately affect the US or China. Global warming is likely more of a threat to China than it is to the US, merely because of the fact that China has roughly four times the overall population density of the United States. Nevertheless, climate change could have worse localized impacts in agriculturally key areas of the US by, for example, triggering long-term droughts, or even desertification, in the Great Plains and Midwest. China's unitary political system may offer Beijing advantages in terms of long-term planning and proactive approaches to climate change impacts. For example, the Chinese government has undertaken massive tree planting and water diversion projects to prevent desertification and deal with regional freshwater scarcity. Similar efforts would be more difficult to launch and sustain in the US, due to tensions between political parties along with often divergent federal, state, and local government priorities. It is broadly likely that climate change is more of a threat to China than the US because of challenges inherent to feeding a larger and denser population, but this is by no means a certain conclusion.

Both countries also face growing dangers from sea level rise. Many key coastal urban areas in China, including the economically crucial Pearl River Delta, face increasing threats from rising seas. While urban conglomerations in the US are more dispersed, several important regions — including major Northeastern cities and much of Florida — face similar threats.

Climate change may have significant geopolitical impacts by altering both Beijing's and Washington's relations with third powers. For example, major disruptions to agriculture in Central America could drastically increase the flow of migrants northward into the United States, with potential domestic political and social repercussions. China may experience greater contention with India and Southeast Asian states over water sharing rights for rivers originating from shrinking Himalayan glaciers.

An overall trend of warming could see desertification in existing croplands and an associated push northwards into areas currently covered by permafrost. While it would be extremely difficult to establish large-scale agriculture in such regions, with sufficient motivation and resources it may be possible to set up farms in extreme northern climates. The vast majority of governments and individuals would be "losers" in a scenario of extremely disruptive climate change. However, Russia and Canada could emerge as *relative* "winners" under such a trend. Canada may experience increased tensions with a hungrier and hotter United States coveting their neighbor's vast and sparsely populated interior. Russia could face similar pressures from China, although nuclear weapons would likely grant Moscow greater leverage in which to negotiate with a land-hungry Beijing. At least theoretically, towards the end of the current century Canada could be forced to reach out to China for strategic balance against the US, while a similar US-Russian axis could form against Beijing. Although such a scenario may seem ludicrous under current strategic alignments, the material implications of global warming could upend long-standing geopolitical relations in unpredictable ways.

Overall, the country that undergoes greater threats and associated disruptions from global climate change will experience a concurrent decrease in overall global power. Based on current indicators, climate change will likely be more disruptive in China than in the US, but such an outcome is not certain. The extent of local, national and global disruptions from global warming are difficult to accurately forecast prior to their actual occurrence. While climate change is overall likely a greater threat to Beijing than it is to Washington, it will probably not be sufficiently disruptive in China (or, more accurately, sufficiently *more* disruptive in China) to prevent Beijing from becoming the world's overall strongest geopolitical power. Of course, in a scenario of extreme and broadly distributed impacts, climate change could be sufficiently disruptive to knock *both* the US and China out of the bilateral contention for the title of the Earth's most influential government. In the absolute worst-case scenario, global warming could conceivably set off a self-sustaining vicious cycle that causes mass starvation, war, economic breakdown, revolution, and migration throughout most countries on the planet, possibly ending the current state-based global order and industrial civilization in its current form.

If perceived as sufficiently threatening, climate change may encourage a degree of mutually beneficial cooperation between Beijing and Washington. Although their contention for overall global power will continue, the need to be the strongest government is (hopefully) less acute than the overriding motivation to prevent mass starvation, war, and global collapse. Both sides, and indeed, essentially all existing national governments, have a common interest in preventing the worst-case scenarios. Beijing and Washington are therefore likely to maintain at least some technological cooperation aimed at preventing or reacting to major climate-change threats. If climate change is sufficiently rapid and disruptive, the two powers could cooperate on geo-engineering efforts to lower global temperatures. As the two most influential countries, the US and China would be well positioned to entice and pressure third powers to accede to their bilateral climate initiatives.

Unfortunately, it is also possible that either Beijing or Washington could weaponize climate change for their own perceived geopolitical aims. This is especially true if global warming is significantly more disruptive in one country than the other. Since China apparently faces relatively more severe threats from global warming, there is a greater likelihood of Washington trying to "use" climate change to its relative advantage against Beijing. Already China, like India, views some climate initiatives encouraged by richer countries as unfair, since the world's relatively wealthy regions became wealthy in large part through the use of fossil fuels. Additionally, election cycles limit the US government's long-term strategic thinking, and many key power centers in the US, at the time of writing, remain climate change skeptics out of economic and political self-interest. The US government is therefore less likely to take climate change as seriously as Beijing. When the Chinese government occupies the position of clear overall power advantage, it may use its influence to effectively impose climate change initiatives on third countries, potentially exacerbating tensions with the US and India. However, the most likely general trend in the coming decades is one of major global powers cooperating against climate change, while "gaming" such initiatives to align with their own perceived interests.

Grey Swan Number Four

(Another) Pandemic Disrupts the Global Economy

The rapid worldwide spread of COVID-19, while shocking, was not exactly *surprising* to many experts. Epidemiologists had long predicted the emergence of a novel pathogen that could create a global pandemic. Many of the same scientific and public health experts believe that another global pandemic sparked by yet another disruptive virus (or bacterium, or possibly a prion or a parasite) new to human beings is essentially inevitable. Furthermore, reckless antibiotic usage among human beings and our livestock could inspire the evolution of a strengthened form of an existing menace. Diseases may enter our populations due to the ever-increasing encroachment of human beings into previously undisturbed ecological systems. As the technology for gene modification becomes more sophisticated and accessible, the possibility of an intentionally weaponized viral agent also increases. Whatever the exact cause, it is extremely likely that humanity will experience another major pandemic in the coming decades. If sufficiently disruptive, the outbreak could shift the course of Sino-US contention from its current path.

Two main factors — intensity and location — will largely determine the impacts the emergence of yet another pandemic on US-Sino relations will have on competition. Here "intensity" is broadly defined as the product of how dangerous and how easily spread a novel illness is. The deadlier and more transmissible a disease is, the greater its impact on global economies and societies. Of course, for most diseases there is something of a trade-off between danger to infected people and the ability to spread, since overly deadly viruses and bacteria may kill their hosts before they can infect new hosts. At any rate the more threatening a disease is, the greater its associated disruptions on global systems. A relatively benign disease akin to a mild cold spreading throughout the globe is unlikely to majorly impact US-China contention; an illness that presents a major threat to human health will have correspondingly larger impacts.

The other key element in considering impact is location. A new disruptive pandemic could emerge in China, the US, or a third country. All other factors being equal, in general the area where the pandemic originates is most likely to experience the most disruptions. A novel transmissible disease originating, say, in Europe or Africa may not significantly alter US-China contention, except to the degree to which the two powers are exposed to travel and economic interlinking in the impacted location. If the disease begins to spread in China, it will most likely be most disruptive within China, and broadly benefit the US government in terms of the bilateral struggle for overall global power. Similarly, a disease originating in and contained to the US may have positive results for Beijing's relative influence.

Largely due to its unified, self-interested, and largely rational political system, the Chinese government currently has significant advantages over Washington in terms of enacting harsh public health measures. Beijing will probably continue to possess these relative strengths in the coming decades. Therefore, all other factors being equal, it seems likely that another major pandemic impacting most or all of the world would help Beijing's relative global influence and power at the expense of Washington's. Nevertheless, China could be the overall "loser" in the event of a sufficiently deadly and transmissible disease emerging within or near its own borders, especially if Washington learned from the missteps of its responses to COVID-19 and rapidly enacted effective countermeasures.

While Beijing currently has an apparent overall advantage when compared to Washington in responding to and minimizing the impacts of a pandemic, its edge may be weakened in the coming decades. Either or both governments may develop artificial intelligence systems or advanced medical technologies that give them greater abilities to counteract or even prevent the spread of a new disease within their borders. Furthermore, China's expanding global economic footprint could create vulnerabilities with regards to novel diseases. For example, a major outbreak of a new disease could, at least in theory, be largely confined to tropical regions of central Africa, South America, or parts of Southeast Asia. Even if China prevented the contagion from spreading within its own borders, it could experience greater secondary and tertiary impacts from disease-driven disruptions in its major trading partners.

Both Beijing and Washington have an overall common interest in preventing global pandemics and minimizing their impacts. The threat of additional outbreaks may therefore help to drive Sino-US cooperation in the public health sphere. Simultaneously, both governments may also seek to use the emergence of any new pandemic and the associated disruptions for their relative advantage. By far the most cost-effective approach to "benefiting" from a pandemic is to minimize its impacts within one's own population, and to a lesser degree, among one's trading partners and allies.

Overall, the likelihood of either Washington or Beijing utilizing intentional biological attacks on the other is extremely low, as such a move would invite universal international condemnation and harsh retaliation. Given current technological constraints, neither side is likely to feel confident in its ability to conduct such an attack with plausible deniability. Nevertheless, both Washington and Beijing will need to consider defense measures to reduce the possibility of intentionally generated pandemics, which may be made by national governments or non-state actors. Effective reactions to novel pandemics could be a deciding factor in their contest for overall relative global dominance.

Grey Swan Number Five

Technology Undermines Mutually Assured Destruction

Technological development will inevitably impact the contours and course of US-China relations. While marginal improvements in existing inventions are unlikely to radically alter bilateral dynamics, certain types of potential technological systems could drastically upend existing trends. Most importantly, any technology that meaningfully undermines, or even overturns, the long-standing dynamic of Mutually Assured Destruction (MAD) between major nuclear powers would increase the possibility of direct armed conflict between China and the US. Any development and deployment of weapons systems that undercut MAD could therefore challenge this book's prediction that Washington and Beijing will never engage in a direct and sustained military conflict.

MAD is an essentially stable system, despite the inherent dangers of miscalculations or errors triggering an enormous catastrophe. All powers under a MAD framework have a very clear self-interest in avoiding a nuclear exchange. A degree of nuclear parity also reduces the risks of conventional military conflict, as neither side can fully guarantee that a clash which started with purely conventional weapons would not escalate into an existentially threatening nuclear exchange.

Several potential technological developments could undermine the balance of mutually assured destruction between major powers, including China and the US, in the coming decades. First is the deployment of a reliable missile-defense system capable of tracking and intercepting (at least) hundreds of incoming warheads. While the US has deployed strategic missile defense systems, their accuracy and reliability in a scenario of an actual nuclear war is debatable, at best. Such systems *could potentially*, in ideal circumstances, successfully intercept a dozen or so ICBMs launched from, say, North Korea. However, they would almost certainly be overwhelmed by a sustained Russian or Chinese strategic nuclear attack. Washington currently has a significant edge over China in terms of missile defense, though it must be emphasized that in practical terms it has little impact on strategic nuclear balance between the countries.

From around mid-century it is at least theoretically possible that either the US, or China, or perhaps even both countries, could develop and deploy systems capable of intercepting full-scale nuclear attacks from a major rival power. However, this scenario is extremely unlikely. In broad military terms "swords" are easier to develop and deploy than "shields." Investments in anti-missile batteries are far more costly and less reliable than simply building up more rockets to exceed the capacity of defensive systems. Relatively crude, "garage engineered" Hamas rockets launched from Gaza were sometimes capable of overwhelming multibillion-dollar, cutting-edge Israeli projectile defense systems during various rounds of conflict. The US or China developing and deploying systems that could guarantee the interception of all missiles launched by an industrialized peer competitor would be even more difficult, likely by an order of magnitude.

Far more possible, though still unlikely, is either China or the US acquiring technology granting overwhelming first-strike superiority. In this scenario, either country successfully invests in systems with the ability to "safely" launch a first strike against all of the other country's nuclear targets, and thus negate the possibility of adversarial retaliation. Weapons systems and command structures capable of such an attack may be possible. For example, China, Russia, and the US have all invested significant resources in developing hypersonic glide craft which may be outfitted with nuclear devices. China and Russia especially have made major advancements in such weaponry in large part because of their desire to negate the capabilities of current and potential future US missile defense systems. These weapons travel much faster than "conventional" ICBMs, and if sufficiently fast and numerous, they could theoretically be used to destroy an adversary's ground-based missile silos before retaliatory launch. Of course, enemy satellites would probably be able to record the launch of hypersonic weapons. A power bent on conducting an overwhelming first strike would also still need to neutralize all adversarial nuclear-armed submarines; new technological advances, such as satellite-based tracking systems, may make such a scenario feasible. Finally, military planners could have to contend with incoming retaliatory strikes by an enemy's strategic nuclear bombers.

All factors considered, if either the Washington or Beijing (or any other national government) one day possesses a combination of even the most advanced missile-defense, air defense, submarine tracking, and strategic hypersonic weapons, a "safe" nuclear first strike against another major global power would still be next to impossible. Firstly, other countries will invest in their own countermeasures and detection systems. Secondly, as emphasized in previous chapters, even a "successful" nuclear first strike would likely result in famine, terror, rage, and unprecedented sociopolitical instability in the "victorious" country. Full-scale warfare between major nuclear powers is only plausible in the event of a series of major errors or miscalculations — which, as evidenced by Cold War history, is a scenario well within the realm of possibility, especially if Washington and Beijing don't sit down with each other (and Moscow, Delhi, and possibly others) to agree to binding limits on their strategic weapons systems.

Nevertheless, there remains one especially intriguing possibility for intentional global warfare breaking out between the US and China at some point in the foreseeable future. If either government was able to carry out a *conventional* first strike capable of destroying the other's nuclear capabilities, it could be tempted to do so. While such a scenario is essentially impossible with current technology, a theoretical combination of hypersonic or space-based weapons in conjunction with an ability to disrupt enemy communications through superpowerful Artificial Intelligence may, someday, grant either the Chinese or US governments the ability to fight and win a war without triggering nuclear Armageddon. Such a conflict, even if technically feasible, would, of course, still majorly disrupt the global economy. Nevertheless, an overwhelming conventional first strike is the most plausible scenario, outside of a limited clash or an accidental nuclear exchange, for bilateral military conflict. China and the US are currently the only countries with the economic, technical, and political resources that could conceivably allow them to develop and deploy the combination of technology needed to achieve total conventional victory against a nuclear-armed peer adversary in the coming decades. However, eventually other powers, such as India, could seek to make such advancements before the end of this century.

Grey Swan Number Six

Various Internal Disasters

Several categories of essentially "random" incidents could strike either the United States or China with sufficient force to disrupt either country's national economy, political system, and global influence. While such scenarios are generally unlikely, they are nevertheless worthy of consideration. Any disaster large enough to cause either the US or China to lose their position as the world's primary or secondary power would likely lead to a lessening of overall contention, as the dominant contender turns to focus on stronger rivals. Of course, it is also possible that a sufficiently disruptive occurrence could knock *both* countries from the top positions of global powers, or even trigger a more generalized collapse in the reigning state-based global economic and political order.

China and the US are susceptible to various natural disasters. For example, a sufficiently powerful earthquake could cause extensive damage to major cities or trigger tsunamis impacting crucial coastal areas of either country. A major earthquake in, for example, California or northern China could spark an economic crisis in either China or the US. In terms of direct threat, China is likely somewhat more imperiled by the possibility of a major earthquake — unlike Washington DC, Beijing is located in a seismically active area. In 1976 a magnitude 7.6-earthquake struck only 90 miles (145 km) east of the heart of central Beijing, killing over 240,000 people. China's urban density and generally lower building quality also pose particular threats in terms of exposure to earthquakes.

The apparent US advantage in terms of minimizing earthquake impacts is relative and subject to the capriciousness of indifferent seismic plates; a sufficiently powerful earthquake in urban areas of the US West Coast could result in an unprecedented national disaster and national economic catastrophe. Coastal areas of both countries, including even the US East Coast, could potentially experience tsunamis caused by distant seismic events. The 2011 Tohoku Earthquake and tsunami killed over 20,000 people in Japan, and caused the Japanese economy as a whole to contract over the course of the year. China or the US could experience even deadlier and more disruptive earthquakes in the coming decades.

Volcanoes are another natural hazard that could cause either country to lose position as a first-rate global power. While earthquakes are overall more of a threat to China, disruptive volcanic eruptions are far more likely in the US. Volcanic activity in China is almost entirely centered on the far northwestern reaches of the sparsely populated Qinghai-Tibet Plateau. In contrast, the US West Coast has numerous volcanoes, and some, most notably Mount Rainier in Washington State, are located near major economic centers. A large volcanic eruption — especially one producing an ash cloud impacting key agricultural areas — could be sufficiently disastrous as to spark an economic crisis in the US, or less likely, in China. Potentially, a truly catastrophic volcanic eruption in a third country could alter weather patterns and cause global crop failures.

Terrorism remains a perennial threat to both the US and China. There is only a remote possibility of a terror attack occurring with sufficient force to cause national-scale disruption in either country. Nevertheless, government *reaction* to a large-scale terrorist incident or series of attacks could cause significant economic and social disruptions, though unless such policies sparked a broader internal conflict, the impacts would probably be limited. Currently, due to its far more extensive global military footprint, and its generally more open social and political systems, the US faces a greater possibility of experiencing significantly disruptive terrorism than does China.

Asymmetrical threats arising from cyber-attacks on critical infrastructure appear to be an escalating danger to both the US and China. While national governments could launch such attacks on their rivals, non-state actors motivated by ideology or economic self-interest will also continue to engage in such activities. Government-sponsored hacking will likely remain aimed primarily at gathering sensitive information instead of causing intentional disruption, since state actors are constrained by the possibility of retaliation (unless they could be sure of complete anonymity and deniability). Non-state cyber attackers do not face such constraints. Using publicly available knowledge to accurately assess the relative vulnerabilities of China and the US arising from disruptive cyber-attacks is extremely difficult. Nevertheless, Beijing will likely have an overall advantage in preventing or responding to disruptive cyber incidents over the coming decades due to its political system, human resources, and the fact that much of its critical infrastructure has been built more recently, with cyber threats in mind.

Either country may experience a meltdown at a nuclear power plant. This form of disaster could lead to economic disruptions in major urban areas, with possible tertiary impacts on the national level. A nuclear meltdown would be especially disruptive if members of the public blamed the catastrophe on official incompetence. In the US, such an outcome would likely be ameliorated somewhat by the two-party system and divested responsibility between federal, state, and local authorities; voters could punish the party or level of government perceived as "responsible" for the failure. In China, a sufficiently disastrous nuclear meltdown, especially one that caused death and disruptions in a major urban area, could result in a broader political crisis, potentially impacting stability on the national level.

By the very nature of their randomness, the calamities discussed in this chapter cannot be accurately forecast.

Additionally, it is important to remember that at least some degree of disruptions from precipitately unpredictable events, including earthquakes, cyber-attacks, and terrorism, are essentially inevitable in both China and the US. Nevertheless, a sufficiently major catastrophe could prompt a chain of events that knocks China, the US, or possibly both countries, from their overall relative preeminent global positions, and therefore undermine the core predictions in this book.

Grey Swan Number Seven
Civil War

Either China or the United States — or possibly both — could face a serious crisis that sparks an internal armed conflict. For the purposes of this analysis, internal armed conflict can be defined as a situation in which an organized group possessing lethal weaponry engages in deadly contention to directly challenge government rule over a sustained period, with the aim of founding an independent political entity or overthrowing the existing order. In order for such a conflict to occur, the insurgents must have a significant degree of at least localized popular support, enabling them to continue the struggle for a period of at least several weeks. Insurgents must also operate parallel administrations, effectively supplanting government control over civilian populations in some areas.

Incidents such as various terrorist attacks in the US and China do not qualify as internal conflict, nor do events like Ruby Ridge (because of the lack of sustained and dispersed conflict) or the 2019-2020 Hong Kong protests (because of the lack of effectively lethal weaponry and an alternative civil infrastructure). Historically parallel incidents that *would* qualify under this definition include the American Civil War, the Taiping Rebellion, and the various rounds of the KMT-CPC Chinese Civil War. Situations akin to the post-Soviet Chechen Wars in Russia, the Maoist insurgency in India, and the Troubles in Northern Ireland also qualify as internal conflicts, although the intensity of these struggles vary significantly. A theoretical war between the PRC and ROC would *not* qualify, since despite being labeled as part of China, Taiwan has never been effectively governed as part of the PRC.

Broadly speaking, there are three factors that determine the likelihood and intensity of internal armed conflict. The first is authority. When a government is seen as lacking legitimate or effective control, challengers may arise. The second key element is identity. Individuals with a specific linguistic, ethnic, or regional identity may organize to forcibly separate themselves from a ruling government in order to establish their own polity. Finally, economic factors are crucial in the emergence of internal wars. Widespread economic hardship frequently precedes attempts at overthrowing national governments, from the French Revolution to the Arab Spring. Of course, these three factors can work in tandem. For example, a government that fails to improve living conditions may face a crisis of legitimacy. Additionally, influential individuals with specific economic circumstances may encourage a particular regional identity to challenge existing national leadership, as in the southern states before and during the American Civil War.

Multiple elements could prompt violent political upheaval in China. There are several parts of the country where local leaders may attempt to break away from central government authority. Around 9% of the Chinese population is made up of non-Han ethnic minorities, most of whom have a strong sense of ethnic and cultural identity. Members of some of these groups, most notably Uighurs, Tibetans, and to a lesser extent Mongols and Hui, have contemporary and historical grievances with the current and former Chinese governments arising from various cultural and sociopolitical tensions.

Terrorist attacks by Uighur separatist groups have claimed hundreds of lives since the early 1990s, with the Chinese government relying on mass surveillance, cultural suppression, and from around 2017, preemptive mass-incarceration to combat the threat and secure its rule. Deadly ethnic riots occurred in parts of Tibet in 2008 and Xinjiang in 2009. These incidents do not quite constitute sustained internal armed conflicts. Nevertheless, in terms of fault lines for sustained separatist conflicts in China, Xinjiang and Tibet remain the most obvious candidates for potential breakaway regions. Other plausible areas for separatist conflict in the coming decades are Inner Mongolia and parts of Northeast China, where ethnic Mongols and Koreans could someday seek to "unify" with their ethnic brethren in Mongolia and Korea. In Korea's case, this is a stronger possibility under a scenario of inter-Korean unification.

There are key linguistic and cultural divisions that could serve as fault lines for sovereignty bids even among the Han majority. Only since roughly the beginning of the 21st century have most Han started speaking Mandarin with their family members; previously, a majority spoke local "dialects" at home. Most of these "dialects" are roughly as dissimilar from Mandarin as Portuguese is from French or Romanian. Contemporarily, outside of parts of far southern China, most Han do speak Mandarin at home to their children, somewhat lessening the potential emergence of linguistically inspired separatist nationalism.

China is large, and even in Han-majority areas there are distinct geographical regions. Local rebels or warlords have effectively seized control of entire provinces or other regions at numerous points in Chinese history, especially during the chaotic conditions that prevailed between the fall of the Qing Dynasty in 1911 and the establishment of the PRC in 1949. Sometimes, these commanders have appealed to various strains of provincial regionalism and claimed to represent local interests against central government tyranny. Additionally, for much of recorded history, China was divided into various warring regional polities, sometimes for hundreds of years, before a dynasty could restore unity. Similar situations could arise again in response to a major crisis in the political center.

China has also experienced numerous failed and successful revolts and revolutions that sought to overthrow and replace the existing central authority, instead of merely breaking away to form an independent polity. Sometimes, as with the war that led to the foundation of the Han and Ming dynasties, the rebellions were led by groups of angry commoners and military deserters who coalesced into a united force that seized control of the country. At other times, dissenting generals or other officials led the revolt. Twice dynasties were formed by non-Han leaders who adopted many Chinese customs to stake their claim to the Mandate of Heaven. Revolutionary religious organizations also launched several notable rebellions.

The link between economic and political conditions in Chinese history is key. Many Chinese governments have fallen, or nearly fallen, in response to widespread hardship. Contemporarily, this is the only scenario that is likely to result in a major internal conflict within the country. While members of some ethnic minority groups have significant resentments, they simply do not have the numerical strength to directly challenge the Chinese state. Many are also divided among themselves; during the riots in Xinjiang in 2009, some Uighurs targeted Mongols and Hui, another Muslim group. Regardless of the specifics of a future Chinese government, it will almost certainly have strong nationalist impulses; indeed, a directly democratic China could very well have *stronger* Han chauvinism than currently is the case. As for the various Han-dominated provinces, they are extremely unlikely to break apart in the absence of an enormous crisis in the political center. Even during the height of the Hong Kong protests, less than a fifth of the city's population advocated for the creation of an independent Hong Kong.

Any remotely likely scenario of internal armed conflict within China in the coming decades is predicated on an economic crisis. For example, rapidly increasing unemployment and/or monetary inflation could spark urban unrest. Next, divisions might emerge within Party leadership for how to best react to the growing protests (note that the preceding sentences essentially outline what occurred during the 1989 demonstrations in Beijing and elsewhere).

An upstart faction may make a bid for total control, and the coup or revolution either succeeds or fails. If a faction could both take power *and* effectively deal with an economic crisis, then it would probably cement its national authority quickly. If, however, one group takes power in Beijing, while its rivals established an alternative power center in another city (say, Nanjing, Guangzhou, or Xi'an), and the two groups were able to attract sufficient support from different military commanders, a civil war of indeterminable length could occur. Finally, there is a scenario in which a "palace coup" is successful at taking power, but not at solving the national crisis that sparked the overthrow of the previous rulers. In this situation a generalized collapse of centralized authority could result, and China could (once more) break apart into rival regional and ethnic-based polities, with relevant powers on China's borders (probably India and Russia, but potentially also Vietnam or Korea) seeking to support various groups out of self-interest.

While they generally garner less public attention and analysis than China's internal divisions, there are also many areas of the US that could seek to break away from Washington's authority if the United States experiences sufficient destabilization in the coming decades. The cultural diversity of the United States has been and is still generally a source of strength, as it encourages inbound migration by talented and hardworking individuals from all over the world. However, in a scenario of severe economic malaise and/or political crisis, this diversity could also present fault lines along which society could split into competing groups.

For example, African Americans have a distinct identity defined, in part, by (legitimate) historical, economic, and cultural grievances against a system dominated by the white majority. A growing Latino population is also culturally distinct, and its geographic prevalence in parts of the country present a potential breakaway region in a scenario of a weakened or fragmented national authority. Many Native American groups not only possess distinct identities and clear motivations to seek self-determination, but they also have existing structures for localized authority in the form of tribal governments. Some natives of Hawaii resent US annexation of their once-independent kingdom. Hawaii's geographic isolation from the US mainland, its distinct culture, and somewhat differing economic imperatives from the rest of the US also make the islands an obvious candidate for a potentially independent polity in the future. None of these examples are meant to disparage these groups as inherently traitorous or somehow "less American" than the white majority. Rather, as always in this book, the aim is objective analysis. In a scenario of collapsing central authority, individuals and groups have historically drawn upon existing regional, local, and/or cultural identities to help fill some of the organizational gaps left by weakened or absent state power.

Perhaps the most dangerous fault lines within US society run parallel to, and in some cases through, its various cultural and ethnic communities. Most notable is the increasingly acrimonious divide between the "left" and "right" of the political/cultural spectrum. For decades, the political and economic elite have exploited and deepened these divisions out of individual and organizational self-interest. On the superficial level, leaders of the two dominant parties appeal to these divisions to garner votes and financial support. On a deeper level, focusing on cultural and identity issues has allowed many key bipartisan aspects of US Federal Government policy to go unchallenged.

Perpetual intervention in foreign conflicts, subsidies to agricultural conglomerates, massive military spending, and increased monitoring of personal communications continue without major opposition from either mainstream party. At the same, a superficial "left vs right" dichotomy fosters robust debate and contention on largely social issues, along with some fairly marginal economic policies.

Whether intentionally or otherwise, the dynamic of effectively using competing group identities to pit the mostly urban, coastal, college-educated, secular "left" against the mostly white, religious, heartland-based "right" has broadly benefited Washington's entrenched elite interests. The system appeared to be fairly stable for decades. However, the COVID-19 pandemic, economic malaise, and the contested 2020 presidential election intensified and exposed the inherent instability of the left-right balancing act. Many individuals on both the "left" and "right" have internalized their political divisions into apparently radicalized tribal identities. They see not only leaders, but also common supporters of the "rival" faction not merely as political opponents but as *existential threats* to their personal safety and US democracy. The intensification and spread of such beliefs is an overall negative indicator for social and political stability in the US.

Economic factors are increasingly crucial factors intensifying internal political divisions in the US. The 2000 presidential election, like the 2020 contest, was deeply contested and controversial, with an outcome that angered tens of millions of Americans and undermined their faith in the political system. However, the 2000 election did not result in any major episodes of civil unrest, much less a highly symbolic storming of the very center of US political power. In 2000 unemployment was at historic lows, there was not an acute public health crisis, and Washington's relative global power was near its zenith.

Another close-fought presidential election resulting in contested claims of legitimacy could spark an internal conflict in the US, especially if it were to occur during a period of widespread economic hardship. Note that long-standing economic, regional, political, cultural, and racial divisions created the conditions necessary for the American Civil War to occur, but the proximate cause for the session of southern states was the election of President Lincoln. Depending on various factors, a sufficiently intense political crisis could result in a peaceful (or mostly peaceful) breakup of the United States into two, or more than two, new countries. However, the divisions between "left" and "right" do not often follow clearly demarcated boundaries, so an entirely peaceful, negotiated division of the US along politically partisan lines seems unlikely. During the Civil War pro-Confederate and pro-Union guerrilla activity occurred on the "wrong" side of the apparent political front lines. A future civil war could be yet more chaotic.

Perhaps the "best-case" scenario for a peaceful breakup of the US would be one in which centralized authority collapses because of a generalized crisis of authority in Washington DC brought about by economic collapse, instead of a contested presidential election. At least theoretically, state governments could simply supplant sufficiently weakened or ineffective Federal authority without even formally declaring formal independence. Otherwise, several states, either individually or in geographic tandem, could declare independence from a weakened central authority. A political collapse somewhat akin to the fall of the USSR is possible. However, it should be noted that although the *initial* breakup of the Soviet Union into its constituent pieces was *largely* peaceful, it did ultimately spark a series of significant notable armed conflicts, including wars in Chechnya, a civil war in Tajikistan, and fighting between the newly independent Azerbaijan and Armenia. The disputed legacy of Soviet collapse, ethnic divisions, and geopolitical contention contributed to the outbreak of direct military conflict between Russia and Ukraine more than three decades after the initial breakup.

As with a scenario of potential civil war in China, rival American factions would make efforts to appeal to the loyalty of the military; however, in contrast to China, much of the American population has easy access to firearms. Guerrilla warfare could break out in numerous areas of the country. In a worst-case scenario, the frontlines between supporters of the rival centers of authority would run within major communities, resulting in violence first against armed rivals, then their civilian supporters. There would be a very real possibility of such violence occurring along ethnic lines in some areas. A cycle of atrocity and "revenge" could spiral out of any faction's control. Canadian and Mexican forces could launch covert or overt interventions in US territory to ensure the security of their border areas and seek geopolitical advantage.

Outside interference in an internal conflict is not limited to a country's immediate neighbors; indeed, Washington and Beijing themselves could play a role in an internal conflict within their rival. Stoking internal political divisions in order to distract or weaken a competing state is a tactic at least as old as recorded human history. Beijing views historical and contemporary US financial and political support for the India-based Tibetan government in exile, demonstrators in Hong Kong, various Uighur groups, and pro-democracy political dissidents as efforts to marginally undermine the CPC's authority. US officials have also accused China of encouraging social and political divisions within the US. If, as is likely, relative power continues to shift to Beijing's advantage and if, as is also likely, overall US-China rivalry continues, the Chinese government may seek to more openly support various ethnic, political, or regional organizations broadly opposed to the US Federal Government.

During this coming century civil war within either the US or China is far more likely than interstate war between the two powers. Nearly any form of sustained internal conflict would greatly weaken either government, potentially for decades. The possibility of national unity being effectively destroyed is also within the realm of possibility for both countries. Therefore, Beijing and Washington may be tempted — especially if bilateral antagonism increases significantly — to try to bring about a civil war within their rival. Such an outcome could help secure one's own position as a globally dominant power. While such moves would be dangerous, they would be far less dangerous than initiating an open and direct military conflict.

Covert and deniable support for dissidents or rebels would likely be more effective than open aid. Blatantly supporting political forces within a rival country can backfire, since it allows the government to leverage popular nationalism and dismiss the supported groups as "foreign puppets." Indeed, this is a common tactic in China (and increasingly in the US) for delegitimizing dissenting groups outside the one (or two) party political mainstream. Even in the case of internal conflict, open foreign support for a particular group can backfire, as its rivals use such support to appeal to popular nationalism. For example, some analysts believe that NATO support for the previous Afghan government helped pave the way for ultimate Taliban victory, since the Taliban could appeal to nationalistic sentiment by denouncing their opponents as foreign pawns.

A sufficiently prolonged and disruptive civil war within the US or China in the coming decades would likely knock either national government from its position as a first-rate global power. All other factors being equal, an internal conflict in one country benefits the relative power of the other. However, as previously emphasized, both countries share deep economic ties, and it is entirely possible that a civil war taking place in one country would cause sufficient economic upheaval as to trigger a political crisis and internal conflict within the other. In the event of *both* China *and* the US experiencing simultaneous civil wars, other national governments would seek to fill the resultant vacuums in regional and global power — unless, of course, they too were caught up in a generalized global cataclysm.

Only one scenario of internal conflict in the US or China over the coming decades would *not* bring about major changes to US-China global rivalry. That is a scenario in which a revolution topples the current Chinese government and then quickly reestablishes effective national authority. The leaders of the new political system, regardless of specific political ideology or methods, would continue to have the same broad national imperatives as previous Chinese governments. Regardless of whether or not they allowed open dissent and competitive national elections, they would seek to maintain territorial integrity and expand China's global influence. The emergence of a hypothetically democratic China would have essentially no impact on overall US-China contention for relative global influence, except to make Washington's ideological justification for its global role more awkward. In fact, a Chinese government held directly accountable to its population could be *more* internationally assertive than the current PRC, since it would need to appeal to a population with deep-rooted nationalistic, and indeed civilizational, pride.

Conclusion

So What?

The purpose of this book is to provide objective analysis of complicated trends. The reader should (hopefully) now possess a decent overall understanding of the fundamental factors driving competition between Washington and Beijing, the likely paths along which this competition will develop over the coming decades, and the scenarios that could derail the forecasted course. This work has been descriptive rather than prescriptive. It focuses on what *is* and what *will likely be*, rather than questions about what *should* occur from an ethical or ideological perspective.

Nevertheless, there are *enormous* ethical and political issues arising from the current state of US-China competition and the likely path on which bilateral relations will move in the remainder of this century. How should individuals, organizations, and national governments react to these trends? Which policies will best serve a country's national interest and the well-being of its people? These are questions which must be addressed not only within China and the United States, but in all societies across the globe. With the exception of the Sentinelese Islanders and other isolated groups, every human society will make economic and political decisions that will be shaped by, and also help to influence, the development of Sino-US rivalry. In the event of the plausible worst-case scenarios for the outcome of the rivalry — nuclear war or unchecked global climate change — even the Sentinelese will experience the consequences of decisions made in Beijing and Washington.

I will not presume to be in a position to make any specific policy recommendations. Political decisions are complicated, they are dependent on the interests of the parties making the decision, and they can backfire spectacularly, even when undertaken with the best of intentions. I will, however, provide some general advice to those entrusted with the responsibility of guiding their societies, countries, and humanity as a whole into a safer and happier future. Avoid emotional policymaking. Acquire objective information. Base your decisions on reality instead of wishful thinking. Make allowances for unexpected developments. Use empathetic analysis. Understanding an opponent's viewpoint does not mean excusing their behavior, but rather trying to rationally understand *why* they have engaged in such behavior and trying to anticipate their next moves. Plan for the long term. Perhaps most importantly, avoid the sunk-cost fallacy, and be willing to change course if policies are not working as intended.

Those of us without the burden of making large-scale collective decisions must also base our analysis on reality instead of rhetoric to survive and thrive in the coming decades. Government statements can be useful in terms of signaling desired outcomes and possible future actions, but what officials *do* is always far more important than what they merely *say*. Remember that, despite enormous efforts to convince you otherwise, *people are not their national governments*. This is true no matter where you live or what form your government takes. The well-being of yourself, your family, and your neighbors is not necessarily equivalent to the interests of the government ruling over you. Indeed, even a government's *perceived* objectives are often not the same as the true, long-term national interests, as proven by thousands of years of recorded blunders, failings, and monumental tragedies. You are likely to experience increasing efforts to convince you that a foreign government is the biggest threat to your safety and freedom, especially if you live in a major global power or one of its allies. Never forget that, for the majority of the human population across vast expanses of history, the national government that was most threatening to their well-being was, in fact, their own.

CHANGEMAKERS BOOKS

Transform your life, transform our world. Changemakers Books publishes books for people who seek to become positive, powerful agents of change. These books inform, inspire, and provide practical wisdom and skills to empower us to write the next chapter of humanity's future.

www.changemakers-books.com

Current Bestsellers from Changemakers Books

Resetting Our Future: Am I Too Old to Save the Planet? A Boomer's Guide to Climate Action
Lawrence MacDonald

Why American boomers are uniquely responsible for the climate crisis — and what to do about it.

Resetting Our Future: Feeding Each Other Shaping Change in Food Systems through Relationship
Michelle Auerbach and Nicole Civita

Our collective survival depends on making food systems more relational; this guidebook for shaping change in food systems offers a way to find both security and pleasure in a more connected, well-nourished life.

Resetting Our Future: Zero Waste Living, The 80/20 Way The Busy Person's Guide to a Lighter Footprint
Stephanie J. Miller

Empowering the busy individual to do the easy things that have a real impact on the climate and waste crises.

The Way of the Rabbit
Mark Hawthorne

An immersion in the world of rabbits: their habitats, evolution and biology; their role in legend, literature, and popular culture; and their significance as household companions.